# Zero Waste Sewing

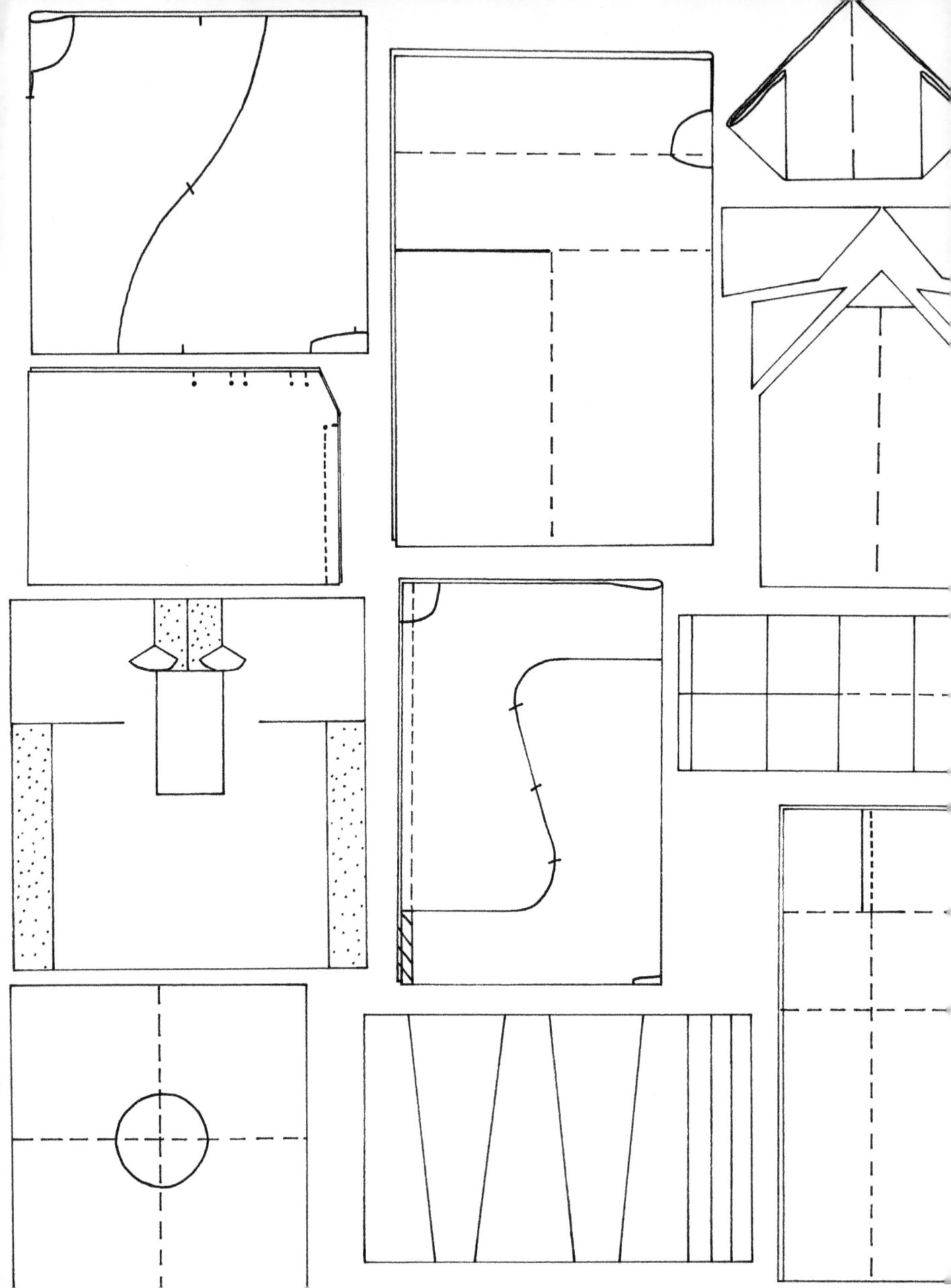

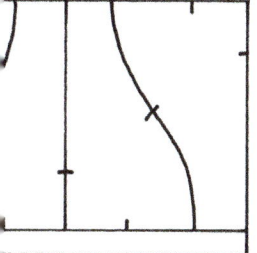

# Zero Waste Sewing

*16 projects to make, wear and enjoy*

Elizabeth M Haywood

COOATALAA PRESS

By the same author
*The Dressmaker's Companion—A practical guide to sewing clothes*

First published in 2020
Cooatalaa Press
PO Box 1014
Clare 5453
Australia

Text, illustrations and photographs copyright © 2020 by Elizabeth M Haywood
Cover photographs and cover by Stu Nankivell www.bluegoanna.com.au

All rights reserved. This book or any portion thereof may not be reproduced or used in any manner whatsoever without the express written permission of the publisher except for the use of brief quotations in a book review or scholarly journal.

www.zerowastesewing.com
#zerowastesewingbook

ISBN-13: 978-0-646-80802-4

 A catalogue record for this book is available from the National Library of Australia

# Contents

6 All projects at a glance
8 Introduction
10 Making the projects in this book

### A top from a square
14 tie front top
22 hooded blouson
30 yo-yo top
34 side drape top
38 geometric top

### One seam
44 introduction to one seam
48 simple dress
54 extra: jacket
56 coat dress
64 cardigan jacket
69 moebius scarf
70 hooded robe
76 hooded coat variation

### Tessellated
78 introduction to tessellated
80 boho dress
87 boho caftan variation
88 wrap skirt
94 wrap trousers
102 dress + coat
114 playsuit

127 Sewing techniques
135 Making zero waste patterns
138 Further reading
140 Index
141 Acknowledgements
142 About the author

**14** Tie front top
Sizes 8-20

**22** Hooded blouson
Sizes 8-20

**30** Yo-yo top
One size

**34** Side drape top
Any size

**38** Geometric top
Sizes 8-16

**48** Simple dress
Any size

**54** Extra: jacket
Sizes 8-20

**56** Coat dress
Any size

**64** Cardi jacket
Any size

**69** Moebius scarf

**70** Hooded robe
Any size

**76** Hooded coat
Any size

**80** Boho dress
Any size

**87** Boho caftan
Any size

**88** Wrap skirt
Any size

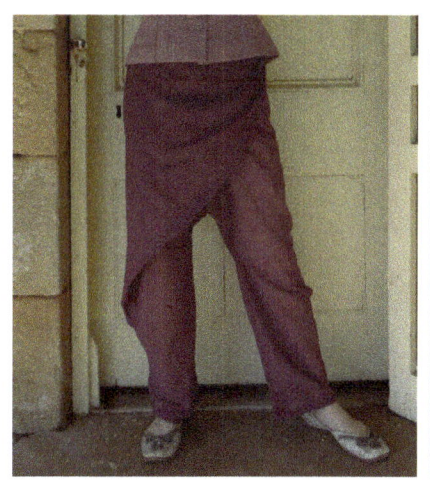

**94** Wrap trousers
Any size

**102** Dress + coat
Any size

**114** Playsuit
Sizes 8-16

# Introduction

Zero waste sewing is making clothes without wasting any fabric. The pattern pieces are designed to completely fit within the dimensions of the fabric like a giant jigsaw puzzle; there are no offcuts and no waste.

While the phrase zero waste is modern, the concept has been around forever; it's as old as the practice of wearing clothes. It's inherent in traditional and folk clothes, where fabric was hand loomed and precious. Think of kimonos, sarongs, kilts, ponchos, saris, caftans, peasant clothes, norse/viking clothes. Note that the idea isn't to use *less* fabric; it's to not waste any.

Zero waste clothes can use all the fabric either in one whole garment, parts of another garment or across a series of garments.

Unfortunately, zero waste patternmaking isn't used much in the fashion industry. Designing zero waste clothes requires the fashion designer to also be the patternmaker or at least have a knowledge of patternmaking. In addition, experience of cutting layouts is needed because the designing, patternmaking and cutting layout all happen together. The designing actually happens as the pattern and layout develop. This is around the other way from how clothing is currently produced, where the designer makes a sketch, the patternmaker translates it into a pattern, and a different person makes the cutting layout (known as a *marker*) prior to cutting, using the specified fabric and pattern. With sustainable fashion studies being offered to fashion students, we may see zero waste patternmaking more in the future.

Zero waste patternmaking has two great benefits. The first is, as the name says, no waste.

It's estimated that 15% of the fabric used to manufacture clothes[1] ends up in the scrap bins and from my own factory experience I'd say that's about right. 15% doesn't sound like much, but globally it results in an estimated 164 million square metres of fabric waste *per day*,[2] 60% of which is synthetic. All the resources used to make that fabric are therefore also wasted - water, oil, human labour, transport, dyestuffs, etc.

The responsibility to dispose of the waste is the manufacturer's. Some factories sell their scraps but most of it ends up dumped. All of this pre-consumer textile waste is simply costed into the garment's price. It becomes an environmental and ethical problem in high volume factories situated in countries without waste management systems.

Factories don't waste fabric on purpose. They operate on tight margins and are extremely conscious of fabric utilization. However, factories also don't have a choice because the design, pattern and fabric have already been decided on by their customer. Because the textile waste is the factory's problem there is little incentive for the fashion designer or clothing label to be concerned with it.

The great thing about zero waste patternmaking is that it completely eliminates pre-consumer textile waste—the problem of waste is designed out.

[1]Rissanen, 2005; Feyerabend, 2004; Abernathy, 1999; Cooklin, 1997. Home sewing undoubtedly wastes more, although scraps are often kept for other projects.
[2]Gugnami, A. and A. Mishra, 2012.

The second benefit of zero waste patternmaking is as a design tool.

This, to me, was an unexpected and exciting aspect of zero waste clothes: some of the most innovative pattern cutting can result from the design parameter of zero waste. The pursuit of less waste results in more creative patternmaking and far more interesting clothing.

Fashion design is traditionally presented as inspiration + market research + fabric and colour selection + sketching. However, designing fashion through patternmaking has much untapped potential. It can yield interesting new silhouettes and design details that maybe would not be realised through traditional fashion design.

Designing in this way can be a hard path for some designers to embrace, because the destination is unpredictable and can't be controlled. Serendipity - making fortunate discoveries by accident - plays an important part in zero waste patternmaking. It's by *doing* and seeing what emerges that brings the design direction, rather than making a sketch and handing it to the patternmaker to make a pattern for it.

There are many different ways to set about making zero waste patterns, just like there are for making regular patterns, and some approaches are discussed at the end of this book.

Zero waste patternmaking does have some challenges:

✂ The most obvious is that the garment is designed for a particular fabric and will have to be redesigned if the fabric is a different width.

✂ Some fabrics easily lend themselves to zero waste and others don't. For example napped, one-way fabrics and border prints are harder to use (but could be more rewarding).

✂ An occasional criticism of zero waste clothes is that they're too conceptual/simple/avant garde/minimalist and more suitable for the catwalk or fashion student's grad parades. Yes, there is a temptation to make zero waste clothes very basic because it's easier to do or to accommodate more sizes. Having said that, patterns don't have to be complex to be effective; some are brilliant in their simplicity.

✂ Grading patterns (that is, making all the sizes) isn't as easy. Or rather, the process is different. Regular patterns are easy to grade afterwards but zero waste patterns need to have the sizing thought about from the beginning.

So, is zero waste patternmaking the future of fashion? It's early days yet. While it's an old idea, it's new for manufacturing and is still being experimented with. I see it as one part in the quest to make fashion more sustainable. I also see great potential as a creative new approach to fashion design.

The projects in this book began out of my own curiosity to see if making zero waste clothes was difficult. I found it's no harder than making regular clothes, only far more interesting and fun! Some of the projects in this book are traditional/folk sewing layouts, some were inspired by catwalk fashions but many of them I made by doing. I could have kept on going...

If you're dipping your toe into zero waste sewing, creating a slow wardrobe for yourself, or just looking for a new sewing adventure, there's plenty in this book to try, inspire, wear and enjoy.

# Making the projects in this book

The projects in this book are all drafts, meaning the actual pattern is made by you. Some require you making a paper pattern or template but most are drafted straight onto the fabric using tailors chalk.

I want to emphasise that this is a different way of working for most of us; usually we buy a paper pattern to sew a garment.

You may be unaccustomed to using tailors chalk. The key to using it is to regularly sharpen it so that it maintains a fine edge. Stand over a bin and scrape the sides of the chalk with a blade. If you don't like using tailors chalk, try a chalk wheel or an erasable pen. Test it first to make sure it's removable afterwards.

Please read through all the instructions including the end notes before you begin cutting and sewing, to make sure you understand them. Due to their unusual shapes, some garments are best cut and sewn all in the same day—otherwise when you come back to it later it may not make any sense.

## Sizing

Most of the drafting instructions in this book refer to body measurements where possible, but sometimes a size is quoted from this chart. The sizes are roughly equivalent to Australian retail sizes. Pick a size closest to your body measurements, and note that you may be a different size for tops and bottoms.

These measurements are all taken standing up.

Take the measurements with a dressmakers tape measure over close-fitting garments or underwear.

**Bust** refers to the fullest part of your bust. Keep the tape measure horizontal around your body.

Your **waist** is the slimmest part of your natural waistline. It's above your belly button and below your ribcage. It can be helpful to tie a narrow ribbon or tape around your torso as it will naturally find the narrowest circumference.

**Hips** are the fullest part of your seat/bottom, approximately 20cm below your natural waistline. Stand sideways to see the fullest part and measure around the hips at this level.

If you're between sizes and the pattern says (for example) *measure half your bust, plus 5cm*, use your actual bust measurement to make the pattern, then pick the closest size for the given neck/armhole depth/etc measurements.

Unfortunately, not every project is available in every size; the limit of the fabric width means sometimes it isn't physically possible.

## Unit of measurement

This book uses metric measurements.

**To convert seam allowances:**

| | |
|---|---|
| 3mm = ⅛" | 1.5cm = ⅝" |
| 6mm = ¼" | 2cm = ¾" |
| 1cm = ⅜" | 2.5cm = 1" |
| 1.2cm = ½" | 5cm = 2" |

| | 8 | 10 | 12 | 14 | 16 | 18 | 20 | 22 | 24 | 26 | 28 |
|---|---|---|---|---|---|---|---|---|---|---|---|
| Bust | 87cm 34¼" | 92cm 36¼" | 97cm 38¼" | 102cm 40⅛" | 107cm 42⅛" | 112cm 44" | 117cm 46" | 122cm 48" | 127cm 50" | 132cm 52" | 137cm 54" |
| Waist | 69cm 27⅛" | 74cm 29⅛" | 79cm 31" | 84cm 33" | 89cm 35" | 94cm 37" | 99cm 39" | 104cm 41" | 109cm 43" | 114cm 45" | 119cm 46⅞" |
| Hips | 92cm 36¼" | 97cm 38¼" | 102cm 40⅛" | 107cm 42⅛" | 112cm 44" | 117cm 46" | 122cm 48" | 127cm 50" | 132cm 52" | 137cm 54" | 142cm 56" |

**To convert centimetres to inches:**
Divide the centimetres by 2.54 to give inches.

**To convert metres to yards:**
Multiply by 1.094. One metre is 1.094 yards or 39.37". Roughly, one yard + 3" = 1 metre.

## Seam allowances

All the seam and hem allowances are included. **Seams are 1cm** unless otherwise stated. Neck edges faced with purchased 12mm bias binding have 5mm seam allowances. Hems are generally 1cm-2.5cm but can be more or less, depending on the length garment you want.

## Fabric

The fabric widths mostly used in this book are 115cm (45"; really 45¼") and 150cm (60"; really 59"). Fabrics don't always come in the advertised width; they may actually measure up to 5cm either side of it. A few of the patterns in this book need an exact fabric width, but most can be made with approximately the correct width. If you're a smaller size, you may be able to use a fabric a few centimetres narrower in width, and if you're larger, try and pick a fabric the correct or wider width.

*Important:* **when the fabric quantities say "exactly" an amount, buy 5cm-10cm more so that you can accurately straighten the cut edges.**

*Also important:* **ensure that the fabric won't shrink—pre-wash and iron it if necessary.**

Use beautiful, good quality, fabric that you love. Cheap fabric doesn't honour your investment of time and effort, but quality fabric is a joy to sew and wear. Choose quality zips, interfacing, thread and trims as well.

You might not need to buy new fabric. Many of the garments in this book were made from thrift-shop fabric, either dress lengths, furnishing fabrics or old household linen. You might already have something at home, maybe in your fabric collection or sitting unused in the linen cupboard.

## Creating a straight edge without using an L-square

A straight cut edge on the fabric is required for every project in this book. *Note that the fabric quantities assume an already-cut, perfectly straight edge. Allow extra for this when buying fabric.*

Here are 3 methods.

### Fold the fabric

Suitable for stiff, firm fabrics such as denim. Fold the fabric in half as shown. Measure from the folded edge to the cut edge at several points, then connect the points with a ruled line and cut.

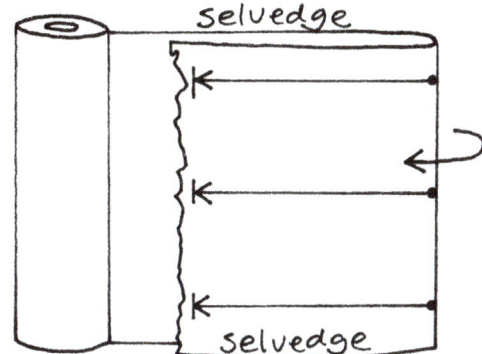

### Pull a thread

This works very well for fine fabrics. Snip the selvedge, find a crosswise grain thread and gently pull it. Ease the fabric along the thread, then cut along the pulled thread. If the line breaks before you reach the opposite selvedge, cut up to the break then find a new thread to pull. You can also do this along the lengthwise grain if you have a piece of fabric with no selvedge.

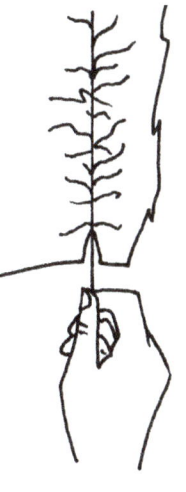

Making the projects in this book

## Tear off a strip

Make a snip in one selvedge. Grasp both sides of the snip firmly and rip quickly across to the opposite selvedge. If the tear runs off to nothing, cut a new snip farther from the end and try again.

## Some stitching terms clarified

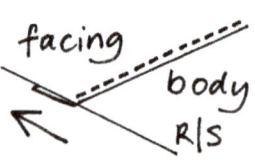

**Understitching** is used on facings and collar edges to control the seam and stop it from rolling to the right side. It's done after the seam has been sewn. The seam allowance is pressed towards the facing (or undercollar) and edgestitched. I use understitching on nearly every garment I make.

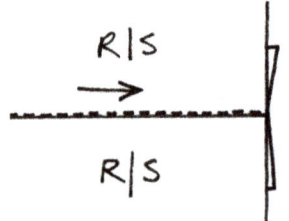

**Stitching-in-the-ditch** is a line of stitching used to hold down a seam onto the fabric behind it. The seam can be pressed open (as illustrated) or closed. The stitching is hidden in the "ditch" of the seam.

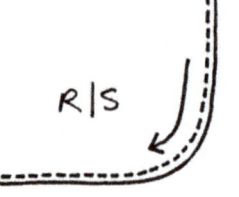

**Edgestitching** is a type of topstitching, where the stitching is about 2mm away from the edge.

## Abbreviations

CF and CB are Centre Front and Centre Back. W/S and R/S are Wrong Side and Right Side.

## Going zero waste

Try and extend zero waste thinking into your sewing room. Maybe you already do this. For example, use what you have instead of buying more. Buy thread on cardboard cones instead of plastic ones, if possible. Save interfacing scraps. Buy notions by the metre instead of pre-packaged. You'll no doubt find, as I did, that it's really hard to go absolutely zero waste. You'll have trimmings from straightening the fabric's edge, levelling hems, cutting back seam allowances, and so on. There will also be overlocker trimmings, thread ends, unpicking threads, and odd ends of things like bias binding. I can only make suggestions for using these. Some people make tiny accessories such as earrings. Others incorporate them into papermaking (which is then used for swing tags, stationery or sold), or make stuffing for cushions or bolsters. I knew a woman who gradually stuffed a pouffe over several years. If you have children they might like fabric scraps for craft or sewing. Strips of fabric are sometimes used by weavers to make new fabrics or rag rugs.

## ...and enjoy!

Enjoy the experience! Make time to slow down and create a garment you'll love to wear. Great fabric, combined with careful cutting, sewing and finishing will reward you with a garment you'll wear for years....as well as being able to say *Thank you, I made it myself, it's actually zero waste.*

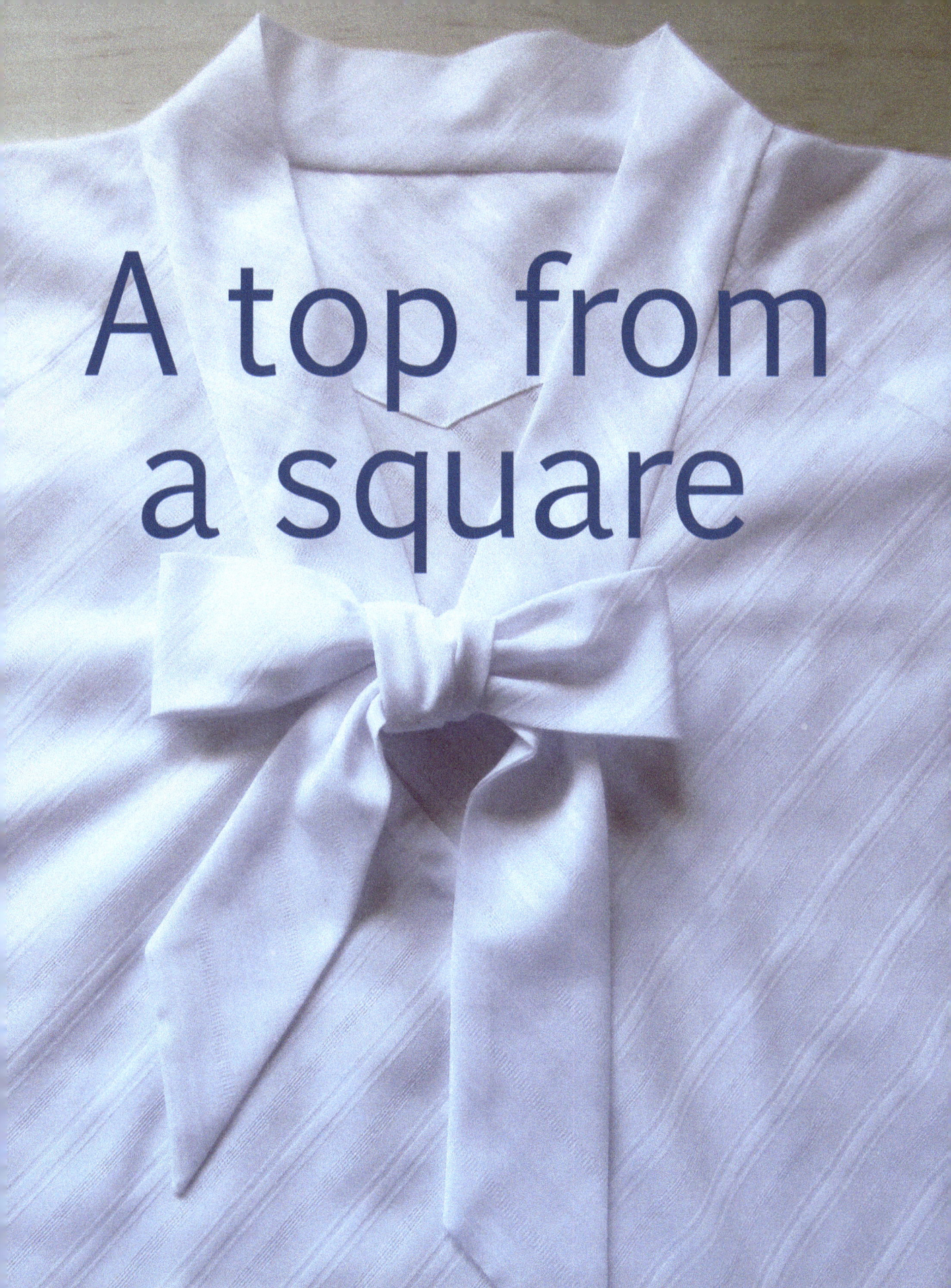

# tie front top

*A bias top with a feminine bow and pretty petal sleeves. The top is cut from an exact square of fabric.*

**Fabric** Woven fabric, 115cm wide. For all sizes, you'll need *exactly* 115cm. If the fabric is a slightly different width, use that length so you have an exact square. Suitable fabrics include lightweight cotton in plain, stripe or pattern. Avoid unstable, flimsy fabrics such as rayon (see *Notes* on page 21).

**Notions** Thread.

**Sizes** 8-10-12-14-16. Note that a size 16 top will also fit a size 18 or 20 body, just with less ease.

**Finished length** Approximately 65cm, all sizes. The top can be made slightly longer if the tie is made narrower.

**Seam and hem allowances** 1cm seams and hems are included.

Zero Waste Sewing

## To cut

**1.** Iron the 115cm x 115cm square of fabric diagonally in half, with the wrong side facing inwards. Press the crease firmly.

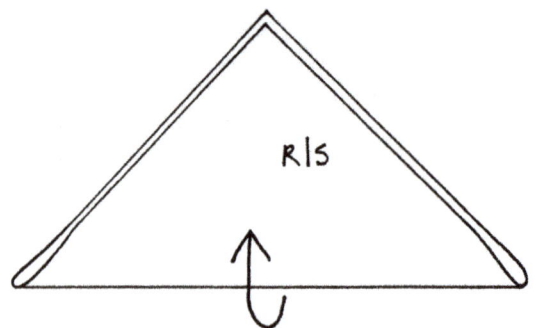

**2.** Press in half again, lightly. Trim the edges if required so the edges are sitting perfectly on top of one another. Unfold the fabric back to Step 1.

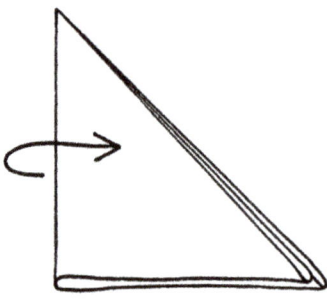

**3.** Using tailors chalk, draw in a line 6cm from the folded edge. Cut. This will make the neck tie.

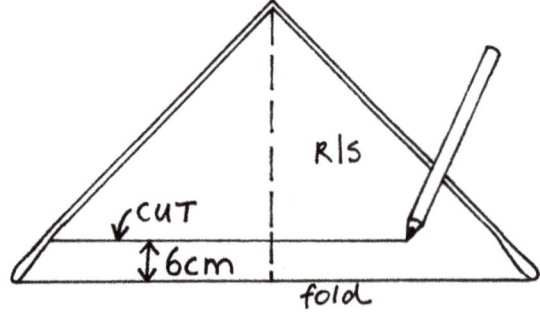

✂ The neck tie is 5cm wide finished. If you want a slightly longer top, cut the neck tie narrower. It can be cut at a minimum of 3cm wide for a 2cm wide finished tie.

**4.** Draw in the body. Make it half the bust measurement, plus 7.5cm. For sizes 8-16 this is 51 - 53.5 - 56 - 58.5 - 61cm (that's 25.5 - 26.7 - 28 - 29.2 - 30.5cm each side of the central fold). Cut the triangles off the sides.

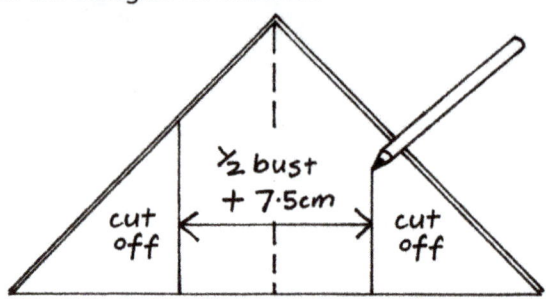

**5.** On the body, mark a horizontal chalk line 9.8 - 11 - 12.2 - 13.4 - 14.6cm long (that's 4.9 - 5.5 - 6.1 - 6.7 - 7.3cm each side of the central fold).

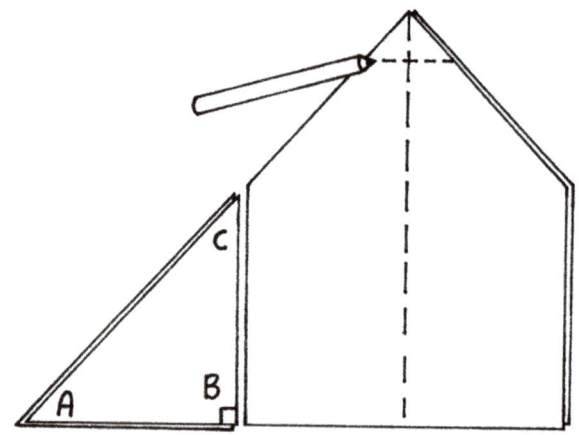

**6.** Make a line of pins 2cm in from the diagonal edge. Position the triangular side piece as shown.

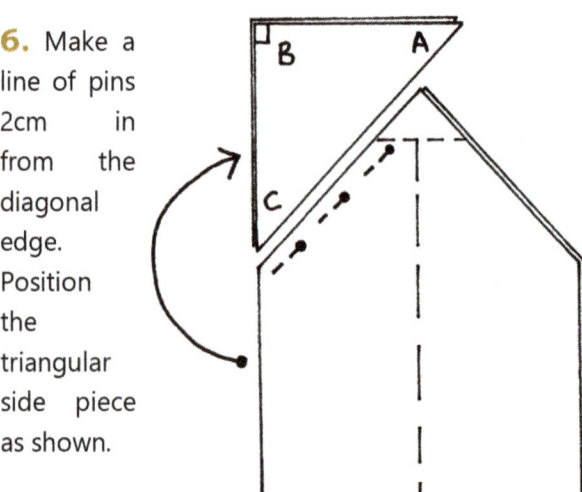

16   Zero Waste Sewing

**7.** Lap the triangular piece over the body so it's next to the pin line. Extend the chalk line (from Step 5) across the triangle.

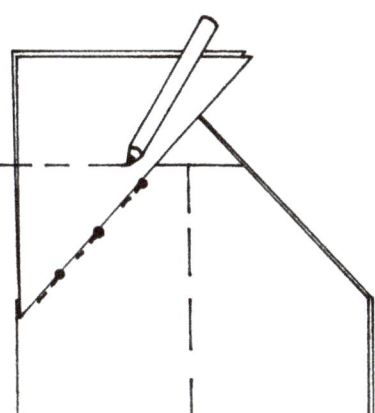

**8.** Slope the line 3cm down as shown, and cut along the line. Repeat with the other triangle.

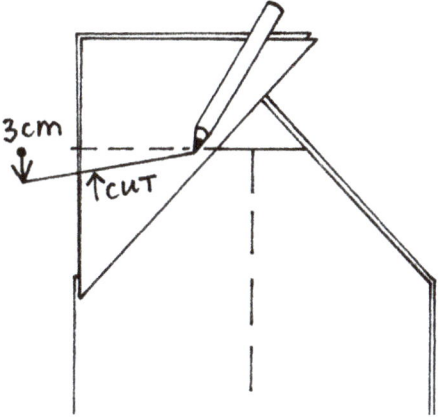

You now have these pieces. The triangles will be sewn to the front and back, and the remaining pieces will become the sleeves.

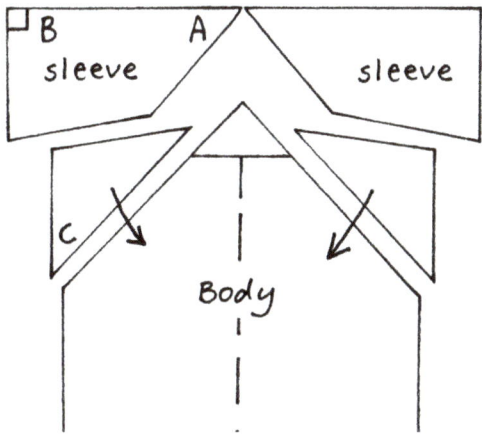

**9.** Sew the triangles to the bodies, matching at corner C. Be sure to match the *stitching* line, otherwise you'll have a step at the side. Overlock the seams and press towards the triangles.

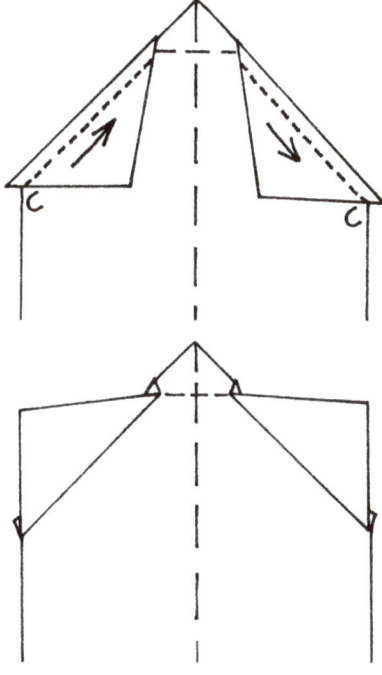

## Cut the necklines

**10.** Do the front first. Fold it in half down the centre. Mark a point 24cm down (all sizes) from the chalk line.

Mark the horizontal neckline width across 9.7 - 10 - 10.3 - 10.6 - 10.9cm.

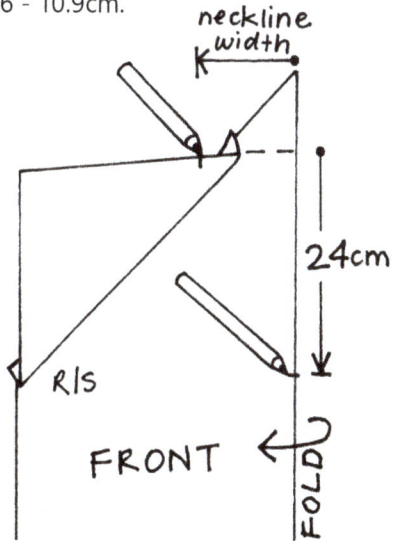

A top from a square

**11.** Draw a curving V up to the neckline width mark. Cut out the neckline and save it.

Mark a notch 5cm up from the bottom of the V; the tie won't be stitched all the way to the bottom of the V because there needs to be room to tie it.

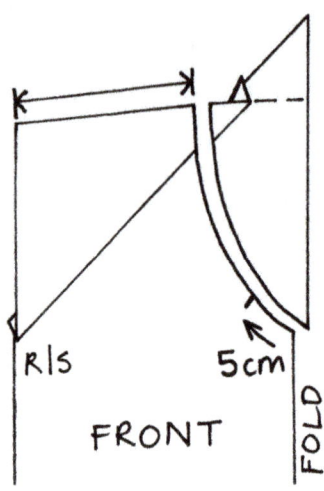

**12.** Measure the length of the front shoulder and make the back the same. Draw in the back neck, lowering it by 2.5cm at the centre back and 1cm at the shoulder. Again, keep the offcut.

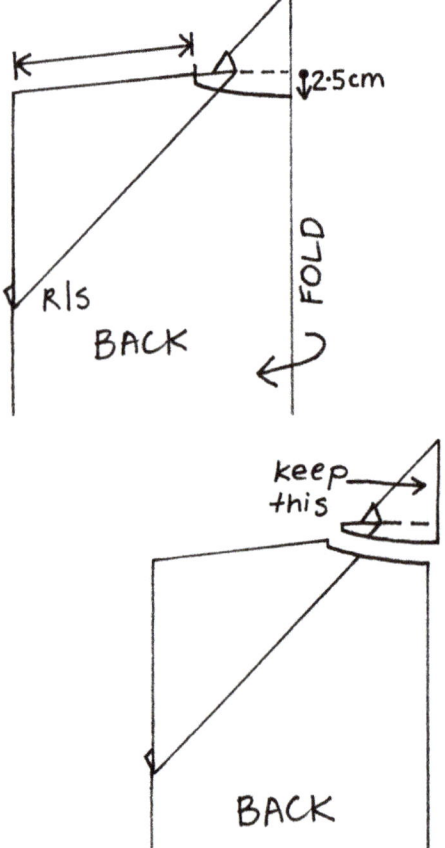

**13.** Before you move the pieces off the table, measure the necklines along the 1cm *stitching* lines and note down the measurements. Stand the tape measure on its side to measure around the curves.

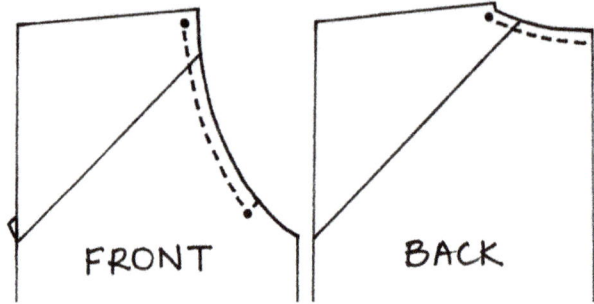

Subtract 5mm from the back measurement and 1cm from the front (a slightly smaller band sits more smoothly around the neck).

Transfer these measurements to the neckband: fold the neckband in half and snip the cut edge with 3mm snips to mark them.

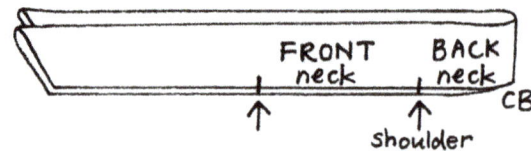

## To sew
**Seam allowances:** all 1cm.

### Front and back neck
**1.** Front V facing: on the front body, take the back neck cutout and lay it under the front V, right sides together. Position the long curved edge 5mm above the notches.

**2.** Stitch exactly from notch to notch, pivoting at the V. Backstitch accurately at each notch.

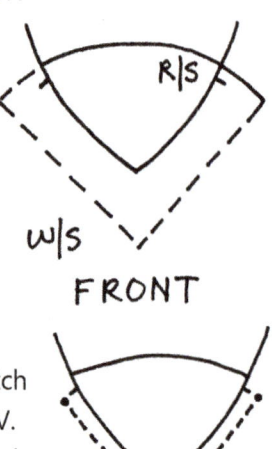

18    Zero Waste Sewing

**3.** Trim away the excess inside the neckline. Snip into the V pivot point and at each notch. Snip the curved seam allowance if required.

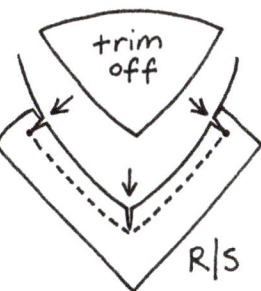

**4.** Turn through and press. Press under the raw edges and tuck in each end. Stitch next to the edge.

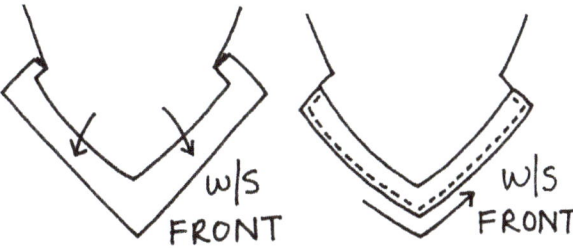

**5.** The back neck has a reinforcing piece rather than a facing. On the back body, lay the cutout from the front neck under the back, wrong sides together. Position the cutout horizontally. Stitch around the edges of the back neck.

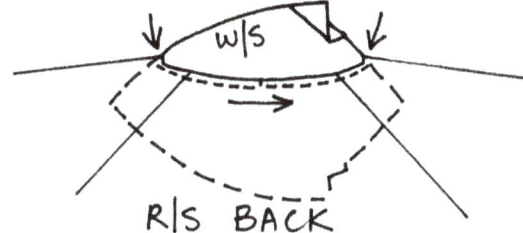

**6.** Trim off the excess. Fold under the edges to give a symmetrical shape. Stitch.

## Shoulders

**7.** Sew the shoulder seams, overlock and press towards the back.

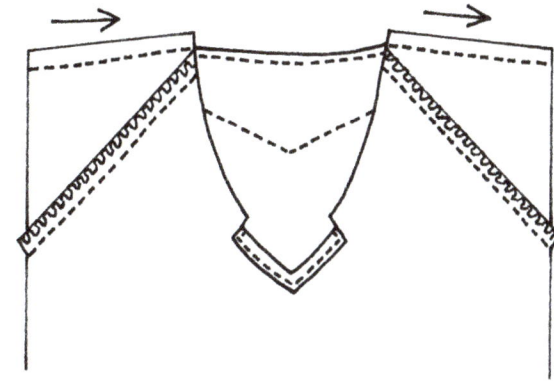

## Neckband

**8.** Open out the neckband/tie and sew one edge to the neckline, right sides together. Match the necktie's notches to the centre back, shoulders and each end. Press the seam towards the tie.

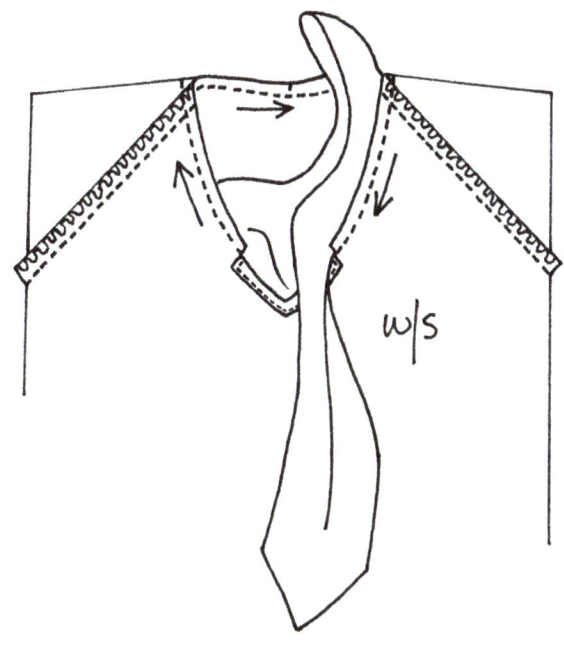

A top from a square

**9.** Bag out the ties: place the right sides together and sew along the edges. Trim the points, turn through and press.

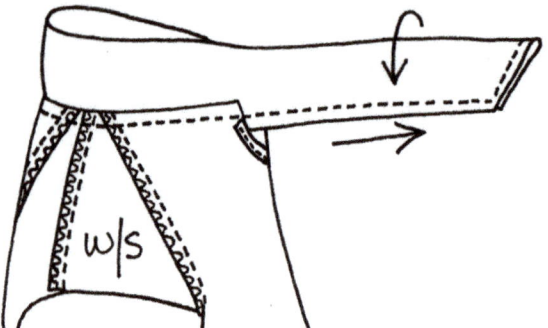

**10.** Turn under the remaining neck edge of the neckband and hand sew into place (recommended) OR pin carefully and stitch-in-the-ditch (see page 12) on the right side of the neck.

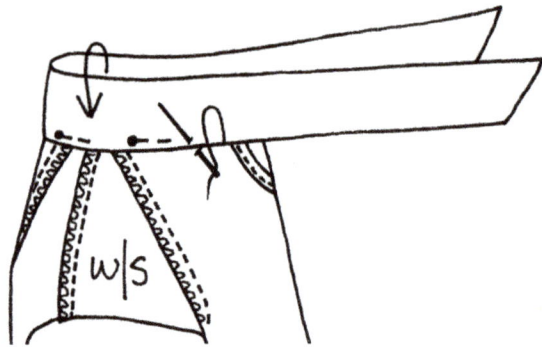

## Side seams
**11.** Mark the underarm point: measure down the sides 24.4 - 25 - 25.6 - 26.2 - 26.8cm.

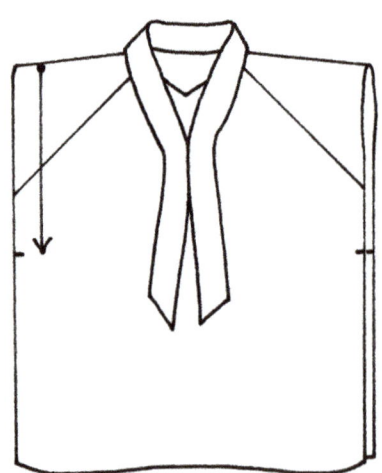

**12.** Sew the side seams. Overlock, running off at the underarm point.

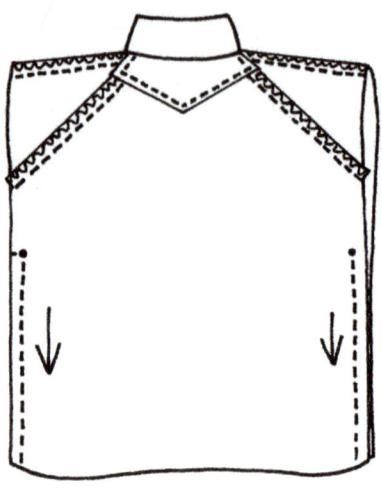

## Sleeves
**13.** Stitch each pair of remaining pieces together as shown, overlock and press.
Hem the diagonal ends and the short edge. The long, unhemmed edge gets sewn to the armhole.

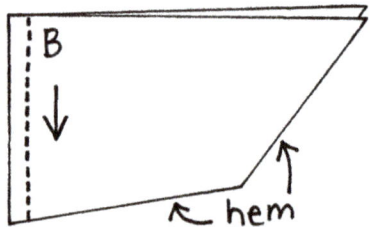

**14.** Fold the sleeve as shown and mark the armhole measurement (from Step 11) with a tiny snip.

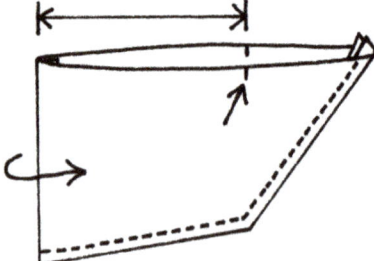

**15.** Lap the ends of the sleeve, aligning the notches. The notches will go to the shoulder and the seam will go to the underarm.

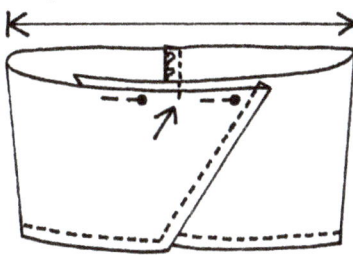

**16.** Sew the sleeve into the armhole opening, beginning and ending at the underarm. Either side can go to the front, but *make sure you've made a mirrored pair of sleeves*. Overlock the seam and press it towards the body.

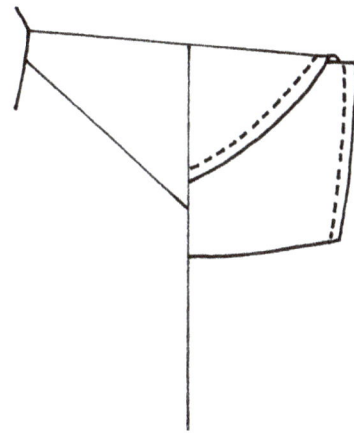

## Hem
**17.** Overlock the lower edge and hem the body with a 1cm hem.

## Notes

✂ Optional: pipe or topstitch the triangular front and back seams.

✂ For a two piece dress, make a wrap skirt (page 88) in the same fabric. Make the skirt with no ties so you don't have too many bows in the same outfit.

✂ Suggestion: for a top without sleeves, just hem the armholes. You might need to sew the underarm higher so your bra doesn't show.
To use up the sleeve sections, stitch them into a headscarf and hem the edges.

✂ Cotton fabric is suggested for this top because it's stable and therefore easy to draw on, cut and handle. However, unstable/flimsy fabrics such as rayon aren't impossible to use, just a little harder. Feel free to substitute a fabric according to your sewing comfort level.

# hooded blouson

*Simple geometric shapes make a modern top with clean bold lines. The side seams conceal deep pockets.*

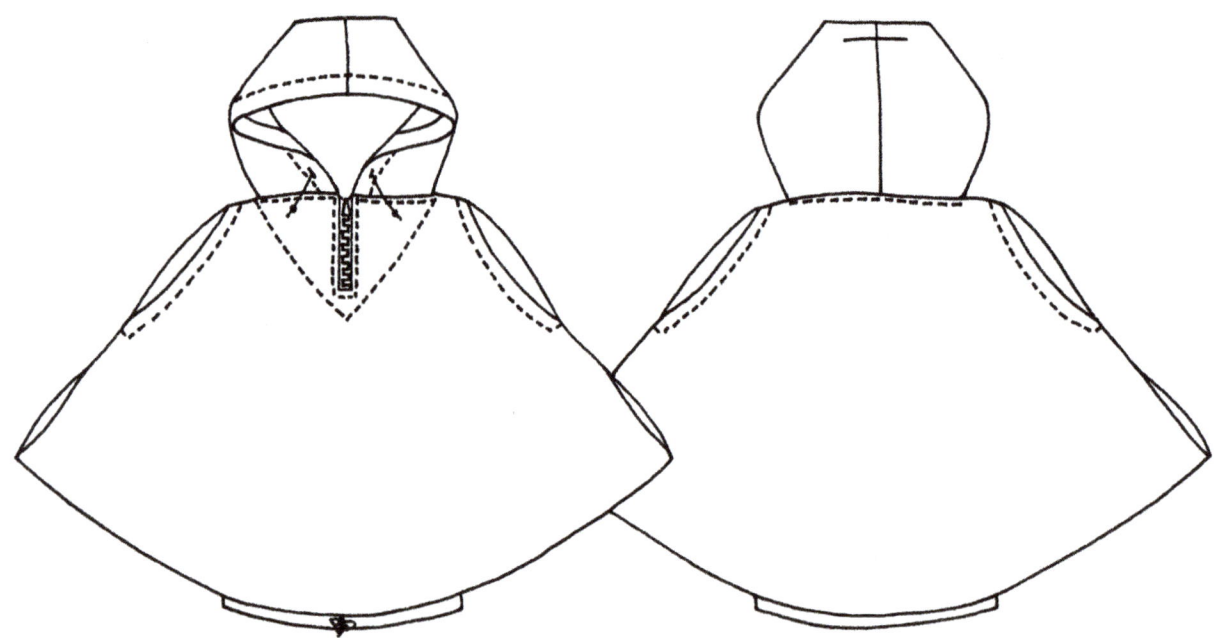

**Fabric** Woven fabric, 115cm wide. For all sizes you'll need *exactly* 130cm. If the fabric is a slightly different width, use that length plus 15cm. Suitable fabrics include medium weight cottons and linens, in plain, stripe or pattern. Nylon ripstop could be used for a windproof top. Ensure the fabric isn't too stiff or crisp or the sides will stick out like wings. Thick, soft fabrics are also suitable (see *Notes* on page 29).

**Notions** For the lower edge: 105 - 110 - 115 - 120 - 125cm of 25mm bias binding and the same of tubular elastic cord. 1 locking toggle with spring. 13 - 13 - 13 - 15 - 15cm chunky zip. Strip of lightweight interfacing 5cm x 30cm. Thread. Optional: 1m of cord for hood.

**Sizes** 8-10-12-14-16. Note that a size 16 top will also fit a size 18 or 20 body.

**Finished length** Approximately 63cm from the shoulder, all sizes.

**Seam allowances** **1cm** seams are included.

## To cut

**1.** Cut off a strip of fabric 15cm wide and cut it in half to use as pocket bags.

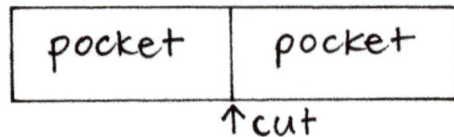

**2.** You should have remaining a perfect square of fabric 115cm x 115cm. Fold it in half diagonally right sides together, and press lightly.

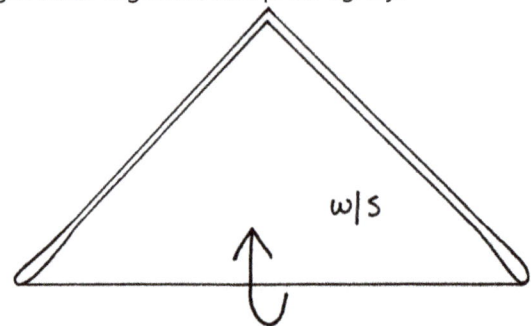

**3.** Fold it in half again so the triangle has a centre line. Lightly press a crease, then unfold.

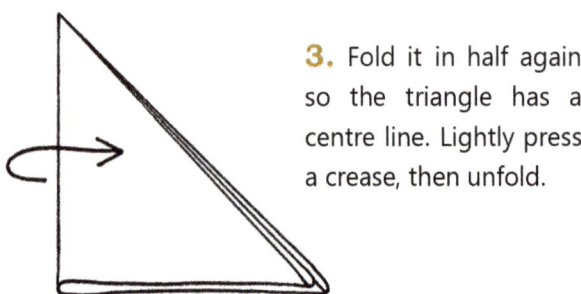

**4.** Draw in removable chalk: half the bust measurement, plus 5cm. For sizes 8-16 this is 48.5 - 51 - 53.5 - 56 - 58.5cm. DO NOT cut anything yet.

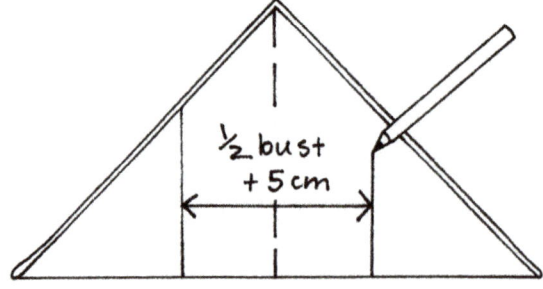

**5.** Fold up each corner so the fold sits on the chalk line. Cut where indicated along the folds.

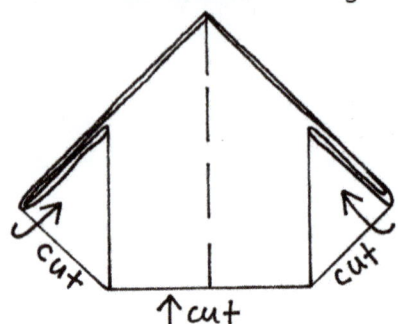

Open out the cut-off bits: the two squares will be used for the hood.

The two large pieces are the front and back.

## To sew
**Seam allowances:** all 1cm.

### Measure for the armholes and sew the neck

**1.** On the front and back, fold down and press the top edge to measure 34.3 - 35.5 - 36.7 - 37.9 - 39.1cm across. This is the neckline.

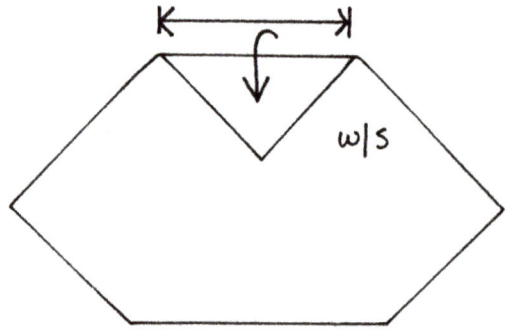

**2.** Measure from the fold and mark a notch for the armhole opening 22.4 - 23 - 23.6 - 24.2 - 24.8cm down.

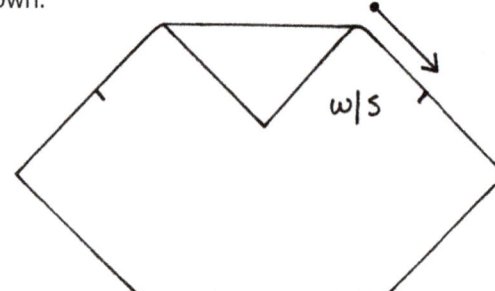

24    Zero Waste Sewing

**3.** Open out the triangular folds.
On the **back**, cut off a triangle 1cm above the fold line. The triangle will be used behind the front zip.

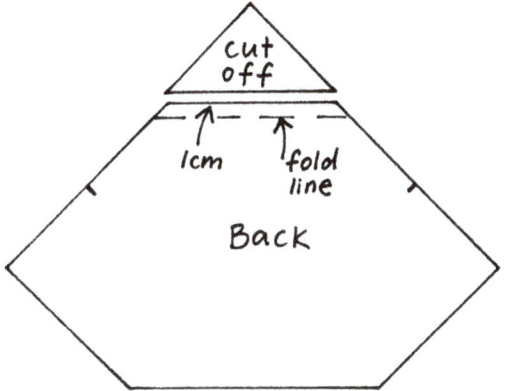

**4.** Overlock:
The lower edge of the triangle.
The top edge of the back.
Each side of the armhole opening, taking the overlocking several centimetres past the armhole notches. You should still be able to locate the armhole notches through the overlocking.

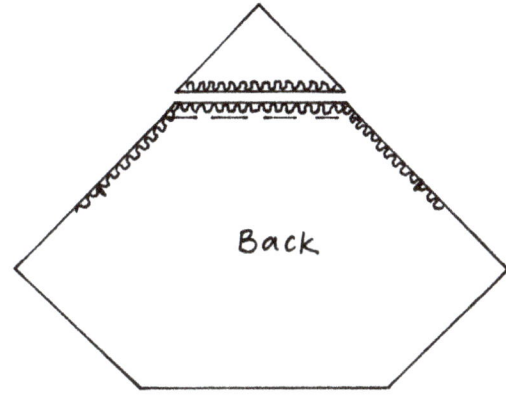

**5.** Press under 1cm as shown (overlocking not shown for clarity).

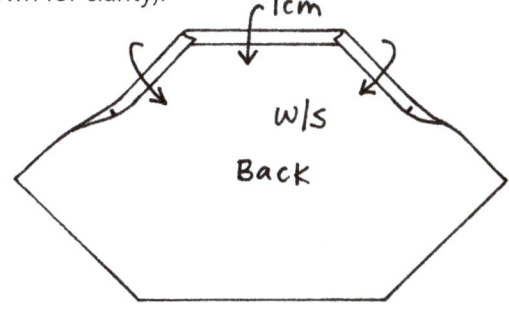

**6.** On the **front**, overlock each side of the armhole opening separately, extending the overlocking several centimetres past the armhole notch and past the neckline fold.

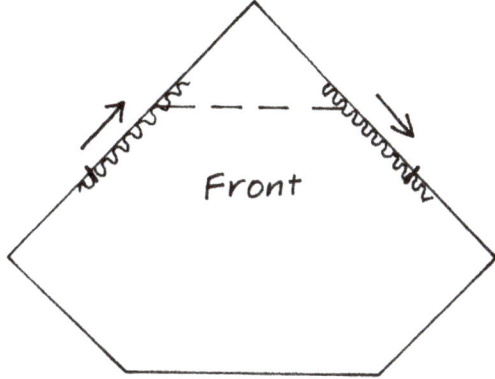

**7.** Press under 1cm along the raw edges of the neckline triangles and the overlocked armholes (overlocking not shown for clarity).

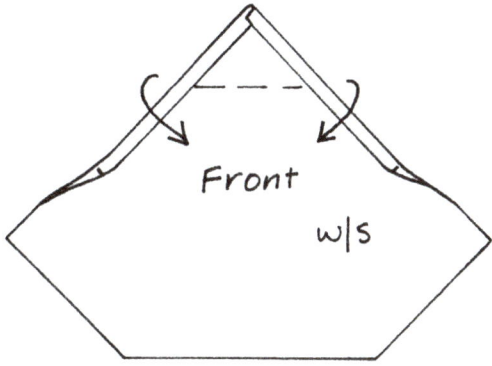

**8.** Fuse the strip of 5cm x 30cm interfacing onto the front. Position it centrally and on equal sides of the fold line.

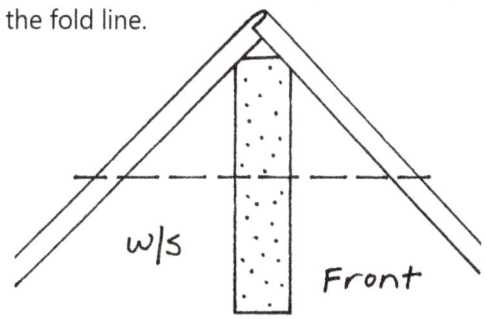

A top from a square   25

**9.** Fold the front triangle right sides together back along the fold you pressed. In the centre, stitch a 1cm wide, 3-sided rectangle the same length as your zip. Use a shorter stitch length for strength.

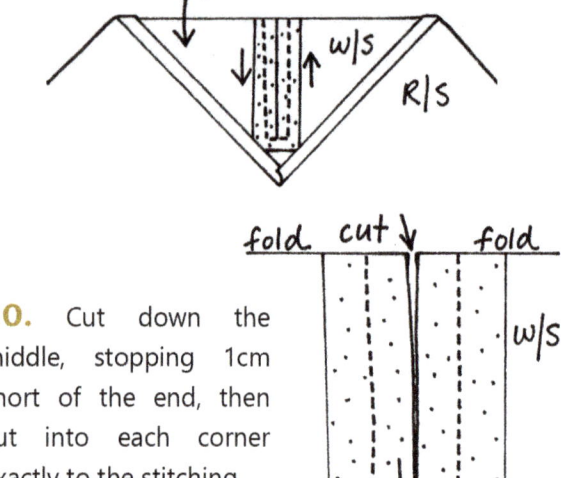

**10.** Cut down the middle, stopping 1cm short of the end, then cut into each corner exactly to the stitching.

Turn through to the right side and press, so you have a narrow rectangular "window" for the zip.

**11.** Fold down the top of the zip tabs and stitch.

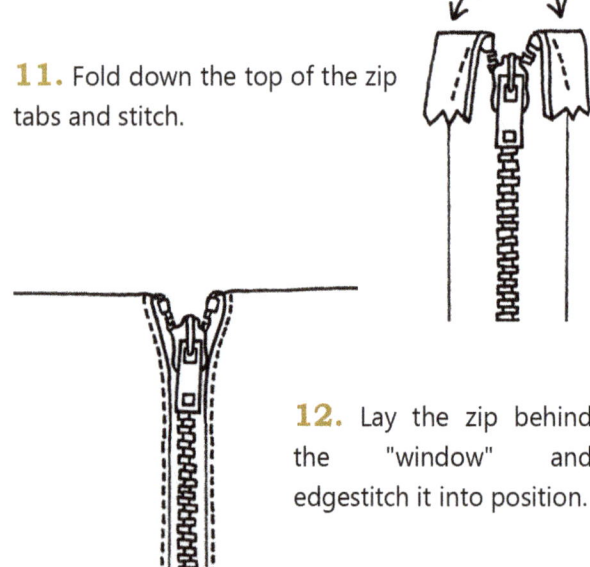

**12.** Lay the zip behind the "window" and edgestitch it into position.

**13.** Place the back and front right sides together. Align the neckline folds and stitch 3cm along the fold to create the shoulder seams, stitching through the pressed-down edges of the armholes.

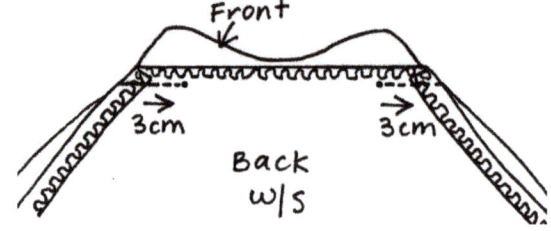

**14.** Lay the neckline flat and stitch the front triangle to the front.

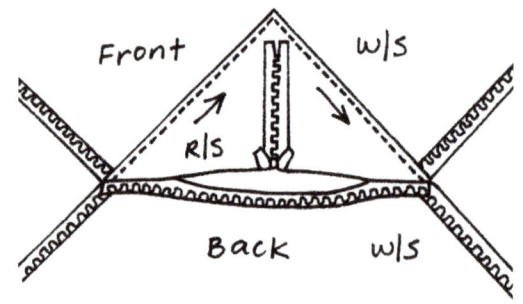

**15.** Take the triangle you cut off the back in Step 3 on page 25. Fold over the top edge 2.5cm and stitch.

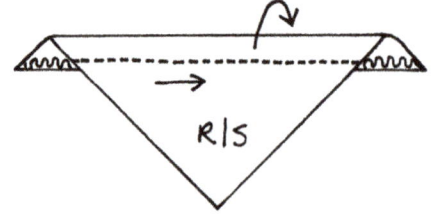

**16.** Trim the triangle to measure 14cm across the top and 15 - 15 - 15 - 17 - 17cm on the sides. Overlock the sides.

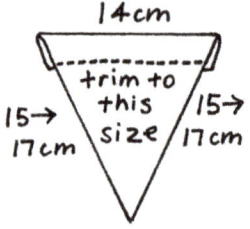

**17.** Sew the triangle behind the zip, stitching it to the zip tape from the back, using a zipper foot.

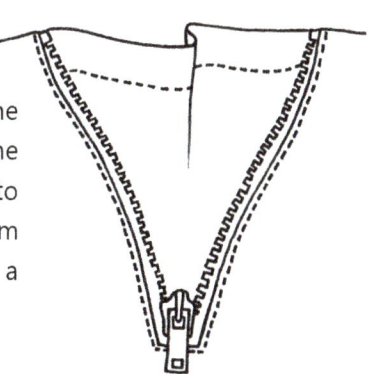

## Make the pockets

**18.** Take each pocket bag piece and stitch a short end each to the front and back, with the right sides together.

Take a **5mm** seam. No need to overlock.

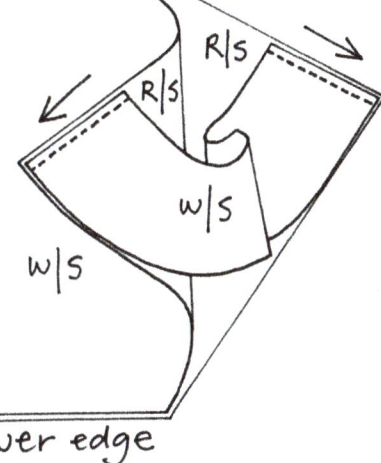

**19.** Press the pocket bag up and understitch (see page 12) on the pocket bag side.

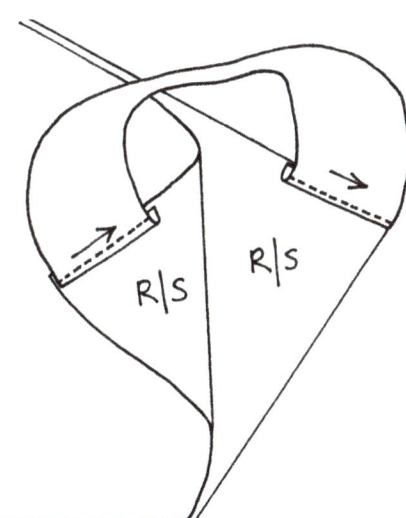

**20.** Sew the side seam below the armhole notch, pivot at the pocket and sew one side of the pocket bag. Overlock, running off just below the underarm notch.

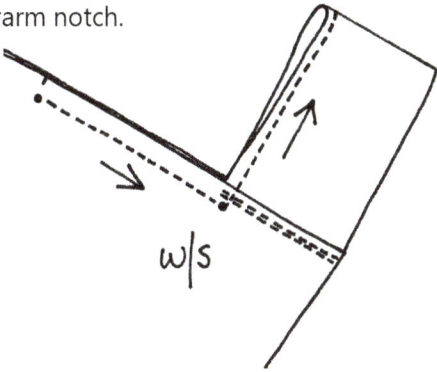

**21.** Fold the pocket down along the 1cm stitching line. Sew the rest of the side seam and pocket together, so the pocket bag is caught into the side seam.

At the raw lower edge, finish the stitching 5mm short of the end. Overlock the seam. Fold the other side's pocket so the garment has a mirrored left and right, and sew it in the same way.

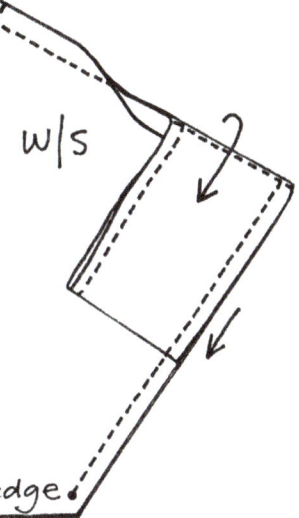

## Armholes

**22.** Stitch around the armholes.

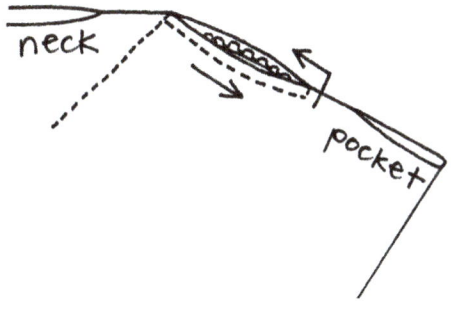

A top from a square

## Hood

**23.** Place the two squares right sides together and sew two sides. Overlock. Optional: sew this as a French seam.

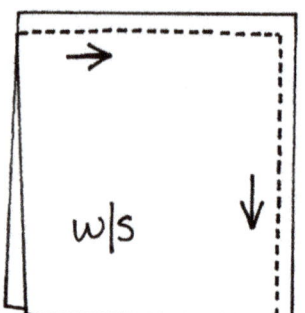

**24.** Open out the point and stitch across the top corner of the hood 14cm across (7cm each side of the seam). Trim off the triangle leaving a 1cm seam allowance and overlock. Save the triangle to place behind the buttonholes in the hood.

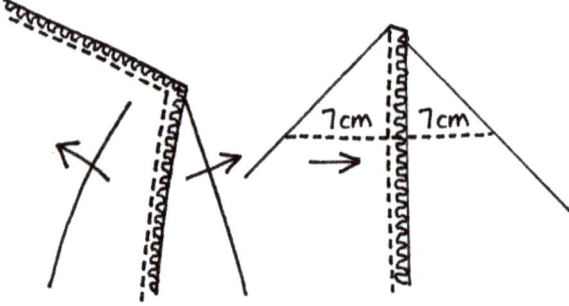

**25.** On the edge that will surround the face, press under 1cm then 2.5cm to form a casing.

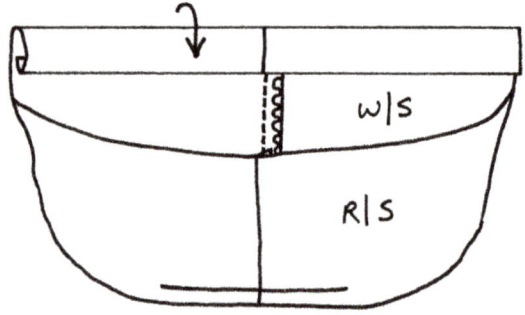

**26.** Open it out and make a buttonhole on each side, centred in the casing and 5cm up. Make the buttonholes through a single layer, backed with the triangular offcuts from the top of the hood.

Make each buttonhole big enough for the (optional) cord to pass through.

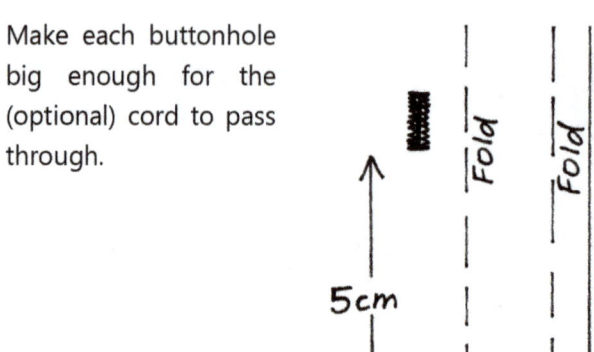

**27.** Stitch the hood casing, holding it taut.

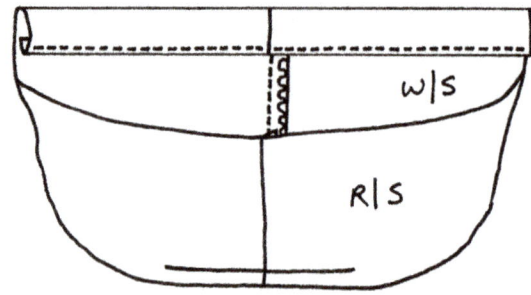

**28.** Overlock the entire raw (lower) edge of the hood.

## Attach the hood to the neckline

**29.** Divide the neck of the hood into quarters and mark with pins. Mark the centre back neckline of the top with a pin.

Sit the hood inside the neckline by 1cm and compare the neckline with the hood size.

Zero Waste Sewing

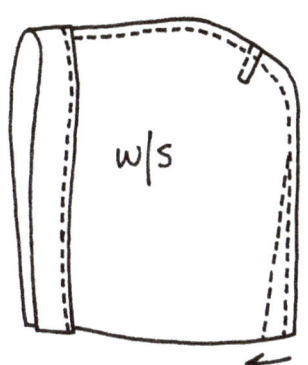

Each size will fit differently. Take in the hood's back neck to fit the neckline. Size 16 should need about 2cm and smaller sizes will need more.

**30.** Edgestitch the hood on with the neckline facing up. Optional: insert a cord through the hood's casing.

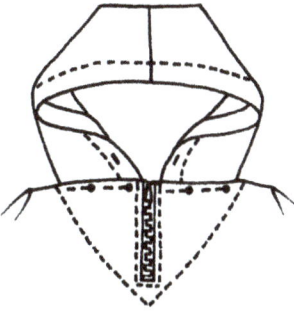

## Waist casing

**31.** Sew the 25mm bias binding to the lower edge to create a casing: mark the centre front (CF) on the body. Begin and end at this point, folding back the ends of the bias. Place the *right* side of the bias binding onto the *wrong* side of the body. Stitch in the binding's crease

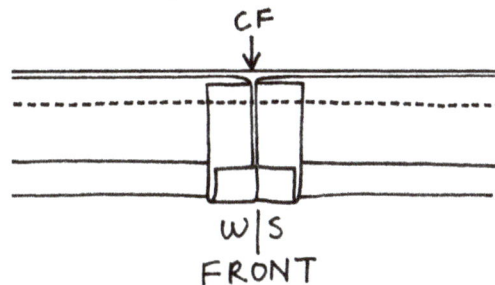

**32.** Press the seam towards the binding. Bring the binding over to the right side and edgestitch it in place.

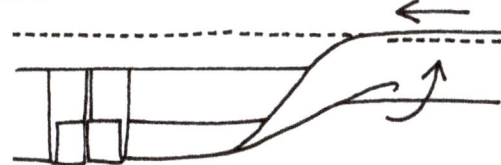

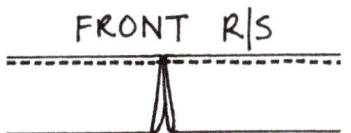

**33.** Insert the tubular cord elastic through the casing and attach a toggle to the ends.

## Notes

✂ Don't want a hood? Use the hood pieces to make pockets instead of a separate strip.

✂ Make the hood detachable: Hem the hood's lower edge. Sew rouleau loops (made from bias binding) to the sides, back and front of the hood. Sew plain flat buttons inside the neckline to attach it to the loops.

✂ For much smaller sizes, experiment with a shorter length of fabric, for example, 1m x 115cm wide, and cut a 15cm wide strip off the selvedge side for the pockets (leaving a 1m square).

✂ Do you have big hands? Cut the pockets wider, say, 18cm or even 20cm.

✂ For very thick, soft fabrics, use a lighter weight fabric for the pockets to stop them being too bulky. You'll need 15cm of lightweight fabric for the pockets and only 115cm of thick fabric for the top. You can also do this if you don't have enough fashion fabric for the pockets.
Thick fabric may require open seams (on the hood etc), and you might need to overlock *before* sewing the seams because an overlocker's foot is too wide for a 1cm seam allowance.

A top from a square

# yo-yo top

A yo-yo, or Suffolk puff, will be familiar to quilters. It's a circle of fabric gathered around the edge and pulled tight, then pressed flat with the gathering on top, forming a smaller circle. The centre of this top is a yo-yo with the gathering on the inside. The top is backless so a bra can't be worn, but the front detail suits smaller busts and is quite secure to wear.

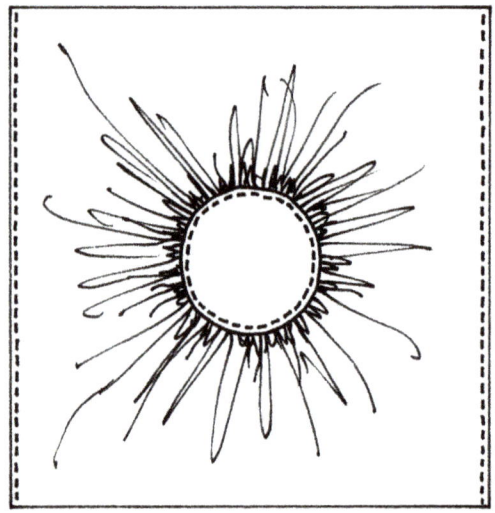

**Fabric** Woven fabric, approximately 115cm square for all sizes. The fabric needn't be exactly 115cm wide; as narrow as 107cm will still tie around a 76cm waist. Suitable fabrics include lightweight and quilting weight cotton, fluid silk satin and rayon, in plain, stripe, check or pattern. If you have a square scarf of a suitable size you could use that.

**Notions** Thread.

**Sizes** One size. It fits any size that can have one side of the square tied around the waist.

**Seam and hem allowances** 1cm seams and hems are included.

## Make a pattern

1. In cardboard (cereal box weight), cut a circle with a 13cm radius. Mark the quarter points around the edge. This is the template for the cutout.

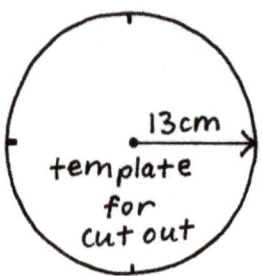

Cut another circle in cardboard with a 6.7cm radius. This is the template for pressing the yo-yo.

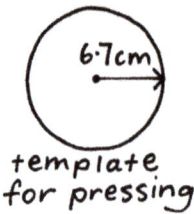

## To cut

1. Take the square of fabric and press it lightly into quarters to find the centre.

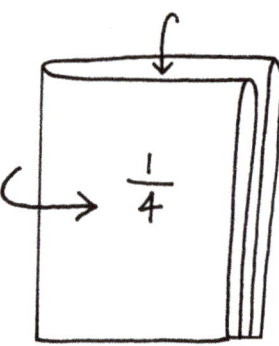

2. Use the larger, 13cm radius, cardboard template to cut out a circle in the centre. Reserve the circle of fabric.

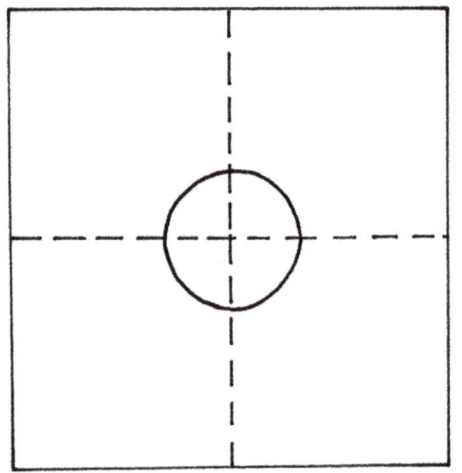

## To sew

**Seam allowances:** all 1cm.

### Make the yo-yo

1. On the circle of fabric, press under 6mm all the way around.

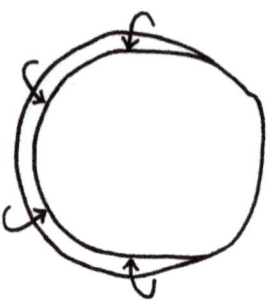

2. Thread a needle with 2 strands of thread and tie a strong knot in the end. Sew small running stitches in the centre of the 6mm hem. Don't finish off at the end; leave the needle dangling.

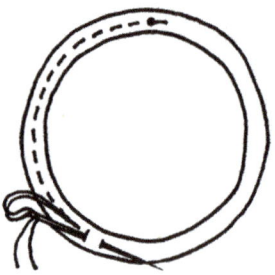

3. Pull up the gathers firmly over the smaller cardboard circle. There will be a hole about 2.5cm wide in the centre. Press the whole thing hard to give a crisp fold line. Remove the cardboard and put back the gathers to how they were pressed. Fasten off the thread. Yo-yo complete.

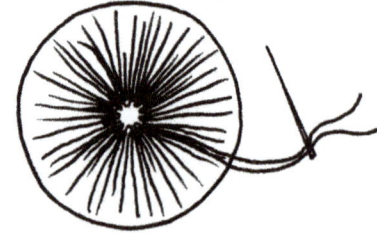

Fold the yo-yo in four and mark the quarters with pins.

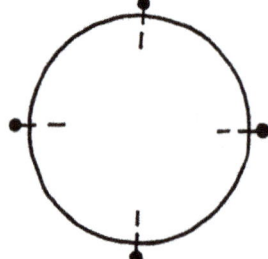

32  Zero Waste Sewing

## Prepare the hole

**4.** On the square with the hole, carefully overlock or zig zag around the hole to neaten the edge.

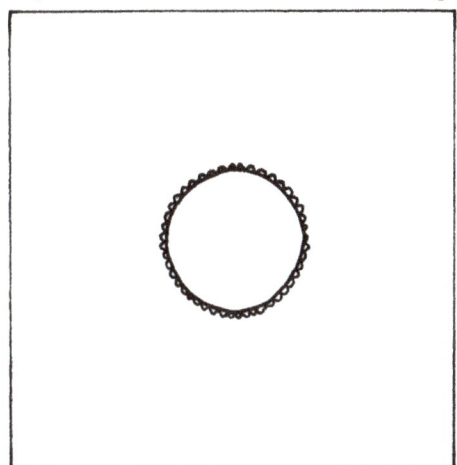

**5.** Machine sew two rows of long gathering stitches around the hole, one 1cm away from the edge and the other between that and the edge.

## Sew the yo-yo in

**6.** With the yo-yo's smooth side facing the front, pull up the gathers to fit behind it, matching the quarter points. Sew in place, stitching on the edge. You could stitch multiple rows of stitching around the yo-yo if the fabric is plain. Alternatively, sew the yo-yo in place by hand.

Hem the edges of the square with a narrow hem. If the selvedges are suitable to leave as-is, you'll only need to hem the two cut sides.

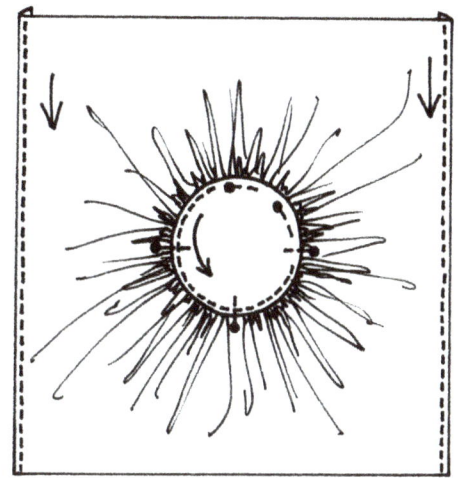

## To wear

To wear, tie the top two corners around the neck like a giant napkin, then tie the lower two corners around the waist, tucking in any excess fabric into the waist folds.

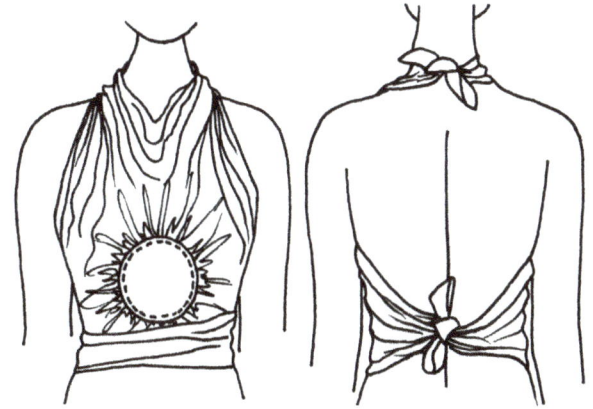

## Notes

✂ The yo-yo can be smaller or larger. My original sample had a 10cm radius cutout and a 5.3cm radius yo-yo. Note that the yo-yo template needs to be slightly more than half the cutout size because the gathering doesn't meet exactly in the centre.

A top from a square

# side drape top

*Fluid jersey paired with simplicity of cut make for a garment that's effortless to sew and wear. This sophisticated tunic is composed of two rectangles, with one armhole in the side and the other in the top.*

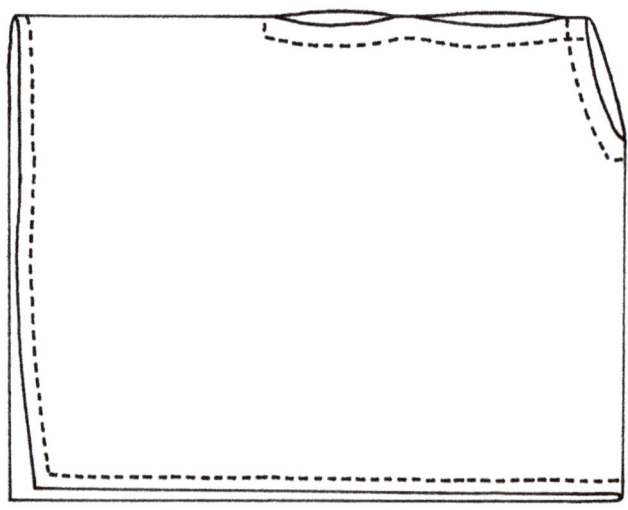

**Fabric** Knit fabric with stretch in one direction only, approximately 120cm wide. If you're very tall you can use wider fabric, for example 130cm or even 140cm. You'll need *exactly* 180cm for all sizes. Suitable fabrics include poly/cotton interlock and t-shirt fabric, in plain, stripe or pattern.

**Notions** 1 set of bra strap holders (home-made or purchased). Thread. Also: stretch machine needle and stretch twinneedle for hems.

**Sizes** Any. Sizes 8-10-12-14-16 are described in the instructions with options for larger sizes.

**Finished length** Approximately 85cm at the shortest part and 118cm at the longest.

**Seam and hem allowances** 2.5cm seams and hems are included.

## To cut

**1.** Cut the fabric in half so you have 2 x 90cm lengths of 120 wide fabric. Lay the two pieces on top of one another, right sides together.
On one side, trim off the selvedges in a 2.5cm wide strip—you'll use these for stabilising the neckline.

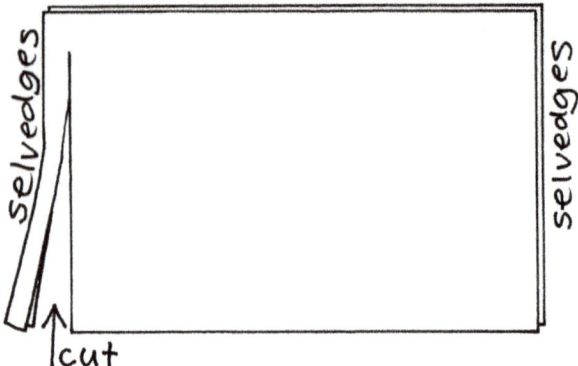

If the selvedges aren't good enough, use a strip of 2.5cm wide woven fabric or tape instead (see Step 3 on the next page).

**2.** From the other side, with the intact selvedge, measure along the top from right to left (including the selvedge in these measurements).
**From "start here":** 7.9 - 8.5 - 9.1 - 9.7 - 10.3cm (add 6mm for each size thereafter).
**Shoulder:** 3cm.
**Neck:** 25.8 - 27 - 28.2 - 29.4 - 30.6cm (and 30.6cm for all sizes thereafter).
**Other shoulder:** 3cm.
**Arm:** 19.9 - 20.5 - 21.1 - 21.7 - 22.3cm (add 6mm for each size thereafter).

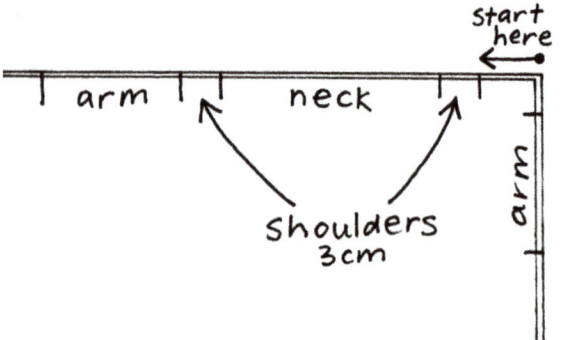

**3.** Measure down vertically:
**Seam allowance:** 2.5cm.
**Arm:** 19.9 - 20.5 - 21.1 - 21.7 - 22.3cm (add 6mm for each size thereafter).

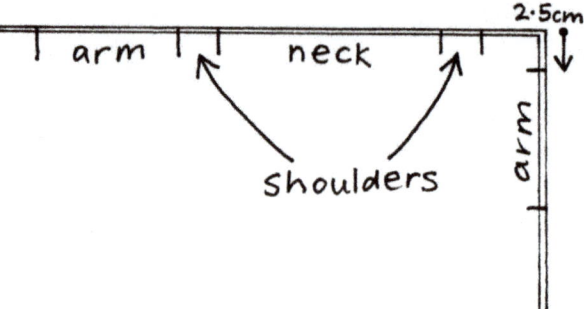

**4.** Mark in the 2.5cm stitching lines with chalk.

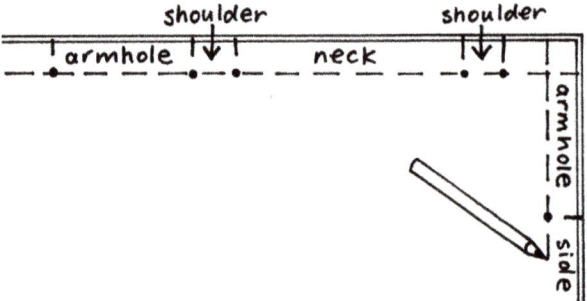

**5.** On the vertical armhole, draw in the diagonal armhole hem line, then trim off the corner 5cm from this line.

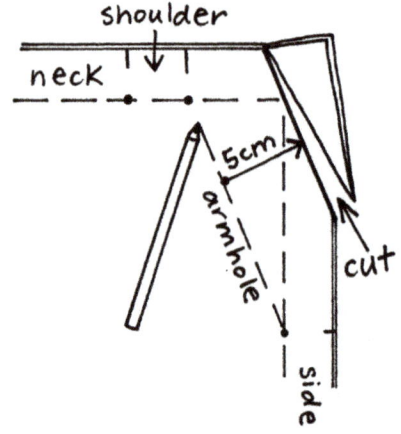

# To sew

**Seam allowances:** all 2.5cm. Use a stretch stitch or mini zigzag unless stated.

## Vertical armhole

**1.** Sew the side seam below the armhole, taking a 2.5cm seam. Press the seam open.

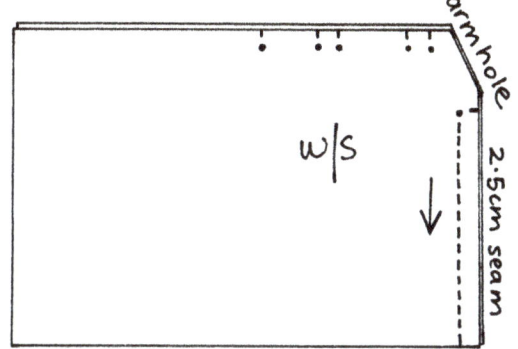

**2.** Fold the diagonal edge 2.5cm then another 2.5cm. Straight stitch down one side, across the bottom, then the other side. This makes the vertical armhole.

Note that a small pleat will form on each side of the V, due to the angle.

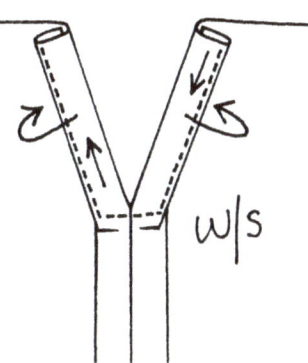

## Neckline

**3.** On the wrong side, sew the 2.5cm wide selvedges to each top edge, extending to just past the armhole. Use a long straight stitch.

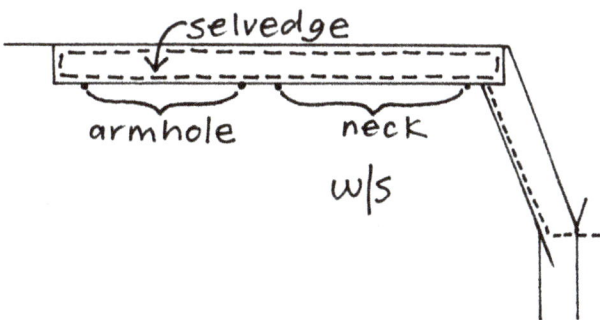

**4.** With the right sides together, sew the shoulders and below the armhole. Take a 2.5cm seam allowance and *just* catch the edge of the selvedge (from the previous step) in as you sew.

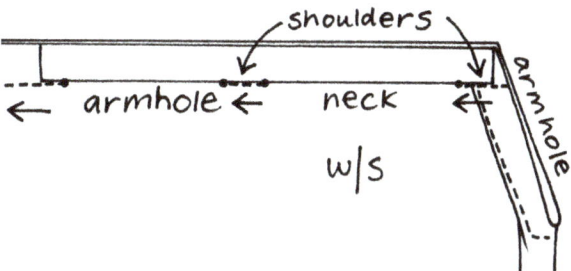

**5.** Press the seam open. Stitch the edge down, pivoting at the underarm of the armhole. Use straight stitch to match the armhole in Step 2.

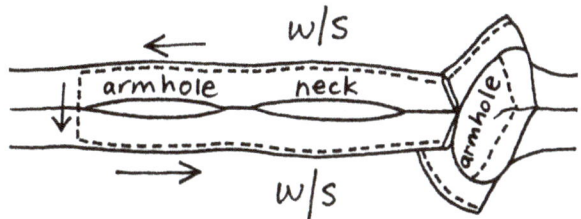

Optional: trim the seam allowance below each armhole to 6mm. There's no need to overlock if the fabric doesn't fray.

**6.** Hem the lower edge and the open side using the twinneedle OR a coverstitch machine if you have one. If the cut edge looks okay as-is, you may decide not to do a hem. Press.

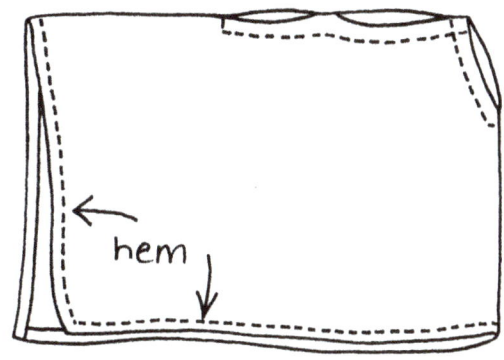

**7.** Sew bra strap holders under the shoulder seams to keep the top in place when it's worn.

A top from a square 37

# geometric top

*An interesting yet very simple cut defines this geometic top with a sculptural neckline. It's made from two squares, two rectangles and two triangles. The back and front are the same. The low underarm is too restrictive for, say, playing volleyball, but there's plenty of across-back movement for driving or sipping champagne.*

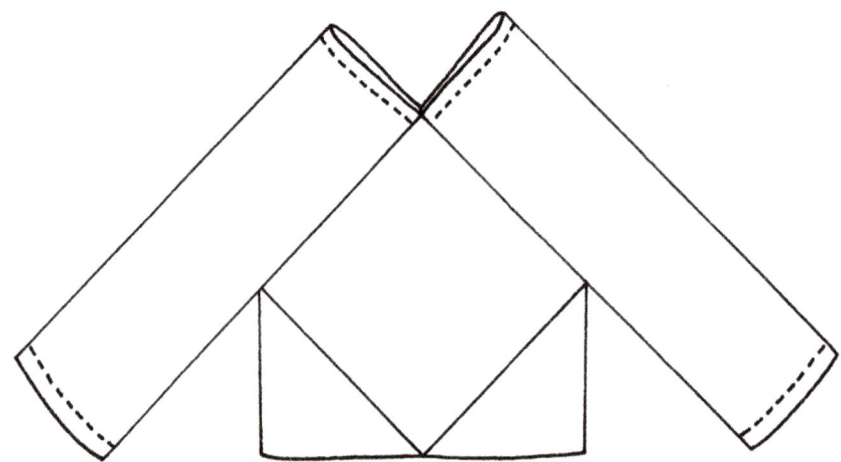

**Fabric** Woven fabric approximately 150cm wide. For sizes 8-16 you'll need *exactly* 65 - 68.4 - 72 - 75.6 - 79cm. The fabric need not be exactly 150 wide; sizes 8-16 will fit on fabric at least 130 - 137 - 144 - 152 - 158cm wide but preferably 4cm-8cm wider. If your fabric isn't wide enough, see *Notes* on page 42. Suitable fabrics include medium weight cotton, linen, silk and taffeta in plains, one or two-way prints and stripes. Avoid very thick fabrics since the armhole junction is bulky, and avoid floppy and very fine fabrics which won't suit the sculptural neckline. Ikat and oriental prints look very good in this pattern.

**Notions** 2 strips of lightweight interfacing for the neck, maximum size 4cm x 40cm. Thread.

**Sizes** 8-10-12-14-16. The armhole becomes too low for sizes bigger than 16.

**Finished length** Approximately 42 - 44 - 47 - 50 - 53cm from the centre front neck. Note that the length *cannot* be altered, however the sleeve length can.

**Seam and hem allowances** **1cm** seams and hems are included.

Zero Waste Sewing

## Make a pattern

**1.** Draw a square on a piece of paper or card, the diagonal of which is equal to half the bust measurement, plus 2.5cm.

Sizes 8-16 will have a 46 - 48.5 - 51 - 53.5 - 56cm diagonal, with a side measurement of 32.5 - 34.2 - 36 - 37.8 - 39.5. See *Notes* on page 42 for how to calculate a side measurement from a square's diagonal.

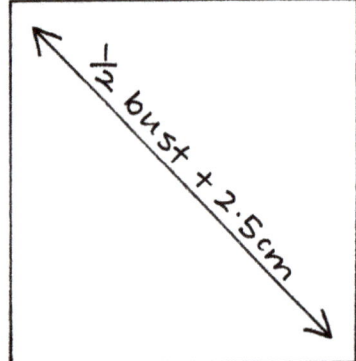

## To cut

**1.** Cut out 4 squares and 2 rectangles. The rectangles are just two squares placed next to each other (the rectangles are for the sleeves).

You should be able to fit four units across the width of the fabric with a strip remaining on the side. The size of the strip (which will be used for facings) will depend the size of the square. If there's no spare fabric at the sides, that's okay.

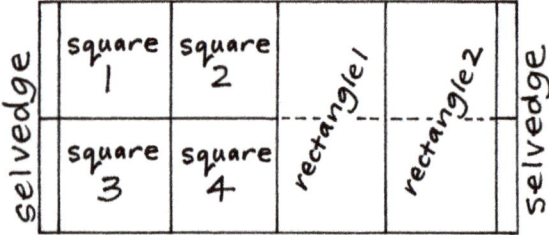

## To sew

**Seam allowances:** all 1cm.

### Sew the body

**1.** Iron two of the squares in half to make triangles, wrong sides of the fabric together. These form the left and right side panels, with the fold at the lower edge in lieu of a hem (they are double fabric in the garment). The top point of each triangle will sit at the underarm.

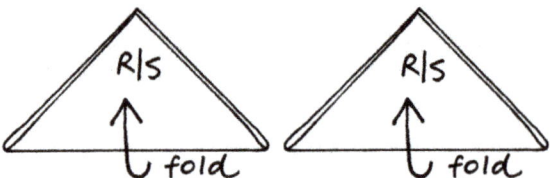

**2.** Lay a triangle onto one of the squares and sew, beginning 1cm in from the edge as shown.

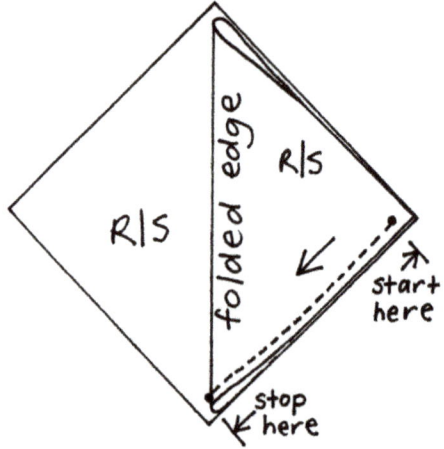

**3.** Repeat with the other triangle. Overlock.

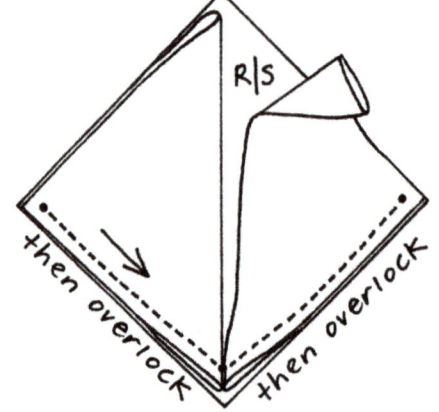

**4.** Open out and press the seams towards the square. The seam allowances at the central point should sit neatly folded on top of one another.

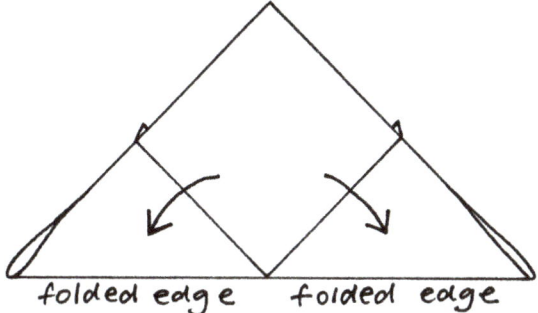

**5.** Lay the second square on top, right sides together, and bring up the second side of each triangle. Stitch, overlock and press as before.
You now have a tube with a pointed top back and front.

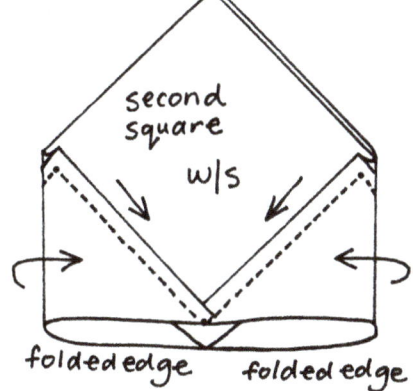

## Sew the sleeves and neckline

**6.** Take the two rectangles, which will become the sleeves.

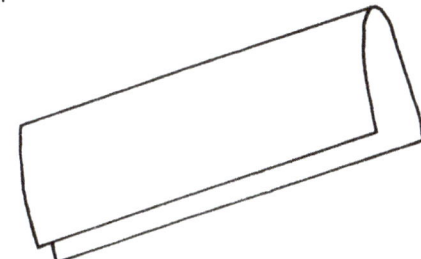

Cut a facing from one of the remainder strips left from cutting out, a maximum of 4cm wide.

Interface the strips if you think they need it (I didn't for the top in this book). Sew a facing to the short end of each rectangle—this will become the neckline.

If you have no strips to make a facing, substitute 25mm bias binding or simply take a 1cm hem.

**To sew the facing:**

Sew the strip onto one of the rectangle's short edges, right sides together. Overlock the other edge of the strip (or not, if it's a selvedge).

Press the seam allowance towards the strip and understitch (see page 12).

Press the facing to the wrong side, out of sight. Leave it just pressed or stitch it in place by hand or machine. Sewing it invisibly by hand is the most elegant solution (do this last if you prefer).

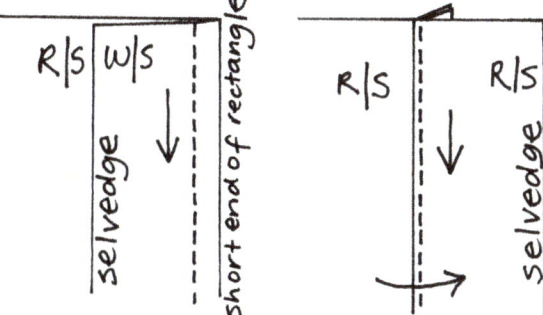

**7.** At this stage you can pin or tack the sleeves to the body and try the top on.

Note that the sleeve lengths will be different for each size. The smaller sizes have bracelet length sleeves, and the larger sizes will require a deep hem. Size 16 will have about a 10cm-12cm hem.

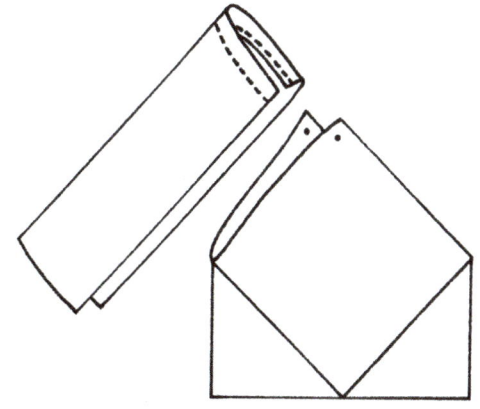

A top from a square

**8.** Sew the sleeve to the back and front of the body. Overlock the front seam now (overlock the back and the underarm seam in one fell swoop in the following step). Repeat with the second sleeve.

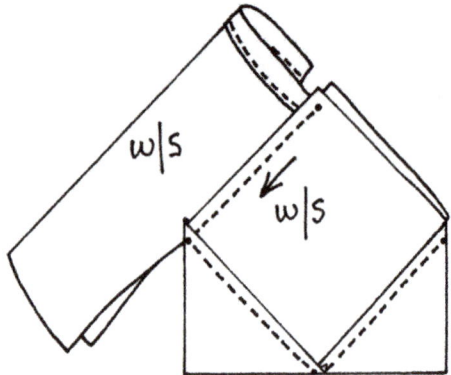

**9.** Turn the top inside out and sew the remaining (lower) part of the sleeve together. The sleeve seam can be tapered if you prefer. Overlock.
Press the armhole seams towards the body and away from the sleeve. At the centre back and front neck, catch the seam junction flat with a needle and thread.

**10.** Try the top on and finalize the sleeve length. Either hem it or sew a facing onto the edge in the same way as you did for the neckline.

# Notes

✂ If the fabric isn't wide enough to fit 4 units across, cut the sleeve rectangles *across* the fabric to give you shorter sleeves. The selvedges can become the sleeves' hems.

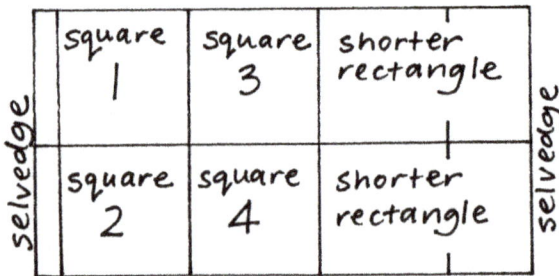

✂ Another idea if the fabric isn't wide enough or if you have odd pieces: a square or two can be pieced to make the most of the fabric. Use pieced squares for the side triangles, with most of the join on the inside. Position the visible join at the back.

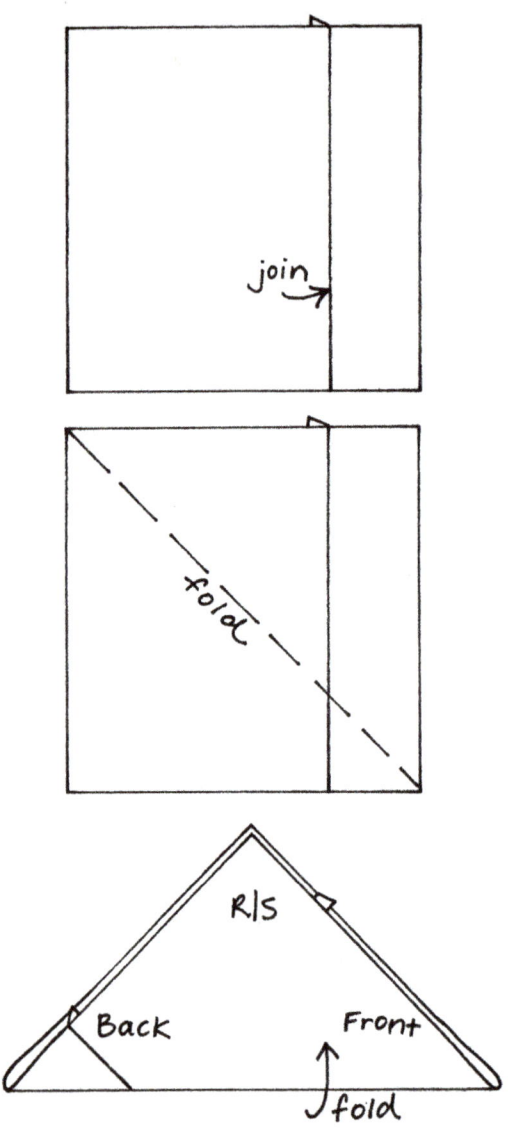

✂ Are you between sizes? Calculate the size of the square based on *your* bust measurement.
The formula to find the square's side from the diagonal is:
(Diagonal measurement)$^2$. Divide the answer by 2. Then find the square root of this.

One seam

# Introduction to one seam

I feel could write a whole book just on variations of this simple, versatile cut.

This is a very old patterncutting concept, reportedly found in garments worn by Bronze Age people recovered from Danish peat bogs. The cut is also known as a bog coat or jacket.

The same cut can be seen in baby clothes of the 18th and 19th centuries and it was the basis of Balenciaga's One Seam coat in 1961. Designers Yeohlee Teng and Maja Stabel use it for contemporary outerwear and Ikea uses it too—we have a one seam child's painting smock at home.

The one seam garment concept can also be knitted, and the seam can be grafted together resulting in a truly seamless garment. Ravelry.com contains many examples of knitted bog jackets.

The idea is very simple. The garment is cut from a square or rectangle of fabric and can be made to fit a man, woman or child. A pattern is unnecessary; the dimensions can easily be chalked onto the fabric and cut.

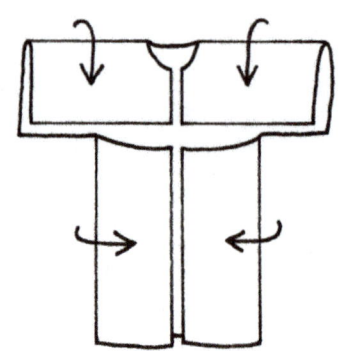

It has a front horizontal seam which is a continuation of the underarm seam. The body width determines the sleeve length.

It can also be cut another way for a seamless front:

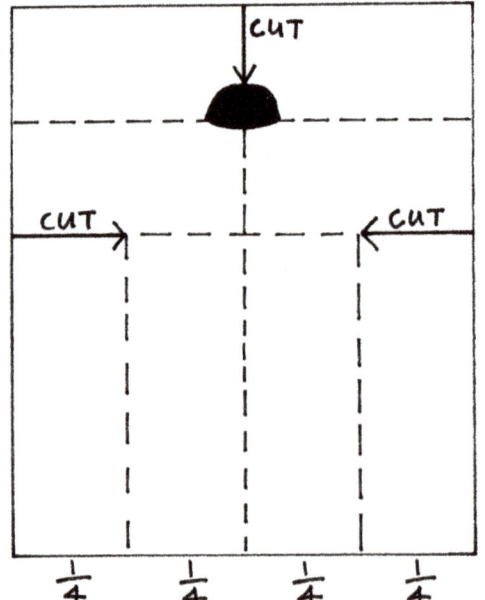

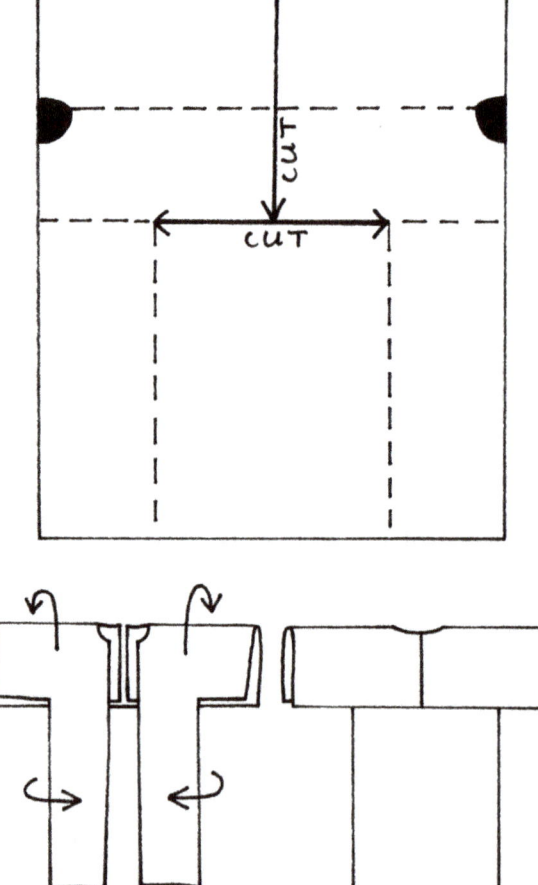

You'll notice in the second version that the upper centre back requires a seam allowance in the centre, otherwise it won't match the lower back unless it's a butted seam. A way to get a seam allowance for this is to add onto each side of the layout. If the width is less than 150cm, it could be centred on some 150cm wide fabric (conveniently, a person's handspan is about 150cm or just under):

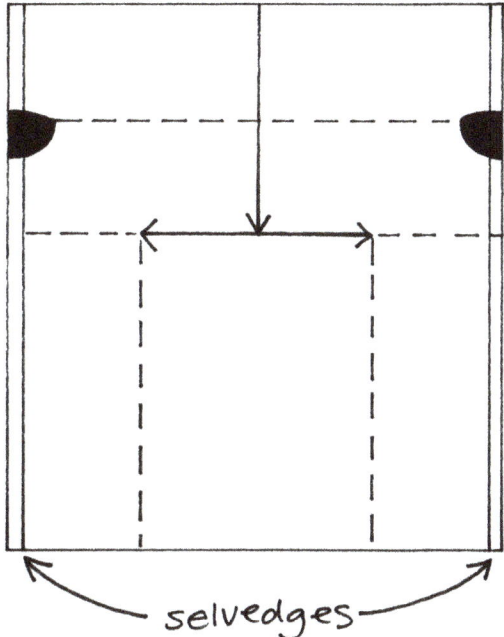

This has the bonus of providing a selvedge at the front, which can be folded back and used for a button stand or a pre-neatened seam allowance.

✂ For all of these layouts, 150cm wide fabric works well for adult sizes. The layout can be positioned either way on the fabric, depending on the width of the layout and the length desired.

✂ Modifications of this cut can have the lower front or lower back cut wider, and pleated or gathered onto the upper. Some of the projects in this book are designed this way.

✂ The armhole depth on any of these layouts can be raised or lowered without affecting much apart from the one seam position. 23cm is about the highest I would make a medium woman's armhole.

## Adjusting the sleeve length

Note that the sleeve underarm is always half the body width. If longer sleeves are desired the layout could look like this:

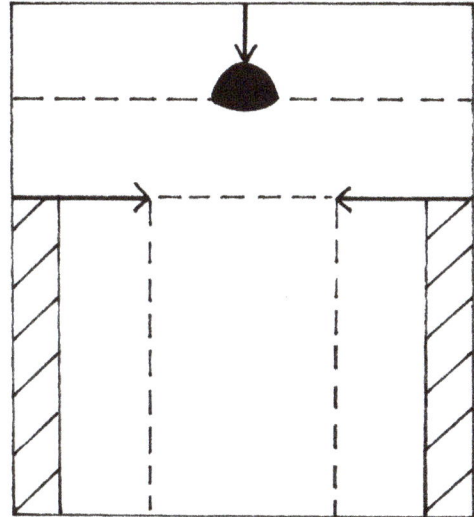

The shaded areas can be used to cut garment details such as belts, collars, pockets and front facings.

It can also be changed for short sleeves, with the garment details cut in the shaded areas at the end of the sleeves.

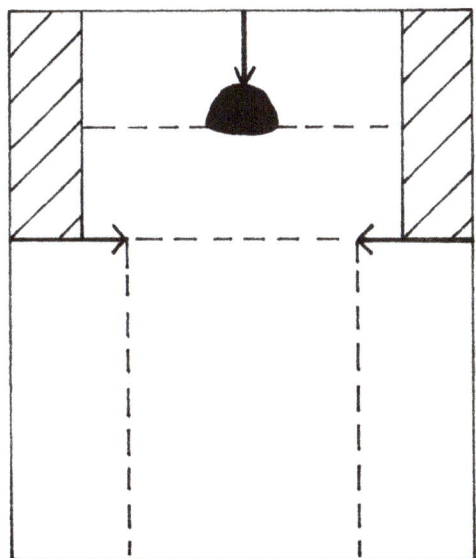

It could even be used for a sleeveless garment:

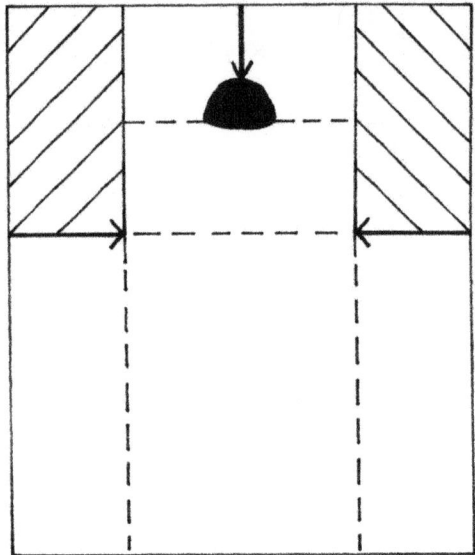

## Sewing the one seam

The one seam is sewn just like a regular plain seam, that is, place the right sides of the fabric together, match the edges and sew. Don't take a seam allowance of more than 1cm or you won't manage the underarm point (the apex of the slit).

I find the best way to sew the one seam is to overlock each side separately first.

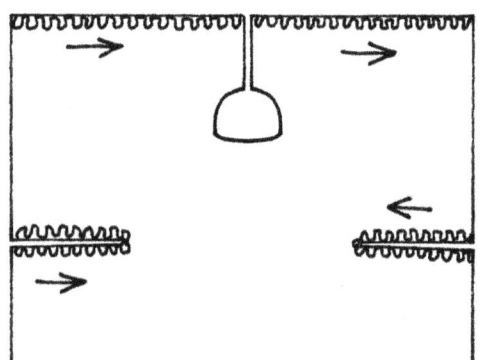

The apex of the slit will be difficult to overlock, but made easier if you can remember to cut it 3mm short of the end when you cut it out. Then, when overlocking, overlock up to the end of the slit and allow the machine to make just one cut (turn the overlocker's handwheel to accurately do this).

Then push all of the fabric to the left and hold the slit's point straight under the presser foot while it overlocks, to make sure you catch it in.

Pin the seam together first, working from each end until you reach the apex of the slit, which is the underarm point. Have the side with the apex uppermost.

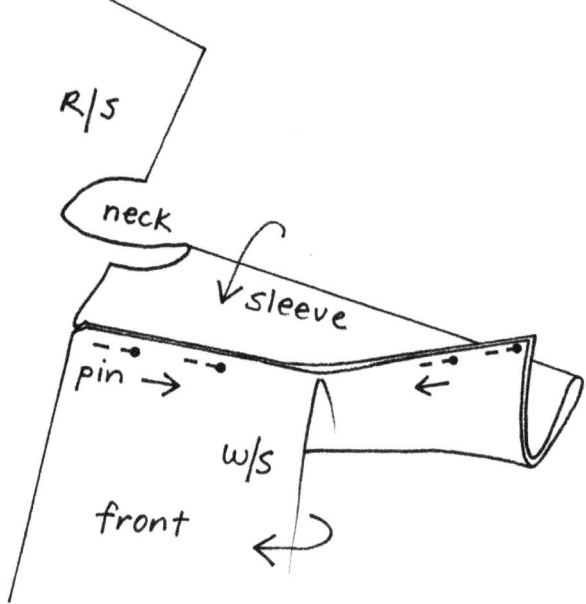

Dip the apex 5mm so you can stitch without pleating the fabric. Keep everything else at the 1cm seam allowance.

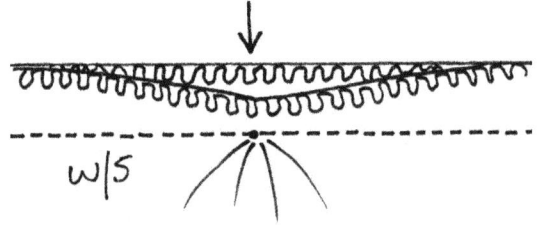

After sewing, press the seam allowance open.

The seam can be topstitched by machine or by hand, piped, bound, embellished or just left plain.

# Fitting notes

Since a one seam garment is dartless, it may hike up at the front due to the bust.

One way to counteract this is to add onto the front, either all the way along or just partially.

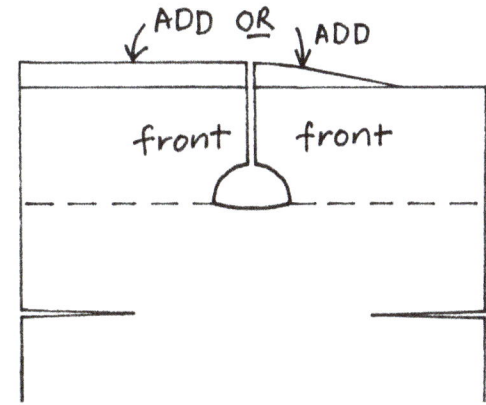

Another solution, which is essentially the same thing, is to move the neck hole further towards the back.
If the neck has already been cut, make the back neck deeper.

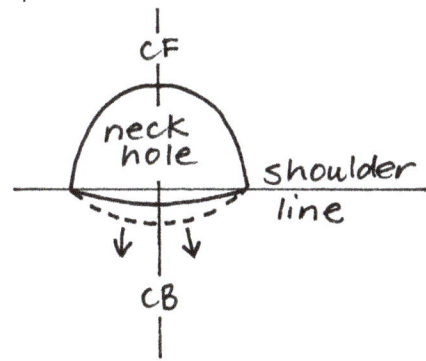

# Changing the silhouette

One seam garments, while cleverly cut, result in a simple T-shape with no shaping. However, it's a good starting point for a zero waste garment and has plenty of design potential.

✂ If the fabric width will allow it, some of the pattern's dimensions can be altered—sleeve depth, body width, neckline and length.

✂ The type and weight of the fabric can change the shape dramatically.

✂ The sleeves can be darted to taper them towards the wrist.

✂ Balenciaga's one seam coat had darts at the hem to give a fashionable cocoon shape.

✂ The sleeves can be gathered into a cuff.

✂ The body can be flared with godets.

✂ Extra fabric in the lower half of the garment can be pleated or gathered into the one seam.

✂ Frills and shirring can soften the rectangular shape.

✂ Shoulder pads? There's no shoulder seam to attach the pads to but they could be secured at the neckline and invisibly hand stitched to the fabric. Shoulder pads could also be attached underneath embellished shoulders.

✂ Create waist shaping with a belt, elastic in a casing, darts, shirring, waist tucks, smocking, eyelets and ribbon, button tabs, elasticized sections, a drawcord or lacing.

# simple dress

*This dress with an 80s vibe is an easy introduction to one seam garments. The idea for it was inspired by the fresh clean lines of American classic sportswear. Hilariously, my early samples looked like nighties, before I twigged that the fabric is the key to making this dress work. It requires a semi-stiff fabric that stands away from the body.*

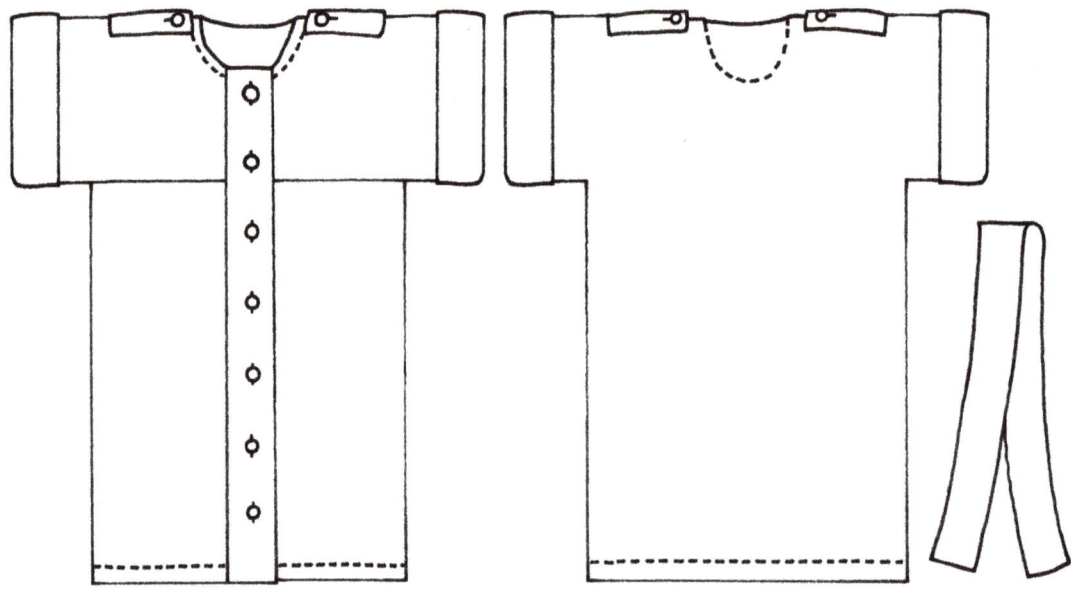

**Fabric** Woven fabric at least 150cm wide. For sizes 8-16 you'll need *exactly* 119 - 124 - 129 - 134 - 139cm. For other sizes, measure your hips and add 27cm. If you don't want a belt, subtract 12cm. Suitable fabrics include denim, firm cotton drill and taffeta. Stripes will run horizontally with the front band running vertically. Unsuitable for checks since they can't be matched.

**Notions** 2 strips of interfacing 12cm wide and approximately 92cm long for the front bands. 9 x 23mm buttons. Approximately 40cm of 12mm bias binding for the neck. Thread.

**Sizes** Any.

**Finished length** Approximately 99cm. If the fabric is wider than 150cm, the dress will be longer.

**Seam and hem allowances** **1cm** seams, **5mm** neck seam and **2.5cm** hem are included.

# To cut

**1.** For the optional tie belt, cut a strip 12cm wide running from selvedge to selvedge.
The remaining fabric will measure your hips plus 15cm. For sizes 8 - 16 this is 107 - 112 - 117 - 122 - 127cm.

Fold it in half so the two cut ends sit on top of one another, as shown. Put the wrong sides together.

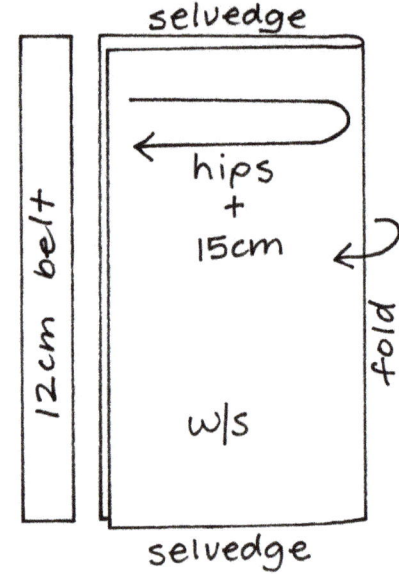

**2.** Cut off two strips along the top, each 12cm wide. These are for the front bands and epaulettes.

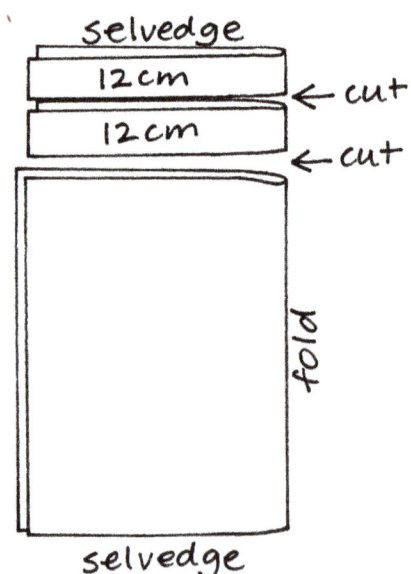

**3.** Using tailor's chalk, draw in the front and back sleeves, each measuring 26.1 - 26.7 - 27.3 - 27.9 - 28.5cm. Add 6mm for each size thereafter.

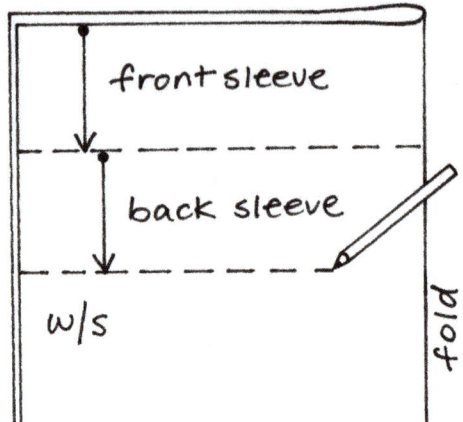

## Draw in the neck

**4.** The neckline can actually be any size and shape you like, however, the **depth** needs to be *at least* 9cm at the front and *at least* 1.5cm at the back.

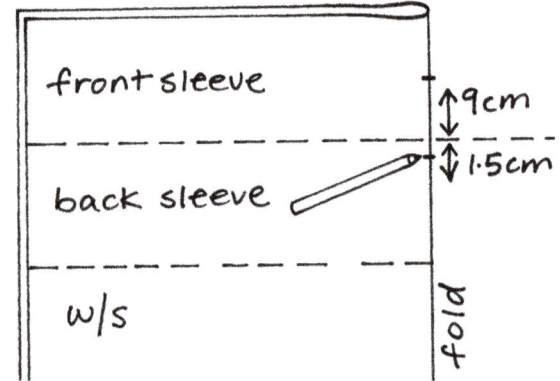

The **width** of the neckline, measured from the fold, needs to be *at least* 6.7 - 7 - 7.3 - 7.6 - 7.9cm and 7.9cm for all sizes thereafter.

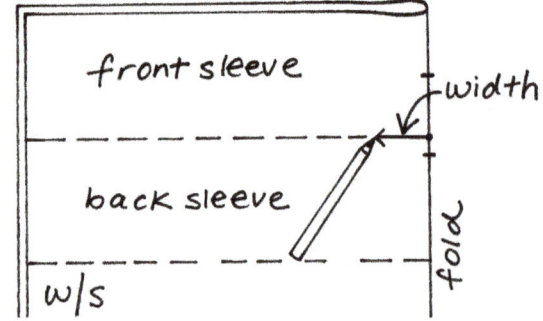

50   Zero Waste Sewing

The neck on the dress in this book was cut at these minimum measurements.

The neckline will be sewn with a 5mm seam allowance (included).

Draw in the shape of the neckline in a pleasing curve.

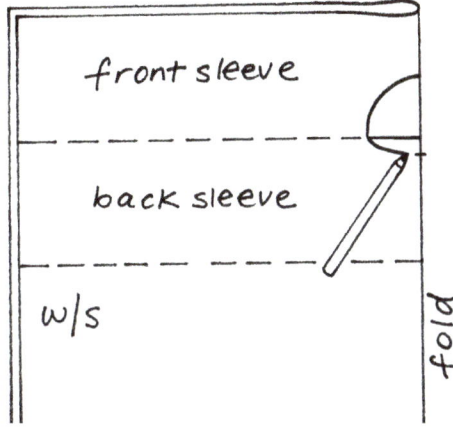

**5.** Draw a vertical line half way through the lower part, below the sleeves.

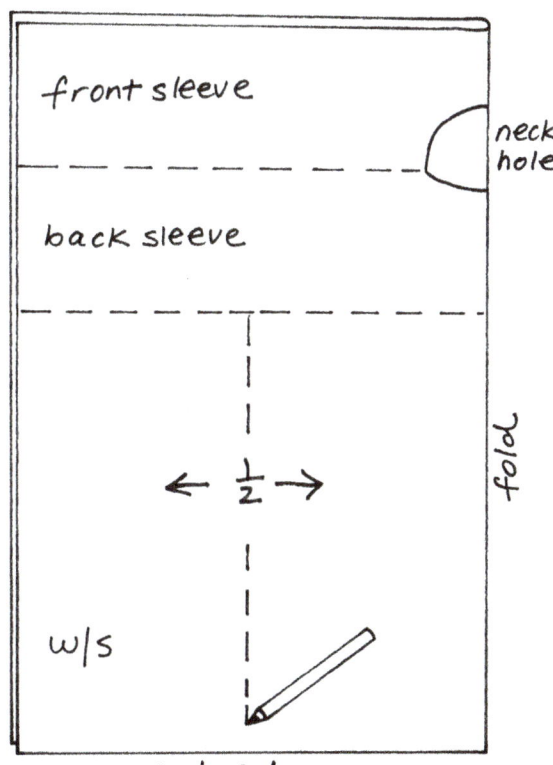

**6.** Cut the lines indicated in pink:

Slit the fold for the upper front and cut out the neck hole *but don't cut through it*—you'll need it later for the back neck.

Cut between (what will become) the back sleeve and the lower front, cutting to 3mm short of the end, to make it easier to sew later.

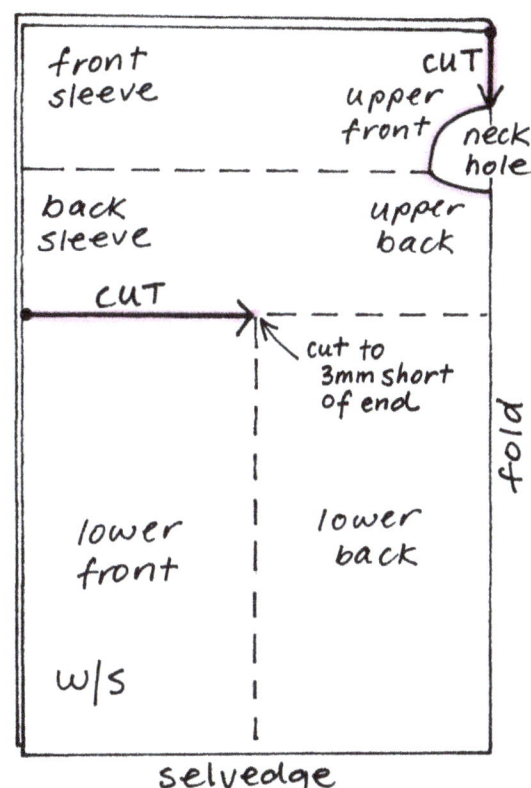

## To sew

**Seam allowances:** all 1cm except 5mm neckline.

### Neckline

**1.** The neckline is sewn first so that you can lay it flat. Follow the instructions for finishing a neckline using bias binding with a facing in *Sewing Techniques* on pages 127-128.

Alternatively, if the fabric is very thick, bind the neck with 12mm or 25mm bias binding.

## Sew the one seam
**2.** Overlock the edges as shown below. See page 46 for tips on overlocking the slits.

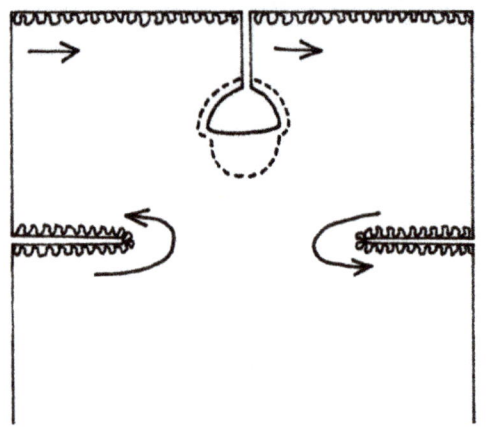

**3.** Fold the dress as shown and sew the one seam as described on page 46.

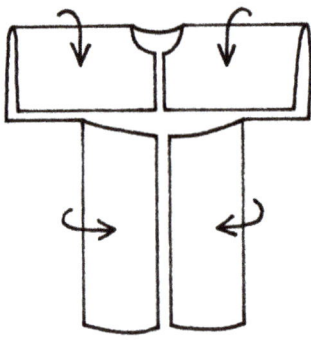

## Hem
**4.** Hem the dress with a 2.5cm hem, or try the dress on and decide on a length to suit *you*. Turn the lower edge under once and hem —you won't need to overlock because there's a selvedge.

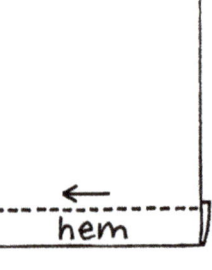

## Front bands
**5.** Iron the front bands in half longways and iron interfacing onto half (the half that will be the outermost side).

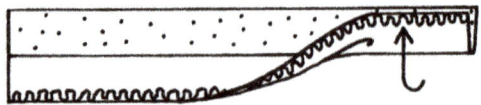

Overlock the long edge of the front band that doesn't have interfacing on it. Since one of these edges will have the selvedge on it, you'll only need to overlock one.

**6.** Pin the band onto the front edge, right sides together. Leave 1cm (that is, a seam allowance) hanging over the top edge so you can finish the top of the band.

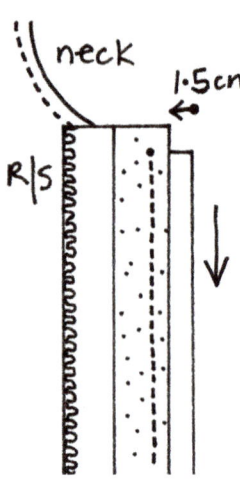

**Important:** step the band's edge 1.5cm away from the front's edge. Why? To preserve the correct centre front. Otherwise the dress will be too wide across the front once the bands are added. The *stitching* line has to be 2.5cm from the front's raw edge because the band is 5cm wide finished. (If this sounds too hard, simply trim 1.5cm off the fronts.)

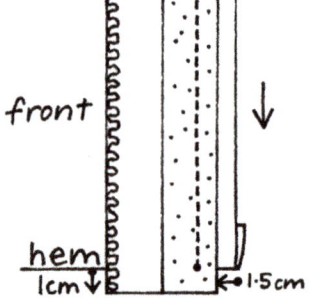

At the bottom, leave 1cm of band hanging over the edge and cut off the rest. Keep the piece you cut off to make epaulettes later.

Sew the band on, stitching 2.5cm from the front's raw edge and 1cm from the band's raw edge (or if you trimmed 1.5cm off the fronts, just match the raw edges and take a 1cm seam).

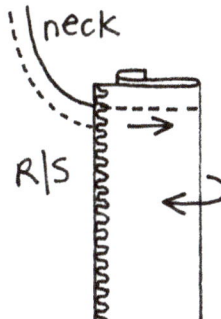

**7.** Bag out the ends of the bands: fold the band back on itself and stitch across in line with the neck. Trim the corner and turn through. Do the same with the lower end of the band.

**8.** Stitch-in-the-ditch (see page 12) to secure the band. Topstitch if desired.

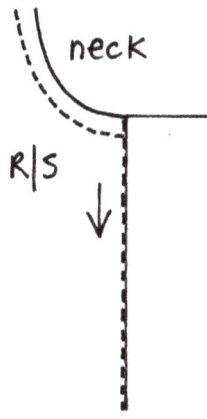

## Make the epaulettes

**9.** Use the cutoffs from the front band, which already have interfacing on them. Fold them in half longways, right sides together, and stitch along one short and one long side.

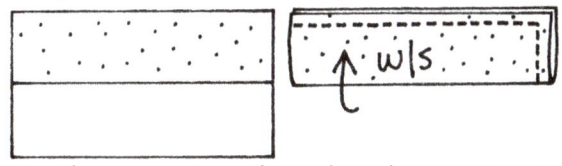

Trim the corner, turn through and press. Topstitch if desired.

**10.** Try the dress on and position the epaulettes. You might need to adjust the length; the ones in this book are 13.5cm finished.

Attach the epaulettes by stitching the raw edge on flat, trimming back to 5mm...

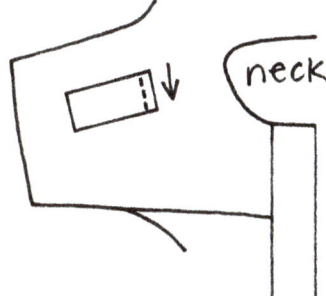

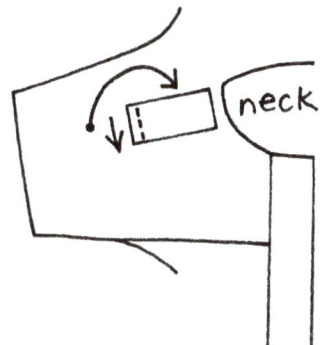

...then flipping the epaulette into place and stitching it down.

## Sleeve hems and finishing

**11.** Try the dress on again. Decide on a good sleeve length and hem the sleeves.
The sleeves in this book were hemmed 13.5cm then turned up 5.5cm to form the cuff.

**12.** Buttonhole and button the front band, positioning the buttonholes vertically about 12.5cm apart. For a concealed closure, use giant press studs instead.
The epaulettes can have a button (with or without a buttonhole) or be invisibly sewn in place.

## Tie belt

**13.** Follow the belt instructions on page 134.

## Notes

✂ You may notice from the cutting measurements in Step 1 on page 50, that a size 10 dress will exactly fit on 112cm wide fabric. If you do this, the dress can be cut at any length.

# Extra: another cutting layout for a jacket (or dress) with no front bands and a back pleat

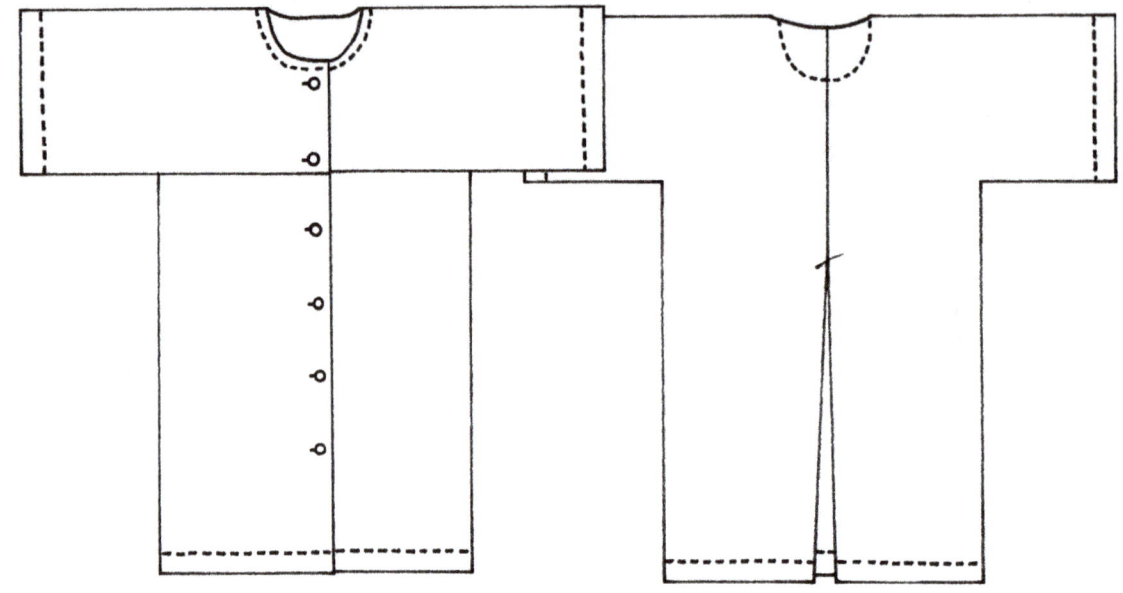

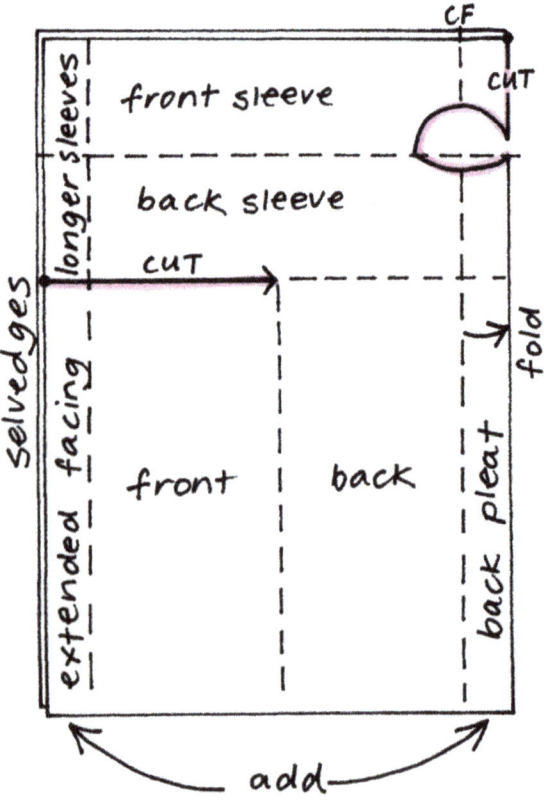

If you've made a Simple one seam dress, you might like to try this variation.

It has longer sleeves and a flattering back pleat. Fabric required: woven fabric, 150cm wide. You'll need the finished jacket/dress length plus 30cm. Note that this garment is cut around the other way from the Simple dress.

## To cut

Refer to the cutting instructions for the Simple dress (pages 50-51), and add an equal amount to each side of the layout to make it fit (centred) on 150cm wide fabric. Up to size 20 should fit. The jacket/dress's length can be whatever you like. Cut a belt from extra fabric if required.

**At the back**, make an inverted pleat (which will be stitched down to the waist).

**At the front**, this becomes an extended facing to make the button stand.

Smaller sizes will have deeper inverted pleats and wider front facings than bigger sizes.

You'll need to mark a "wrap" on the centre front (CF) to give you space for the buttons. (If you folded back each front on the CF line, the edges would just meet, not wrap over.) Mark the fold line 2cm from the CF. Interface the remaining part of the facing.

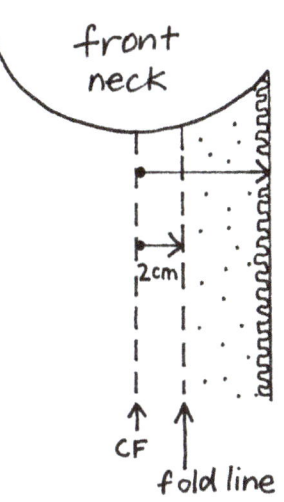

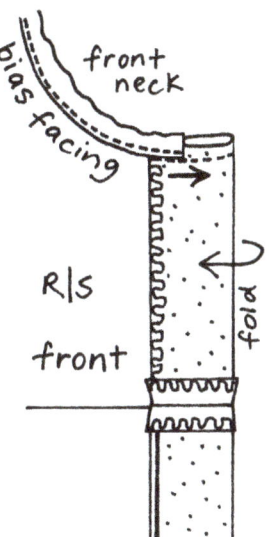

To sew the front neck, fold back the front facing along the fold line and stitch across the top, 5mm down from the top raw edge.

Attach the bias neck facing as described in *Sewing Techniques* on pages 127-128, lapping the end over the front facing.

The jacket shown here has three buttons. The middle one uses the seam as a slit buttonhole.

## Notes

✂ Feel free to cut the neck deeper; the jacket shown here has a neck with a depth of 11cm at the front and a width of 9cm (see Step 4 on page 50).

✂ The neck cutout on this jacket wasn't used as a back neck facing. Instead, the cutout was used to make two welt pockets, finished size 2.5cm x 20cm. A different fabric was used for the pocket linings which were stitched to the fronts so they didn't flap.

# coat dress

*A variation on the simple one seam dress, this version has lapels and is a longer length with longer sleeves. The lapels are formed by an extended front facing.*

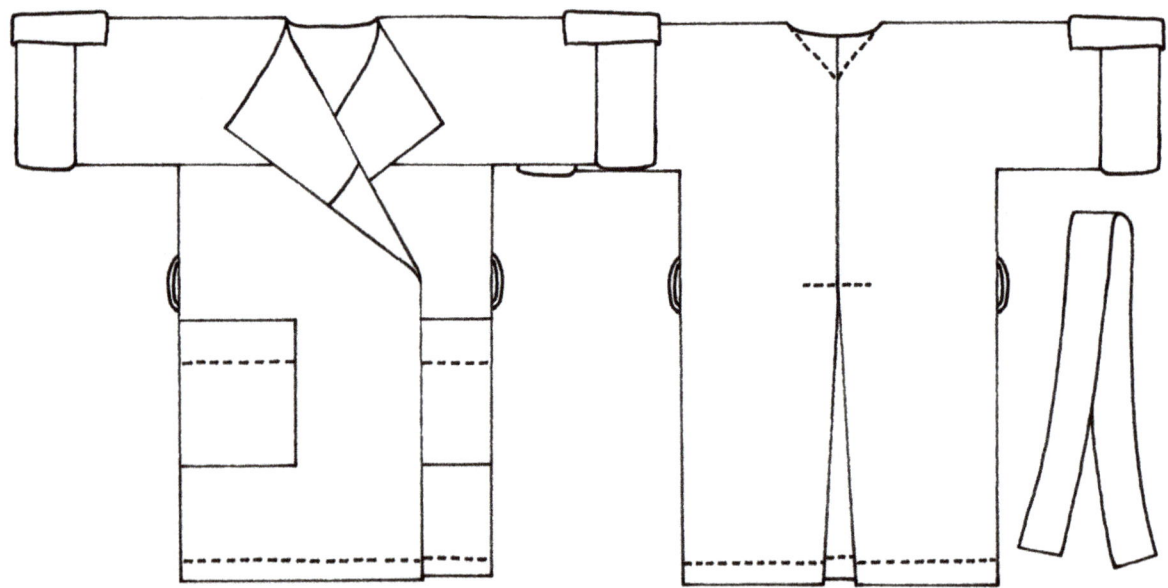

**Fabric** Woven fabric, approximately 150cm wide. For sizes 8-16 you'll need *exactly* 188 - 193 - 198 - 203 - 208cm. For other sizes take your hip measurement and add 96cm. Suitable fabrics include taffeta, denim, firm cotton drill and wool. Choose a semi-stiff fabric. Not suitable for checks since they can't be matched. Stripes will run horizontally.

**Notions** 2 buttons or giant press studs for the waist fastening. 15cm wide strips of interfacing, about 230cm long in total, for the front edges. Two 5cm x 10cm pieces of interfacing for the sleeve tabs. Thread.

**Sizes** Any.

**Finished length** Approximately 110cm long. Note that the fabric's width determines the coat dress's length—the dress will be about 40cm shorter than the fabric's width. If you don't require a belt, the coat dress will be 12cm longer.

**Seam and hem allowances** **1cm** seams, **2cm** for the back pleat, **5mm** for the neckline, **2.5cm** hem.

## Make a pattern

You'll need to make a cardboard template for the neckline.

**1.** On a piece of card (cereal box weight), rule two intersecting lines. The horizontal one is the shoulder line and the vertical one is the centre front (CF).

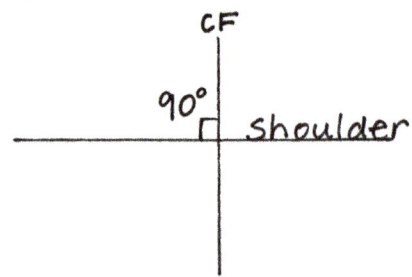

**2.** Draw a second vertical line 5cm to the right of the centre front (CF). The card will be folded along this line later.

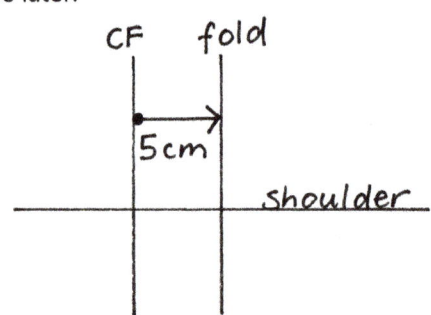

**3.** On the *fold line*, measure 1.5cm down for the back and 9cm up for the front.

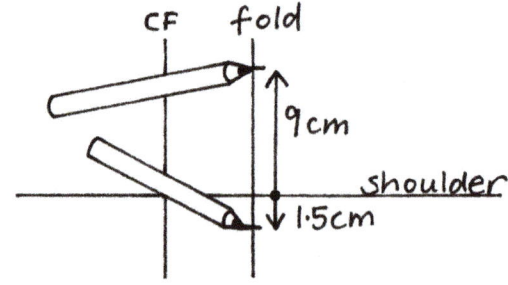

**4.** Measure out to the left of the CF for the side of the neckline. For sizes 8-16, make it 6.7 - 7 - 7.3 - 7.6 - 7.9cm. For all sizes bigger than that make it 7.9cm.

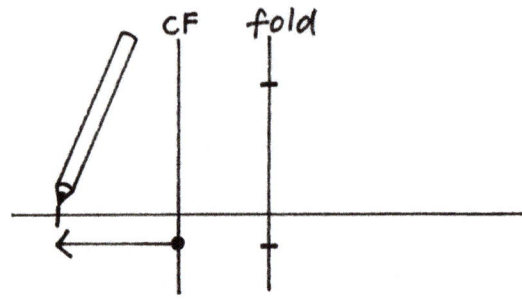

**5.** Draw in a curved line for the back neck.

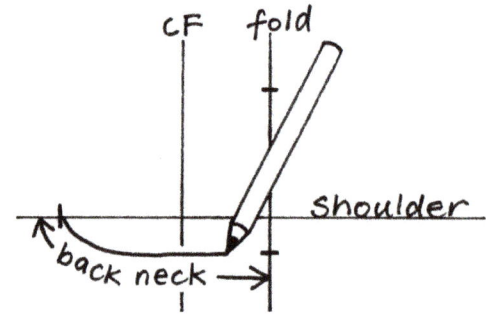

**6.** Connect the other two points with a ruler.

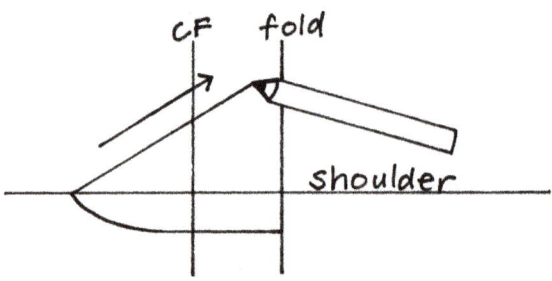

**7.** Fold the card in half along the *fold* line and cut it out through both layers.

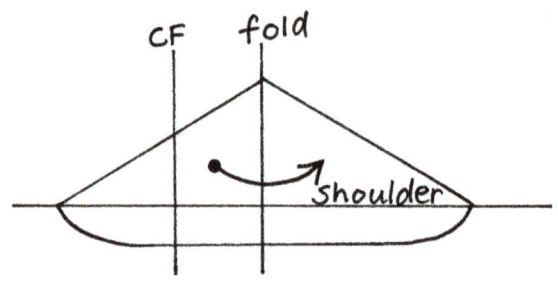

58   Zero Waste Sewing

**8.** Crazy-looking shape, isn't it? Label the shoulder line and the centre front (CF).

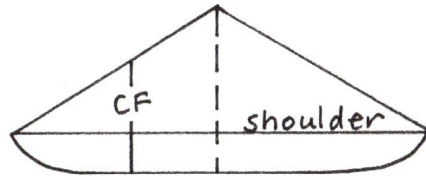

## To cut

**1.** Fold the fabric in half so the two cut edges sit on top of one another, as shown. Cut a 12cm wide strip from the top edge to use for a tie belt (or not, if you don't want a belt).

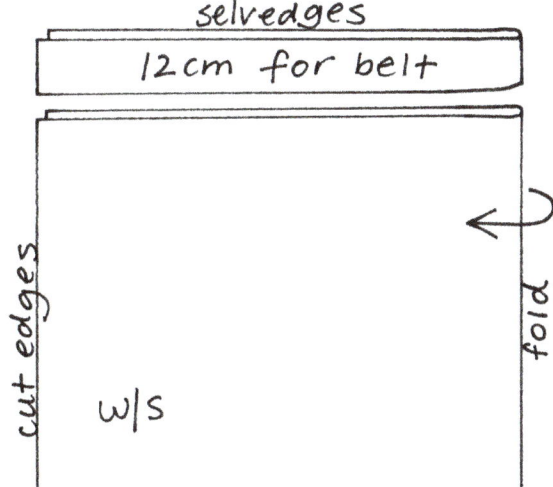

**2.** Using removable chalk, draw in the sleeves down from the top edge. For sizes 8 - 16, make each sleeve 23.4 - 24 - 24.6 - 25.2 - 25.8cm. Add 6mm per size thereafter.

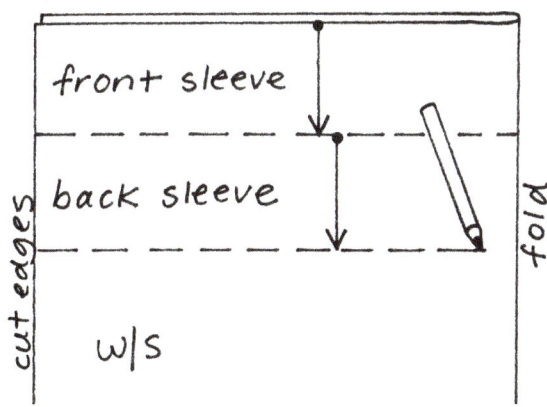

**3.** Draw in 20cm (all sizes) for the back pleat next to the fold.

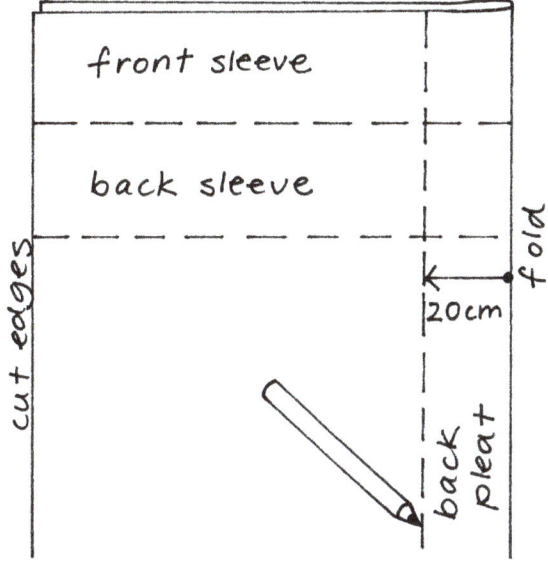

**4.** From this line add a quarter of your hip measurement, plus 4cm. For sizes 8-16 this is 27 - 28.2 - 29.5 - 30.7 - 32cm.

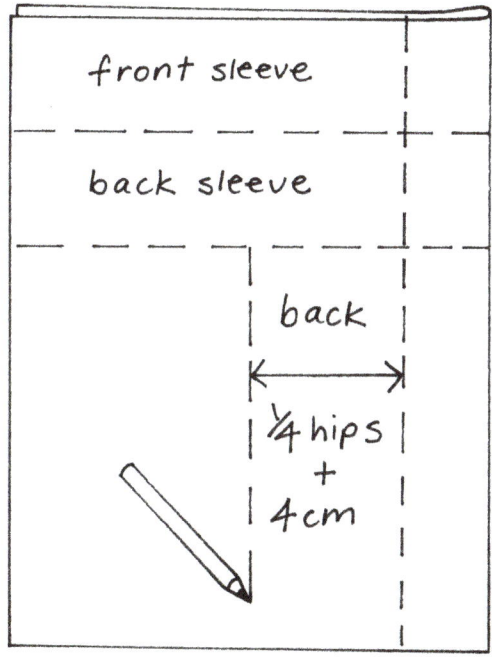

One seam

**5.** There will be a quarter of your hip measurement, plus 4cm, plus 20cm remaining. The 20cm is for the front wrap and facing. For sizes 8-16 this is 47 - 48.2 - 49.5 - 50.7 - 52cm.

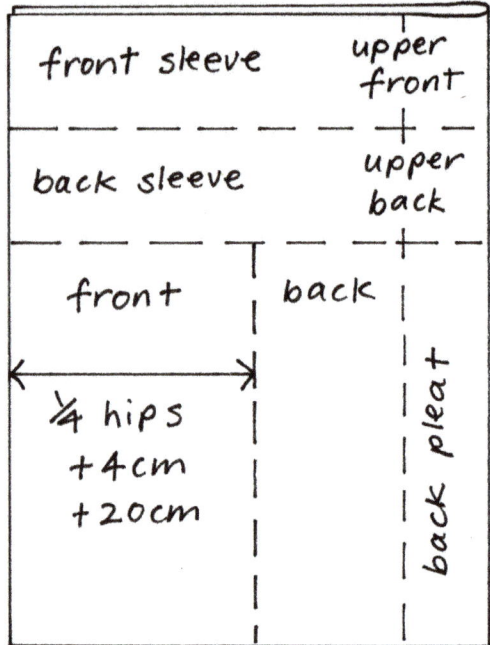

**6.** Sit the neck template on to match the *shoulder* and *centre front* (CF) lines. The corner of the template will sit about 2cm-3cm from the fabric's fold.

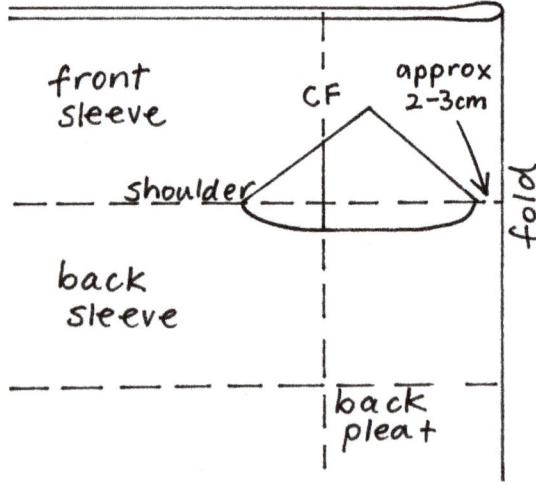

**7.** Cut on the indicated lines. For the neck, cut horizontally level with the bottom of the neck hole. *Don't cut through the neckhole*—you'll need it later for the back neck facing and beltloops.

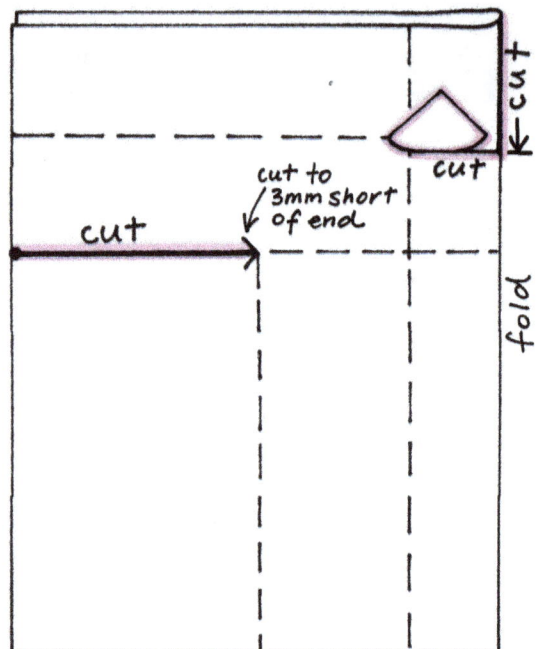

**8.** At the top of the back pleat, cut out a rectangle 18cm wide and 40cm long.

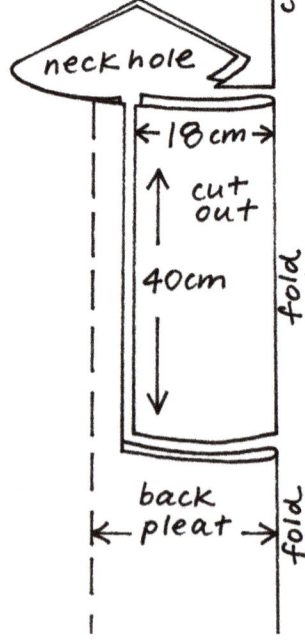

**9.** Lay the 36cm x 40cm rectangle out flat.
Cut 10cm off the top. Cut it into two to give you two sleeve tabs each 18cm x 10cm.
Cut the remaining piece in half to give you two 18cm x 30cm pieces for patch pockets.

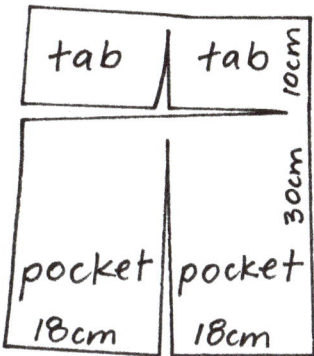

## To sew
**Seam allowances:** all 1cm except 2cm centre back pleat and 5mm neckline.

## Interfacing
**1.** Iron 15cm wide strips of interfacing to the upper and lower front for the turn-back facing/lapel.

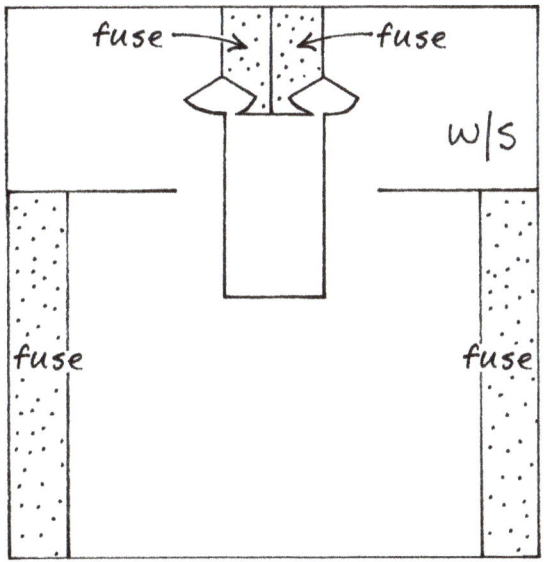

## Overlock
**2.** Overlock all the sides (except the selvedge), the underarm slits, the upper fronts and the rectangular pleat cutout. See page 46 for tips on overlocking the underarm slits.

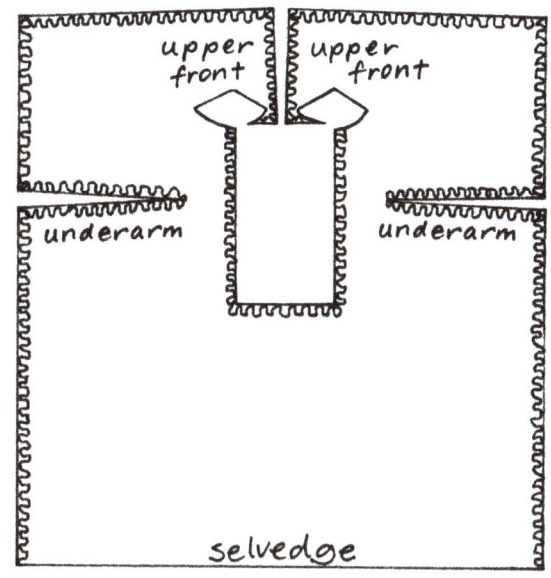

## Back pleat

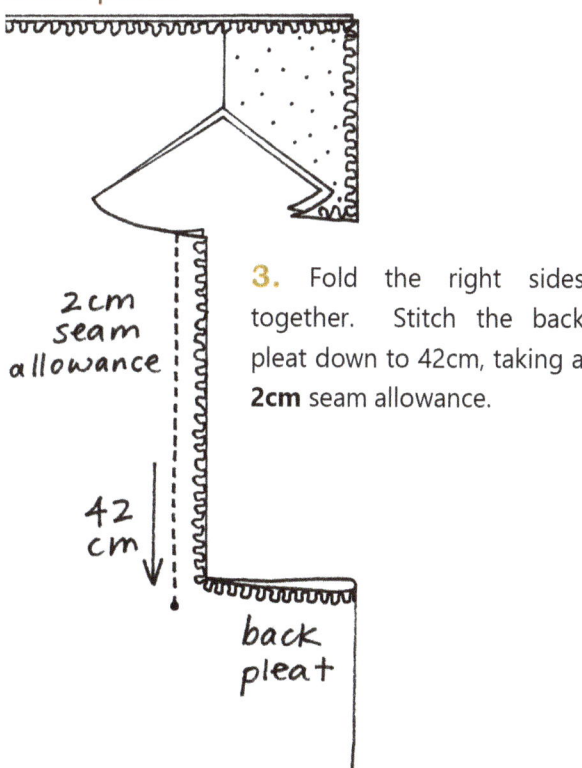

**3.** Fold the right sides together. Stitch the back pleat down to 42cm, taking a **2cm** seam allowance.

One seam

**4.** Press the seam open. At the top, stay-stitch to hold the pleat flat.

At the bottom, stitch across to hold the pleat in place.

Below the pleat, either press crisp folds or leave it unpressed. If you press folds, you may like to topstitch them so they stay folded.

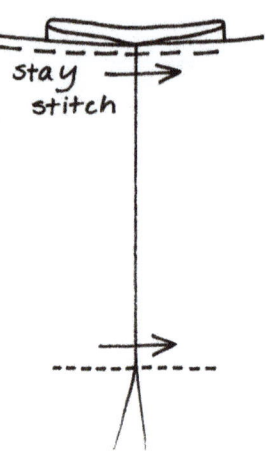

## Neckline

**5.** Take one of the neck cutouts to make the back neck facing. Interface it if needed. Press under the two sides to make it fit the width of the neckline.

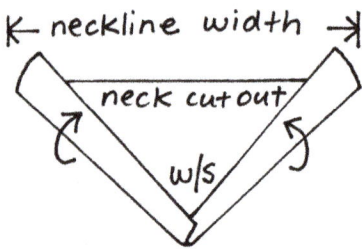

**6.** Lay it under the back neck and trim the top to fit the shape of the back neck.

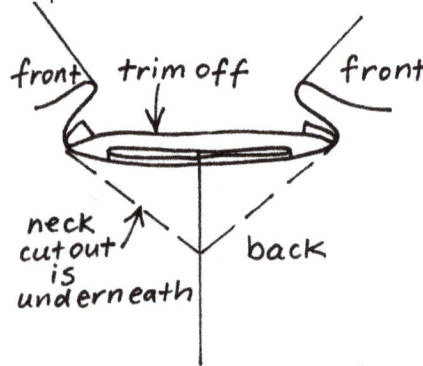

**7.** Lay the back neck facing on the back neck, right sides together.

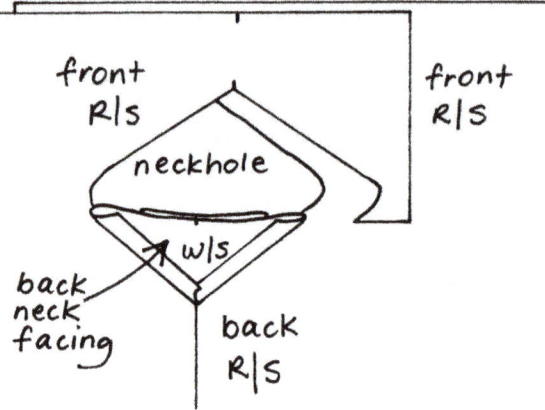

**8.** Fold the upper fronts back on themselves by 15cm, along the edge of the interfacing. Lap the ends onto the back neck facing. Stitch 5mm around the neck edge.

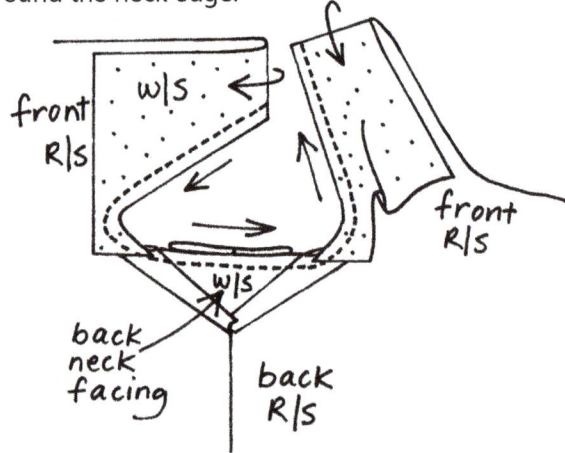

**9.** Understitch the back neck facing, extending the stitching just 1cm-2cm onto the front facing.

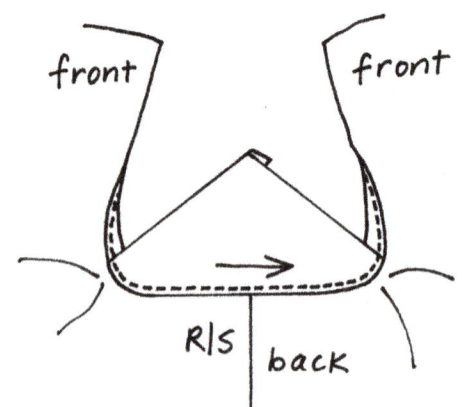

62  Zero Waste Sewing

You'll stitch the facing down with the front facing in Step 11.

## One seam

**10.** Fold the sleeves into position and sew the one seam as described on page 46.

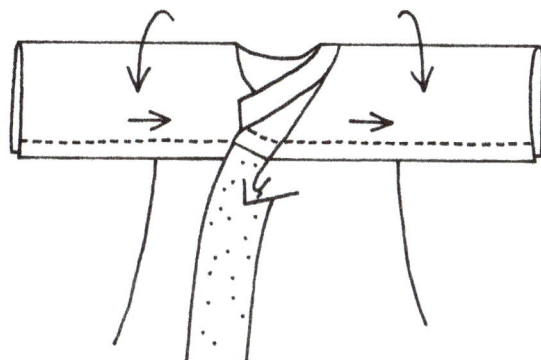

**11.** Press the front facing into position (15cm turned back). Stitch-in-the-ditch (see page 12) along the seamline to secure it.
Machine or hand stitch the back neck and front facings down.

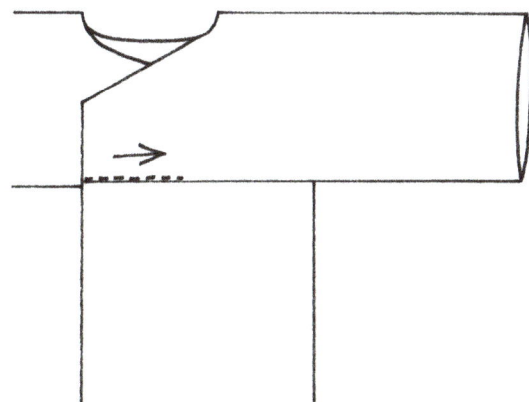

## Sleeve tabs

**12.** Iron a 5cm strip of interfacing onto each tab. Fold each tab right sides together and sew two of the sides. Turn through and press.

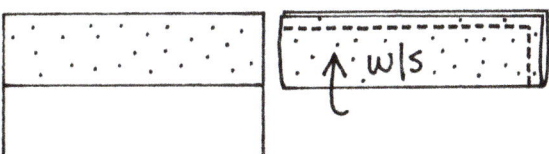

## Tie belt

**13.** Make the belt following the instructions on 134.

## Patch pockets

**14.** Overlock the tops of the pockets and fold them down 10cm.

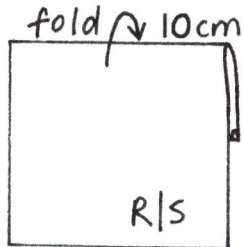

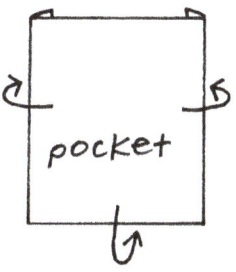

Press under the other three sides 1cm. Try the coat dress on and position the pockets in a flattering position. Sew in place.

## Finishing

**15.** Cut two beltloops from the spare neckhole cutout and make as shown on page 134. Try on the coat dress with the belt to position the beltloops.

**16.** Hem the sleeves with a 15.5cm handsewn hem, then turn up a 7cm cuff. Position the sleeve tab on the edge of the cuff so that 10cm of the tab is visible. Invisibly stitch it in place.

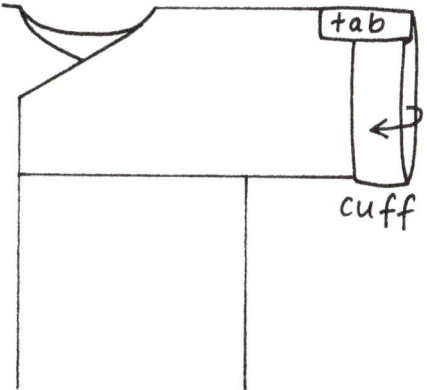

**17.** Hem the coat dress.
Sew buttons and buttonholes or giant press studs to the front at the waist.

# cardigan jacket

*A relaxed, unlined jacket with a soft unstructured collar.*

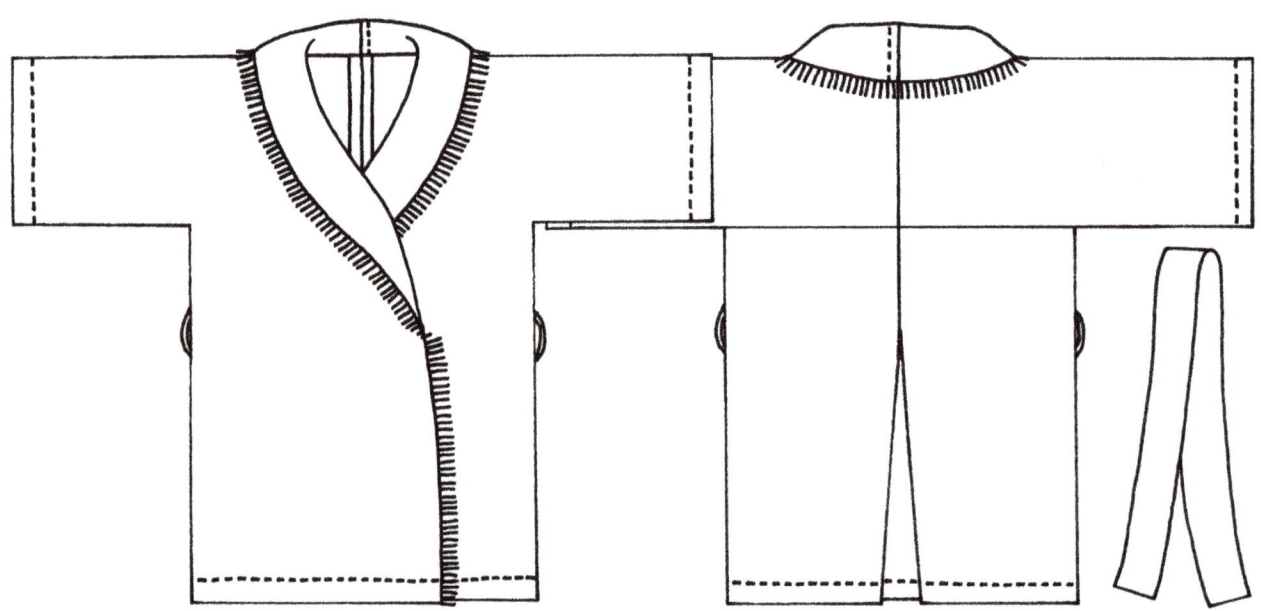

**Fabric** Woven fabric, approximately 125cm-150cm wide. For sizes 8-16 you'll need *exactly* 157 - 162 - 167 - 172 - 177cm. For other sizes, measure your bust and add 70cm. Suitable fabrics include wool. The fabric must look the same on both sides and be able to be frayed to give a fringing for the front edges. Plains, stripes or checks are fine (for checks see Step 1 on page 66). Stripes will run horizontally. You could use a blanket—it may have a fringed edge you can use for the front. Boiled wool or double knit could also be used and the jacket given a bound or stitched front edge instead of fringed.

**Notions** Thread.

**Sizes** Any.

**Finished length** To be decided by you.

**Seam and hem allowances** **1cm** seams, **5mm** neck seam, **2.5cm** hem. The front edges are fringed.

## To cut

**1.** Fold the fabric in half so the two cut ends sit on top of one another, as shown. Put the right sides together. **If your fabric is checked**, fold it along the centre of a check—allow for this when buying fabric.

Using tailors chalk, draw in the sleeves down from the top selvedge. For sizes 8-16, make each sleeve 23.9 - 24.5 - 25.1 - 25.7 - 26.3cm. Add 6mm per size thereafter.

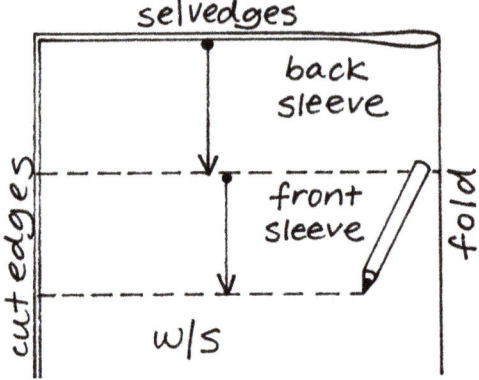

**2.** From the folded edge, mark in a back pleat of 12cm (all sizes).

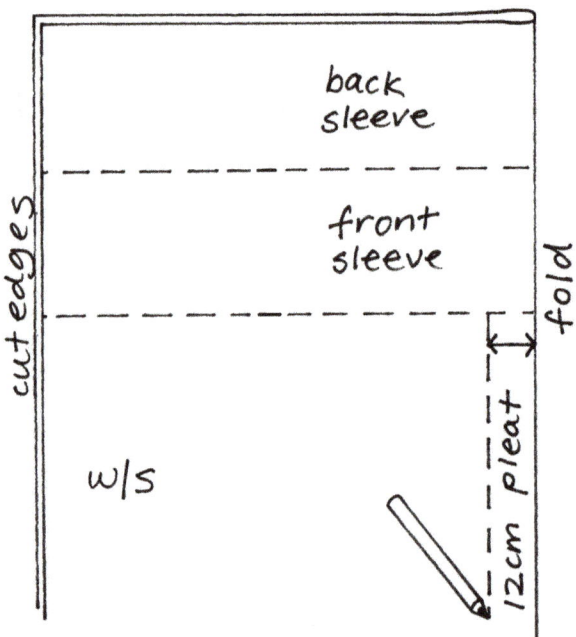

**3.** Mark in a quarter of your bust measurement, plus 4cm, from the pleat line. For sizes 8-16 this is 25.7 - 27 - 28.2 - 29.5 - 30.7cm.

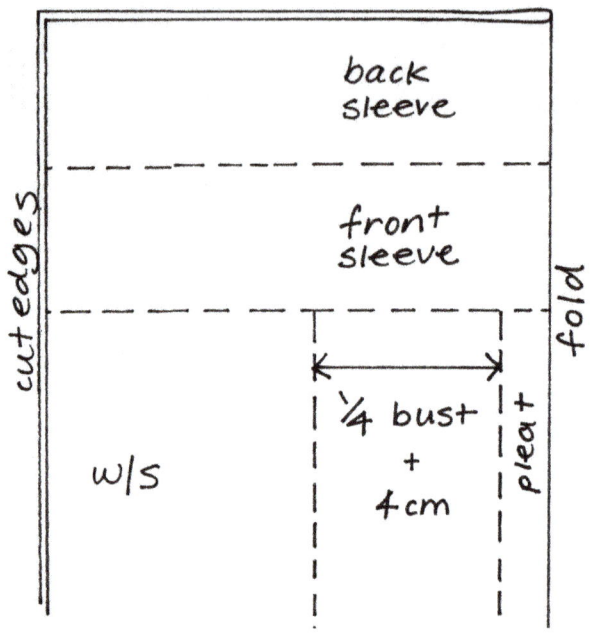

**4.** Mark in the same measurement again to find the centre front (CF). Note that this line is also the upper centre back (CB). There'll be 15cm remaining, for the collar.

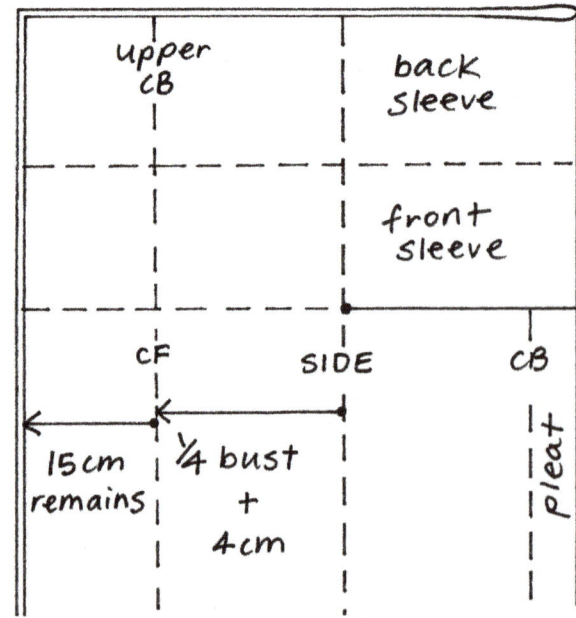

66   Zero Waste Sewing

**5.** Add a 1cm seam allowance to the upper centre back *stitching line*; this will be the *cutting* line.

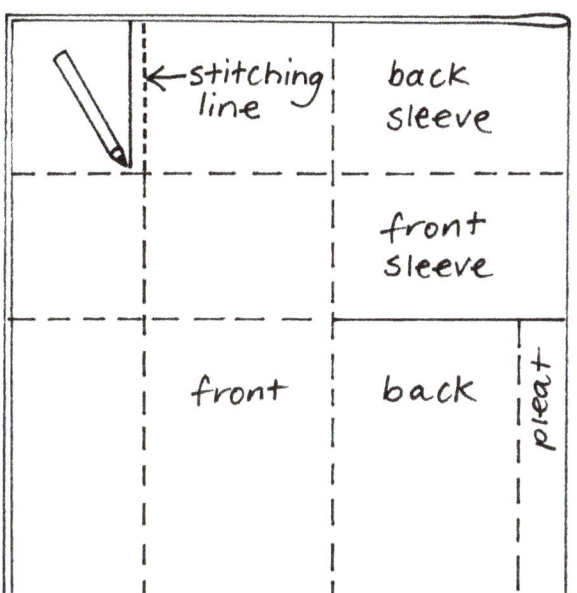

**6.** Extend the *cutting* line at a right angle as shown by 8.2 - 8.5 - 8.8 - 9.1 - 9.4cm for sizes 8-16. For all bigger sizes, keep it at 9.4cm.

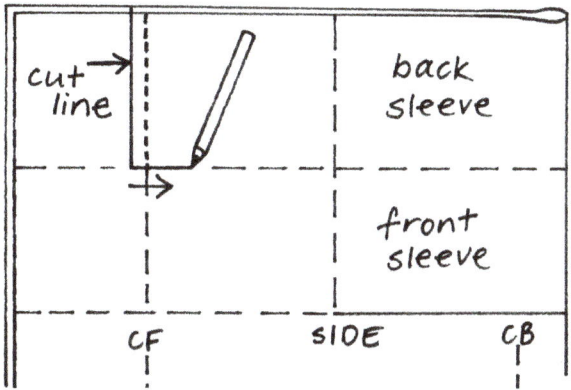

**7.** Cut the lines indicated in pink. Cut the underarm 3mm short of the end to make it easier to sew.

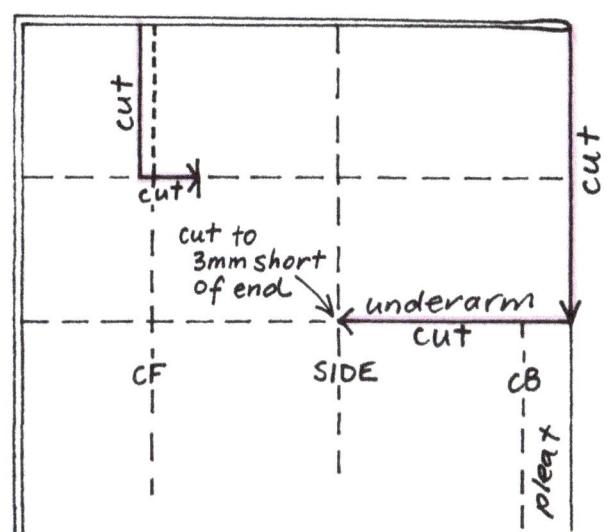

## To sew
**Seam allowances:** all 1cm except 5mm neck seam.

**1.** With the right sides together, sew the back pleat 19cm down to form an inverted pleat. Press. Stitch across the top of the pleat to hold it in place.

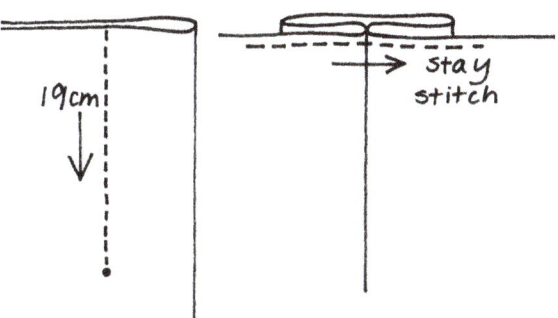

**2.** Sew the upper centre back seam. Press it open and overlock.

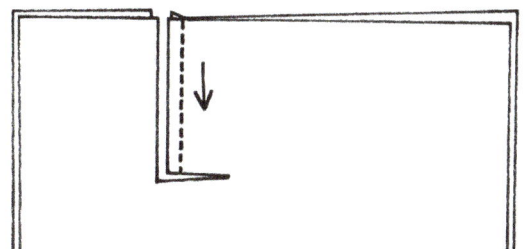

One seam

## Underarm/back seam

**3.** Before sewing the one seam, overlock the seam allowances first, as illustrated. You won't need to overlock the top edge since it's a selvedge. For overlocking advice, see page 46.

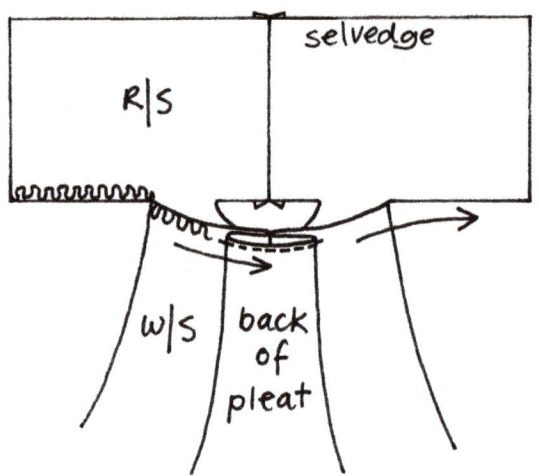

Fold the sleeve down along the shoulder line and sew the seam. Again, see page 46 for advice.

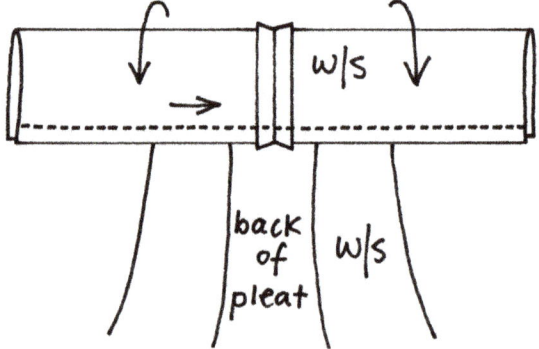

Press the seams open. If the back pleat is too bulky to press open, press that section closed towards the neck and then press the rest open.

## Neck seam and collar

**4.** Pin the neckline to itself, *wrong* sides together. Have the centre back seam in the middle. At each end fold back along the bottom of the line you drew in Step 5 on page 67. Pin a **5mm** seam.

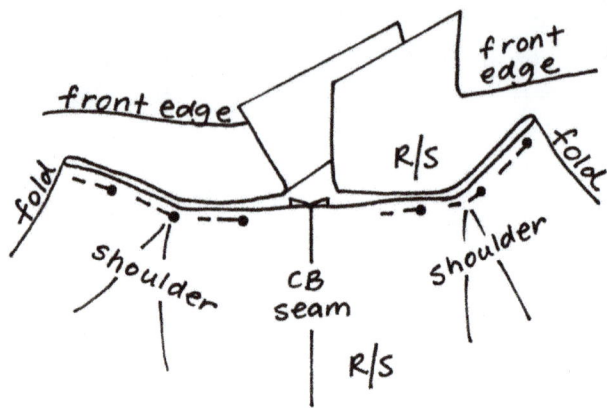

**5.** At the centre back neck, bring the edges together and sew a seam to fit the neckline seam you've just pinned. Trim off the excess leaving a 1cm seam allowance. Press open and overlock. Keep the trimmings for beltloops later.

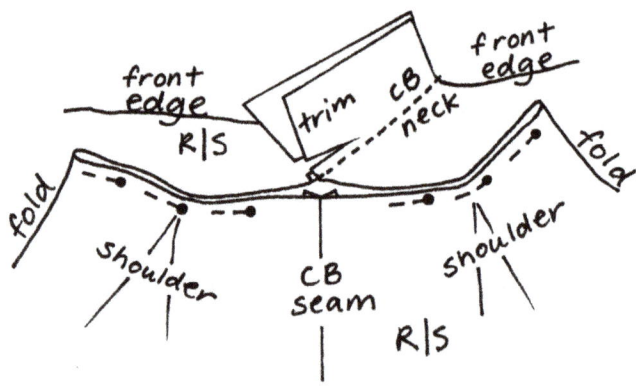

**6.** With the centre back neck seam sewn, stitch a **5mm** neckline seam. Overlock.

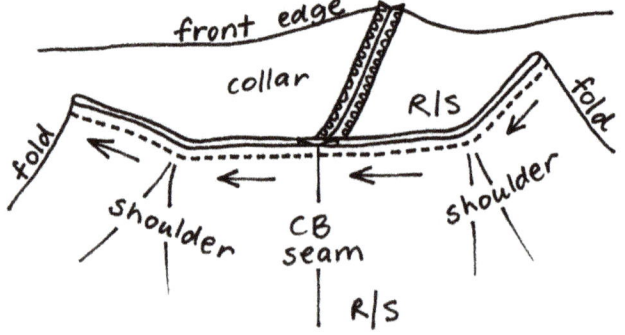

68    Zero Waste Sewing

**7.** Fringe the front edges/collar about 1cm-2cm. Fringe it a little, then try it on to see if it needs more. When you're satisfied, sew a narrow zig zag in matching thread so it doesn't fray any further.

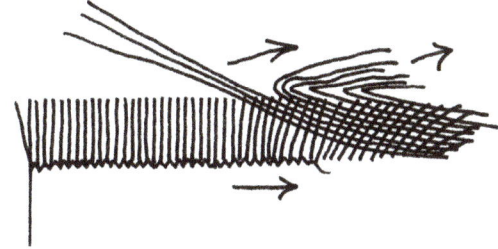

## Hem the body and sleeves

**8.** Try the jacket on to determine the length. Cut off the excess minus a hem allowance and hem the jacket.
A "classic" jacket length brushes the inside of your curled fingers while you stand up straight. The cardigan jacket in this book has a *finishe*d length of 51cm from underarm to hem.

**9.** Hem the sleeves.

## Belt and beltloops

**10.** Cut a strip at 12cm wide from the surplus fabric and make a tie belt according to the instructions on page 134.

**11.** Try the jacket on with the belt and mark the beltloop positions. Make two beltloops using the offcut from the back neck in Step 5 on page 68. Sew the beltloops and stitch them to the jacket.

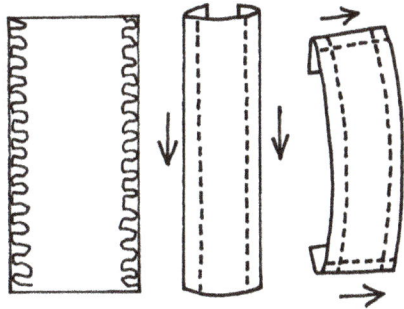

**12.** Review the remaining fabric and decide what to do with it. You could use it to make pockets. If you'd like full-length sleeves you could add it onto the length of the sleeves.

You could use the offcut to make a **moebius scarf**. The piece needs to be 25cm-35cm wide. The one shown is 164cm long and 34cm wide. Take the piece and twist one end 180 degrees.

Join the short ends using a flat felled seam or a neat lapped seam.

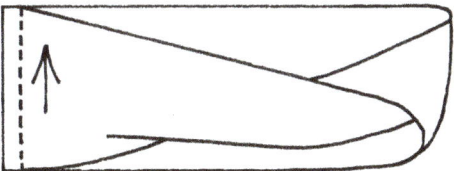

On a moebius strip, the entire edge can be hemmed (or fringed) in one operation. Wear it as a cowl, twisted once over the head.

One seam 69

# hooded robe

*I wondered if the one seam idea could incorporate a hood. While experimenting, I discovered that the hood is the defining unit: the sleeve depth must be the same as the hood height. The hood flows seamlessly into the robe's front but requires a gusset at the back to make it 3D.*

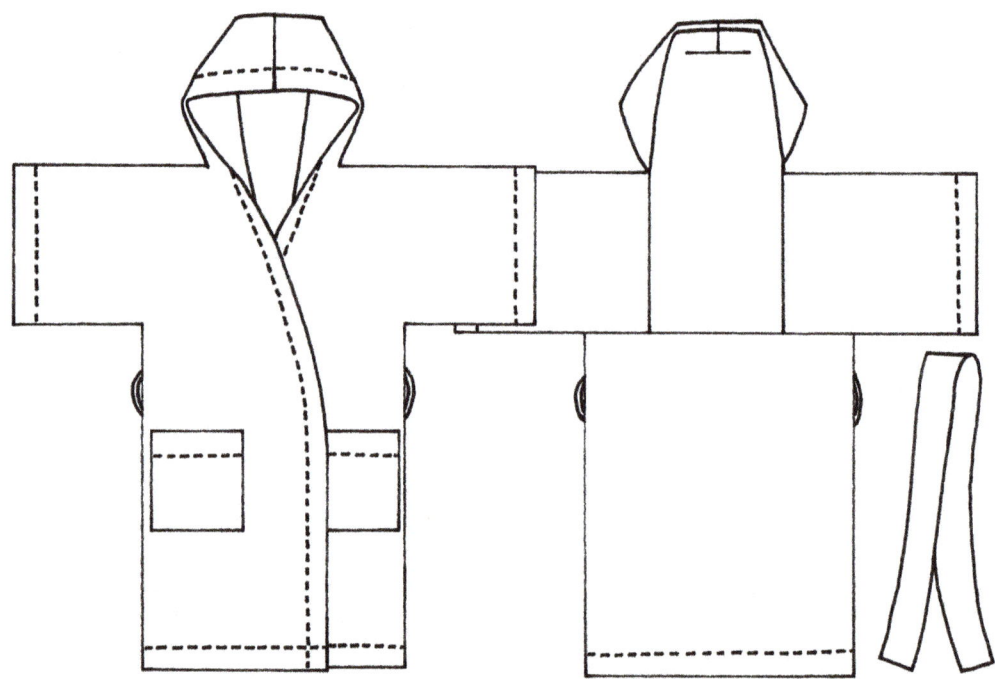

**Fabric** Woven fabric approximately 150cm wide or wider. For sizes 8-16 you'll need *exactly* 193 - 198 - 203 - 208 - 213cm. For other sizes, take your hip measurement and add 101cm. Suitable fabrics include heavy cotton, waffle weave, towelling and fleece. Choose soft, absorbent fabrics. Plains, stripes or checks are fine (for checks see Step 1 on page 72). Stripes will run horizontally.

**Notions** Thread.

**Sizes** Any.

**Finished length** The fabric width determines the length; it will be approximately 35cm shorter than your fabric width. For 150cm wide fabric, it will be about 115cm long. The fabric shown was 141cm wide.

**Seam and hem allowances** **1cm** seams and **2.5cm** hems are included.

## To cut

**1.** Fold the fabric in half so the two cut ends sit on top of one another. Have the right sides together. **If the fabric is checked,** centre the check along the fold—allow for this when buying fabric. Mark a selvedge-to-selvedge strip 18cm wide, next to the cut edge. Cut, giving you two 18cm wide strips.

**2.** The remaining piece of fabric should measure 78.5 - 81 - 83.5 - 86 - 88.5cm across as folded (for sizes 8-16).

Using tailor's chalk, draw in the sleeves each 32cm (all sizes) down from the top.

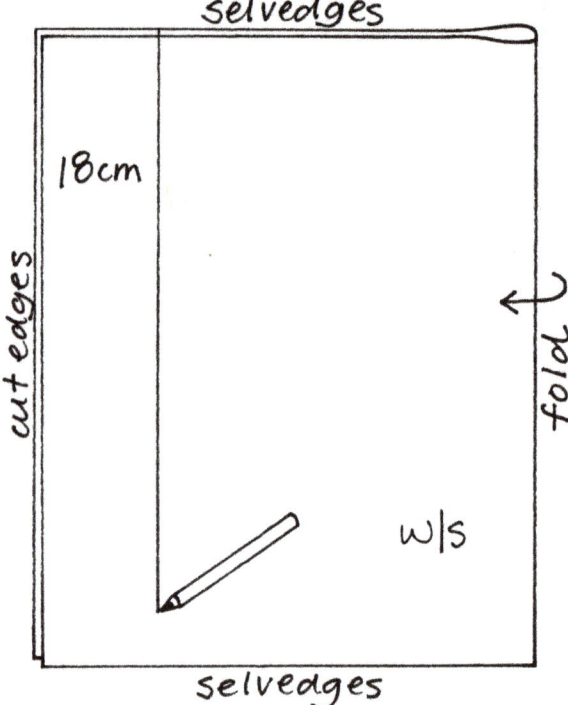

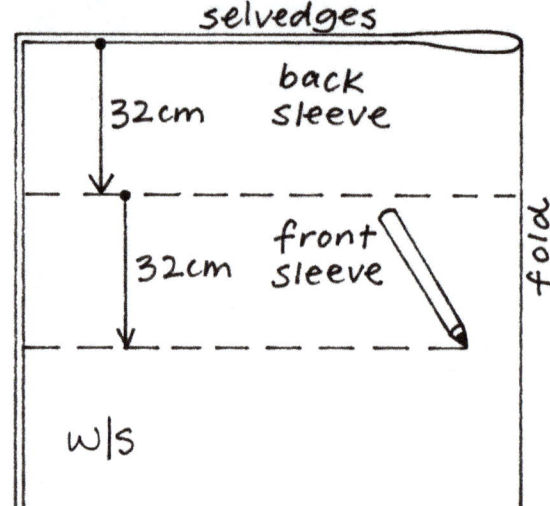

From one strip, cut a hood gusset 18cm wide by 66cm long. Mark the centres of the long sides with a tiny 3mm snip.

Also cut two pockets 18cm x 24 cm.

**3.** Draw in the cut line for the hood, 24cm from the edge (all sizes).

This should leave you with a back sleeve measuring half your hip measurement, plus 7.5cm ease, plus 1cm seam allowance. For sizes 8-16 this is 54.5 - 57 - 59.5 - 62 - 64.5cm.

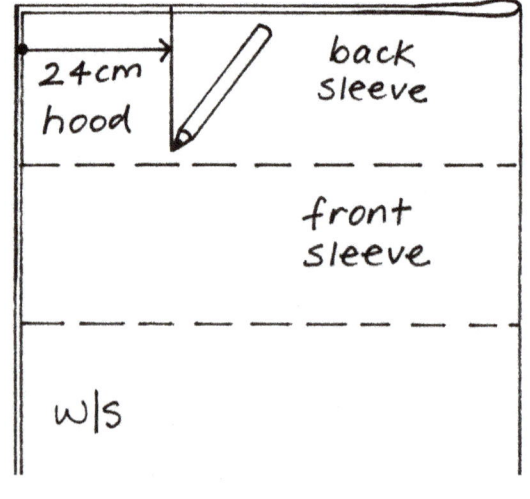

Keep the rest for the belt and beltloops.

72    Zero Waste Sewing

**4.** Draw in the underarm cut line: it's half of (half your hip measurement, plus 7.5cm ease), *plus* 4cm. For sizes 8-16, this is 30.7 - 32 - 33.2 - 34.5 - 35.7cm.

(What's the 4cm for? It's a quarter of the finished gusset width.)

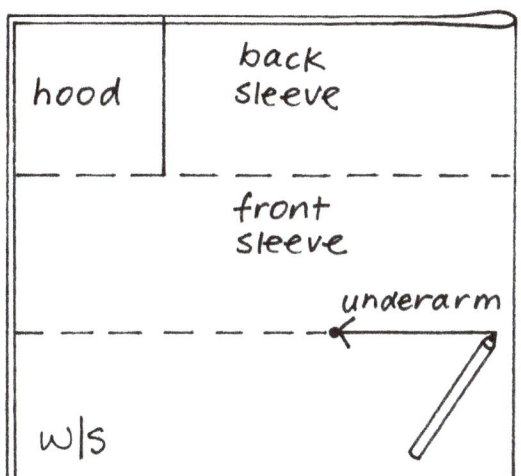

**5.** Cut the lines indicated in pink. Cut the underarm 3mm short of the end to make it easier to sew.

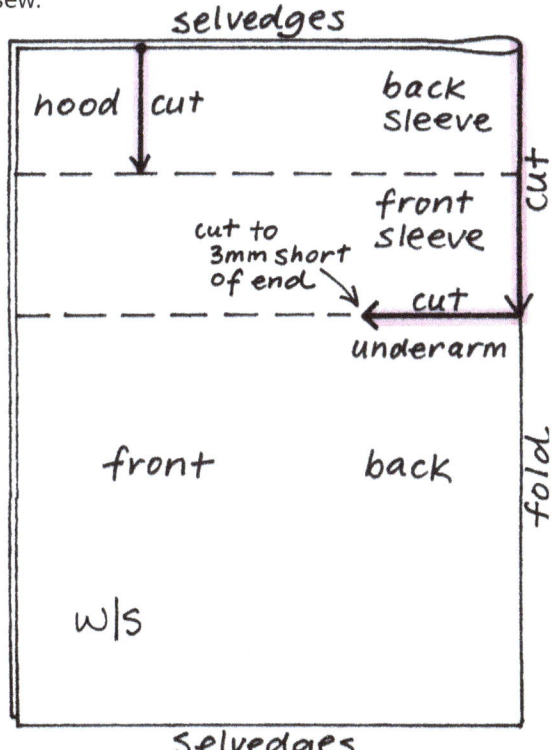

## To sew
**Seam allowances:** all 1cm.

### Hood
**1.** On each layer, mark a dot 1cm lower than the end of the hood/back sleeve slit.

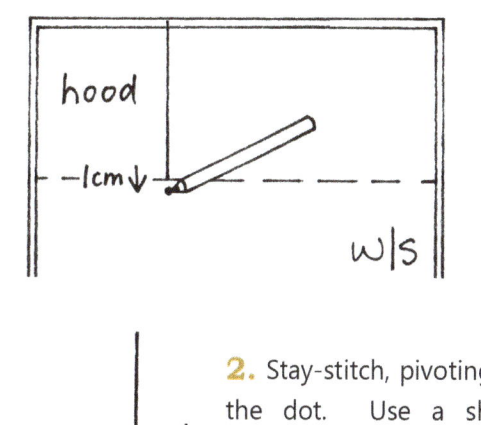

**2.** Stay-stitch, pivoting at the dot. Use a short stitch for strength. Extend the slit to the dot using sharp scissors.

**3.** Take the hood gusset and sew it to the hood/back slit, matching the centre of the gusset with the dot you've just stay-stitched to. Orient the gusset so that its selvedge is NOT on the side with the hood. Sew with the gusset underneath and pivot at the dot.

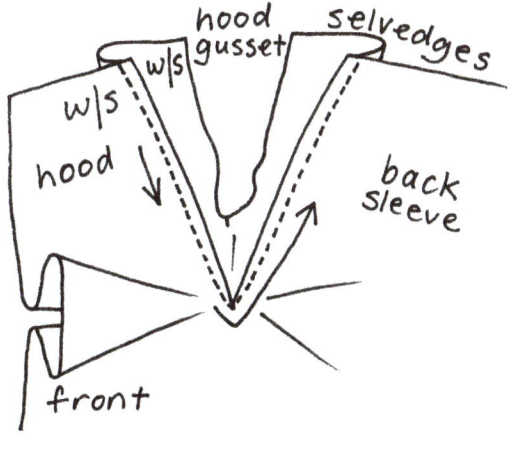

One seam

**4.** Do the same for the other side of the gusset on the other hood/back. Overlock (not shown for clarity). Press the seam away from the gusset.
If the fabric is very thick, press this seam open and overlock each side separately.

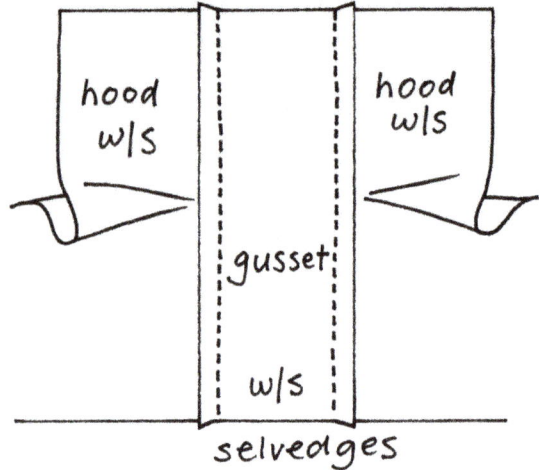

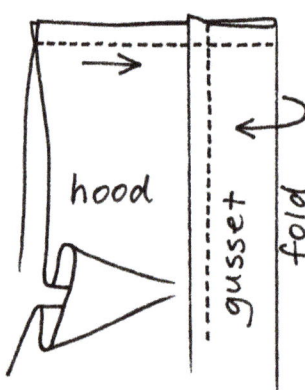

**5.** Fold the hood in half and sew across the top. Overlock. Again, if the fabric is very thick, press the seam open.

**6.** Fold the point of the hood the other way and stitch across where it's 10cm wide.

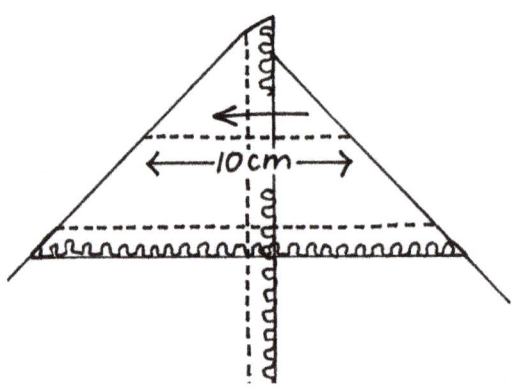

## Underarm/back seam
**7.** Before sewing the one seam, overlock the seam allowances first, as illustrated. You won't need to overlock the top edge since it's a selvedge.
For overlocking advice, see page 46.

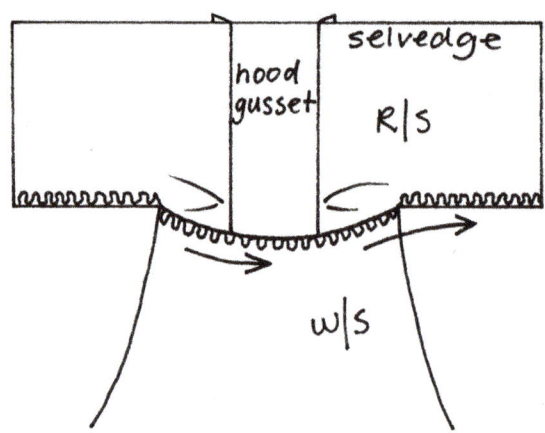

**8.** Fold the sleeve down along the shoulder line and sew the seam.
See page 46 for advice sewing this seam.

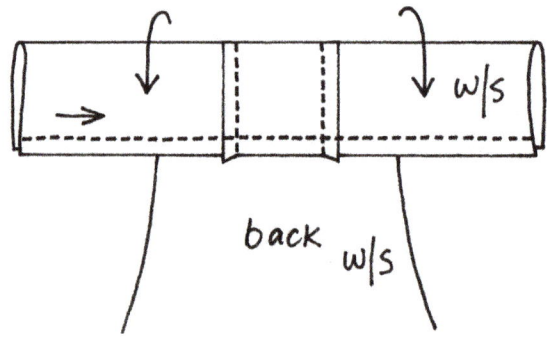

**9.** Hem the front edge, sleeves and lower edge with a 2.5cm hem.

## Belt and beltloops

You should have two strips remaining, 18cm wide. One is 150cm long and the other about 34cm long.

**10.** Cut 5cm off one of them to make beltloops. Overlock the long sides, turn under the edges and stitch. Cut it in half to make two beltloops, one for each side. Try on the robe to position the beltloops.

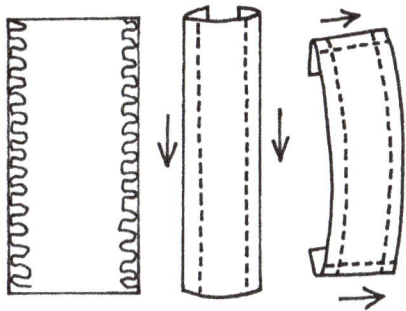

**11.** For the belt, join the two strips together on the short ends and press the seam open. Fold in half longways, right sides together, and stitch. Leave a gap to turn it through.

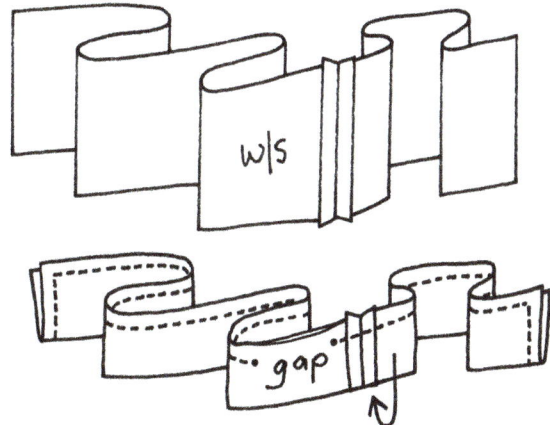

Trim the corners to no closer than 3mm, turn through and press. Sew the gap shut by hand.

The finished belt will be about 180cm long and 8cm wide. For a narrower belt, take a bigger seam allowance (the one in this book used a 1.5cm seam) OR fold the belt in three, to yield a belt about 5.5cm wide.

## Pockets

**12.** Overlock the top (18cm long) edge of both pockets.

If the fabric needs it, iron a 5cm wide strip of interfacing on the top before overlocking.

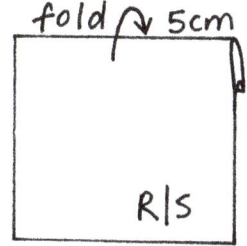

Press down the top 5cm.

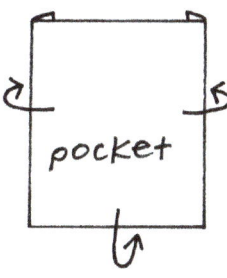

Press under 1cm around the other three sides. Try on the robe to position the pockets in the best place before sewing them on.

The pockets on the robe in this book are positioned 2.5cm towards the back and the rest on the front.

## Notes

✂ In the right fabric, this could make a flattering wraparound dress. To fasten it more securely than just the belt, button the wrapover: add 2.5cm to each front to make a 5cm wide facing and interface behind the button holes. You'll need 5cm extra fabric to do this.

✂ This coat was cut from a blanket using the same pattern.

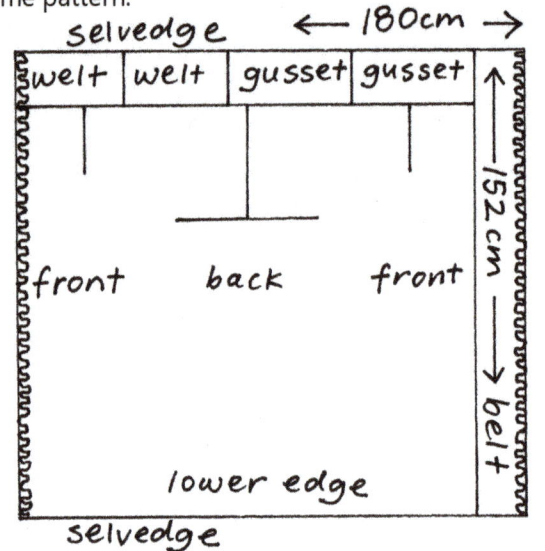

The blanket's size was 152cm x 180cm. One of the selvedges was used for the lower edge. The hood's gusset has a central seam to use the fabric economically. There wasn't enough fabric for patch pockets so the coat has welt pockets.

Consider how you'll handle the very thick fabric. Overlock the seams *before* stitching. After sewing, press them open. Bind the edges with 25mm bias binding rather than make hems. The pocket welts are a single layer of blanket with binding and the pocket bags are made from a thinner fabric.

If the blanket is old, wash it and block it flat so it's square, instead of hanging it on the line to dry—otherwise the edges will warp. Go easy with the steam iron; some wool blankets shrink easily.

# Introduction to tessellated

Tessellating patterns fit perfectly into one another and the interlocking pattern is designed to continue infinitely. Floor tiles, patchwork quilts, honeycomb, jigsaw puzzles and work by artist MC Escher are all examples of tessellating patterns.

This concept can also be used for cutting garments. Essentially, it's top-and-tailing perfectly fitting pattern pieces.

With the tessellated garments in this book (except for the wrap trousers), the *fabric width* determines the *garment's length*, and the garment is cut around the other way from usual. The selvedge can be used for the hem.

Tessellated patterns are easy to make in any size. Because garments grow in width more than length as the sizes increase *and* tessellated garments are cut across the fabric, the garment's width can be changed without worrying about fitting everything into the fabric.

Not all fabrics suit tessellated patterns. It is not recommended to use napped fabrics, one-way prints and stripes, as these will run horizontally. Stripes and checks generally can't be matched at the side seams.

## How to draw a tessellation

It's important to draft a paper pattern before cutting tessellated garments so as to get the curves right.

Tessellated patterns can also be made easily using CAD or a drawing program.

**1.** Draw in the top and bottom widths of the pattern piece (A and B).

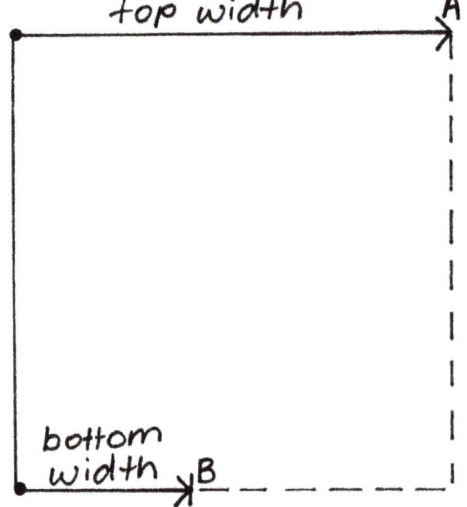

**2.** Mark the horizontal centre.

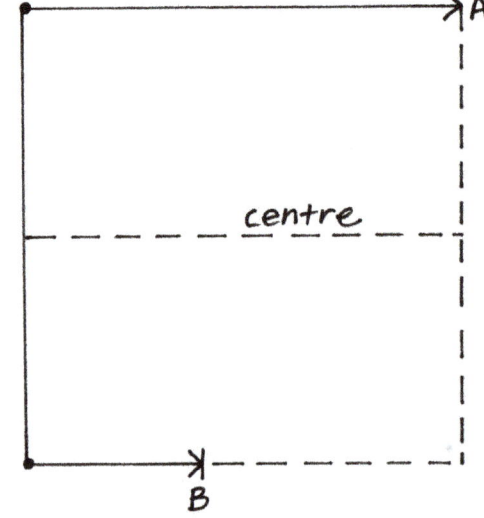

78  Zero Waste Sewing

**3.** Rule a diagonal line between A and B and mark where it intersects the centre (C).

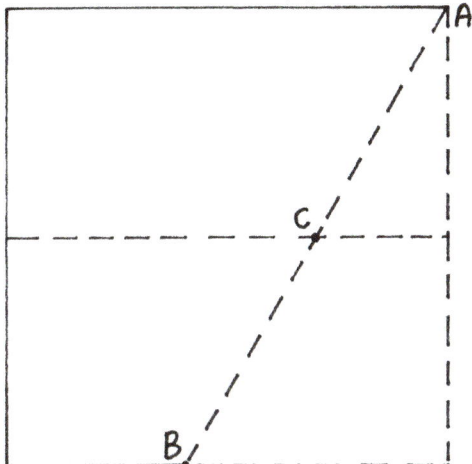

**4.** Draw in the shape from A to C.

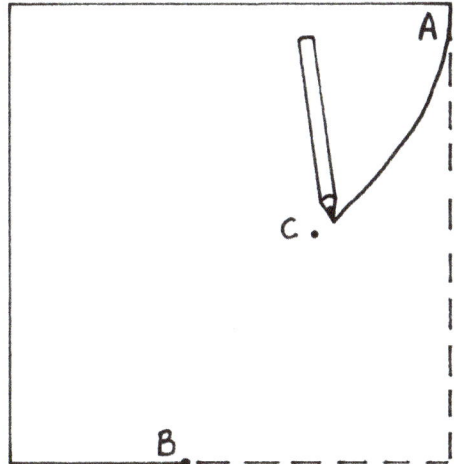

**5.** Trace it off on a separate piece of tracing paper.

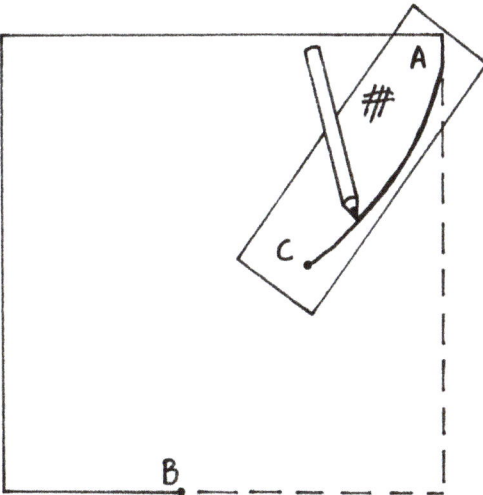

**6.** Flip the tracing paper over and colour lightly in pencil over the back of the line (you're making your own carbon paper).

**7.** Turn the tracing paper back to the right side and place it over A-C again.
Pivot the tracing paper on point C so that point A on the tracing paper is over point B on the pattern. Note that the tessellation is not flipped or mirrored—it is pivoted and swung. Draw over the shape on the tracing paper, imprinting the line through to the pattern.

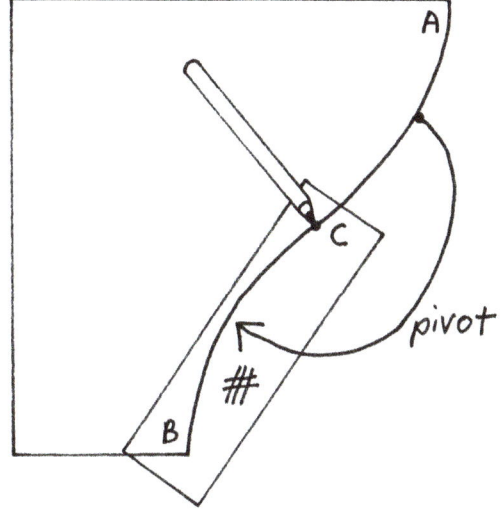

**8.** Add a notch at C to help sew the edges together.

If you're using CAD or a drawing program, simply copy the line A-C, then rotate it from point C until it lands on the right spot.

It's important to remember that tessellation doesn't result in a pair of pieces—it's the same shape rotated. If you need a pair cut, put two layers of fabric right sides together.

Tessellated   79

# boho dress

*A cool dress for hot days by the pool or at the beach. The voluminous sleeves particularly suit tall women.*

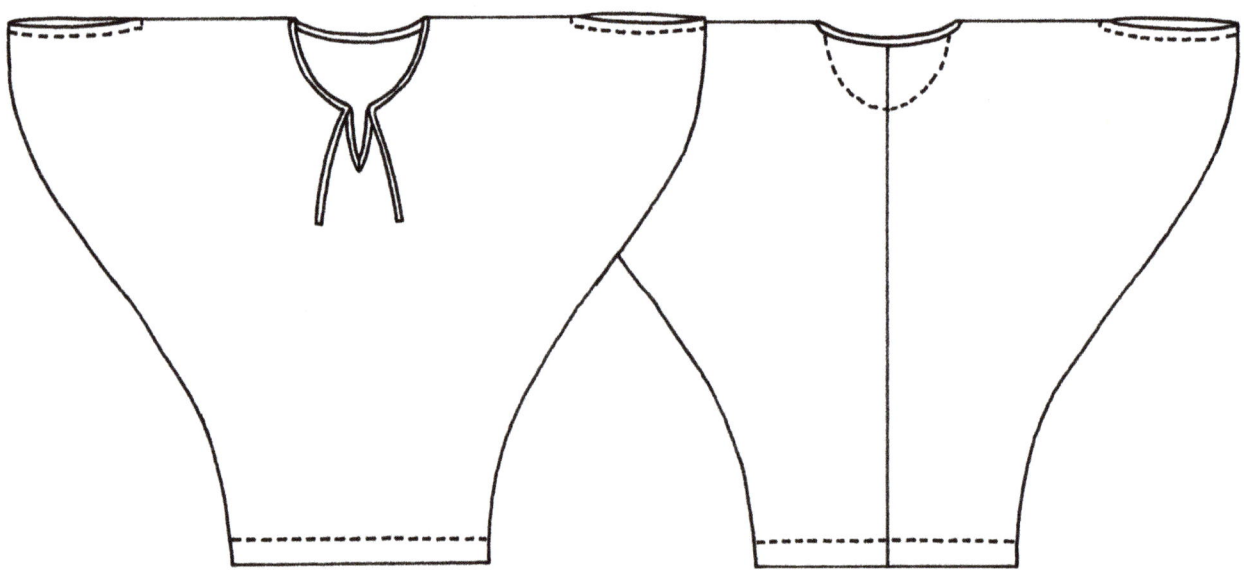

**Fabric** Woven fabric, approximately 112cm-115cm wide or slightly narrower. Note that the fabric's width is the dress's length. For sizes 8-16 you'll need *exactly* 210 - 212.5 - 215 - 217.5 - 220cm. For other sizes, halve your hip measurement and add 164cm. Suitable fabrics include lightweight cotton, soft sheers, voile, rayon and silk. Choose drapey, soft fabrics. Stripes and two-way prints are fine, but note they'll run horizontally and may not match at the side seams.

**Notions** 12mm bias binding for the neckline, approximately 140cm. Thread.

**Sizes** Any.

**Finished length** Maximum length is 108.5cm or shorter if a larger hem is taken.

**Seam allowances** **1cm** seams are included. The neck is bound.

Zero Waste Sewing

# Make a pattern

## Draw in the body

**1.** On a large piece of paper draw a rectangle. Make the **width** 76cm; this is the shoulder seam. The **length** is the same as the fabric's width (115cm or similar).

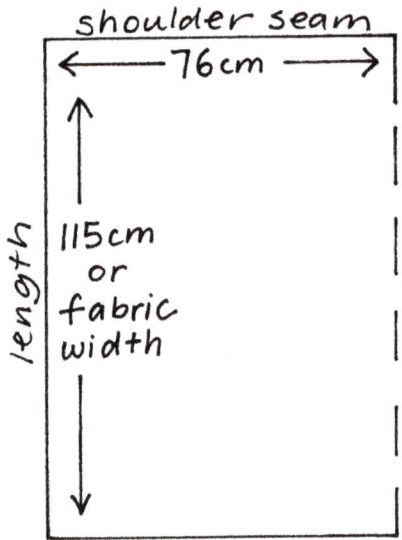

**2.** Add onto the side: a quarter of your hip measurement, plus 5cm. For sizes 8-16, this is 28 - 29.2 - 30.5 - 31.7 - 33cm. Draw in the rest of the rectangle.

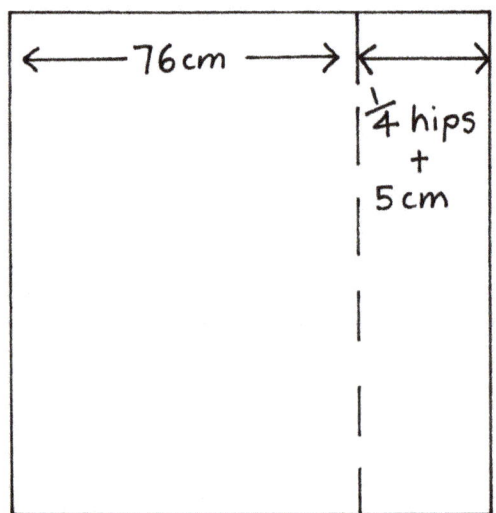

**3.** Measure in the same amount on the other side. Note that you aren't making the rectangle any bigger, you're merely drawing a line inside the rectangle.

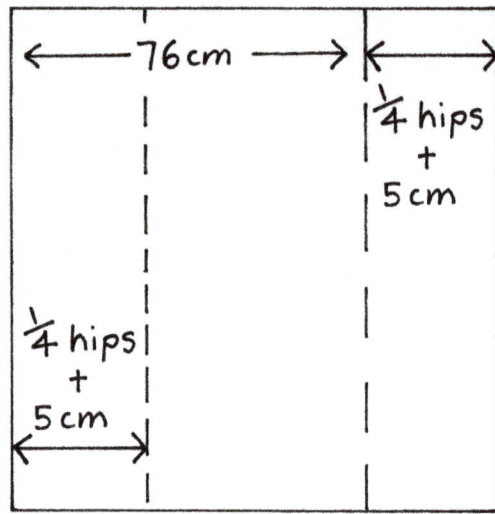

**4.** Fold the piece of paper in half so you have a half way line.

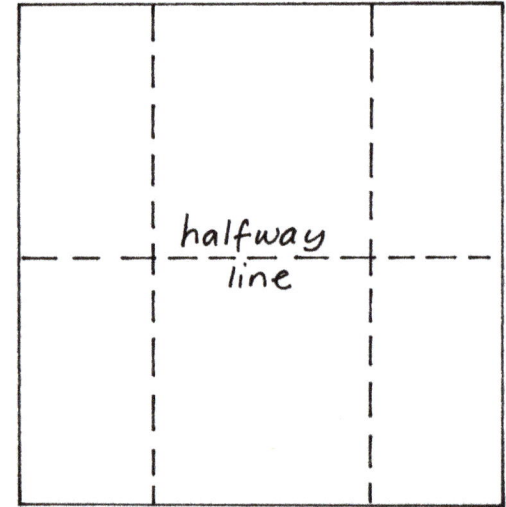

82    Zero Waste Sewing

**5.** Rule a diagonal line between the two sides. Mark where it intersects the half way line.

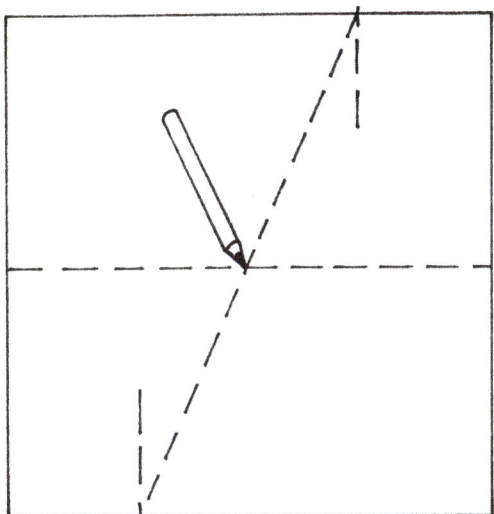

**6.** Draw in a curved line as shown in the upper rectangle. Curve it out about 7.5cm from the diagonal line.

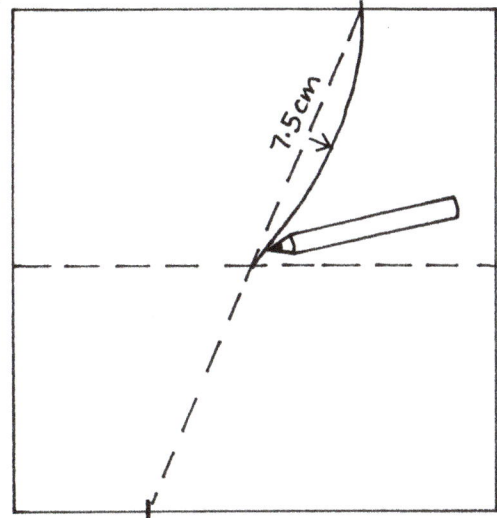

**7.** Pivot the curved line as described on pages 78-79 to make the tessellated shape. Mark the half way point as a notch to help when you sew the seam.

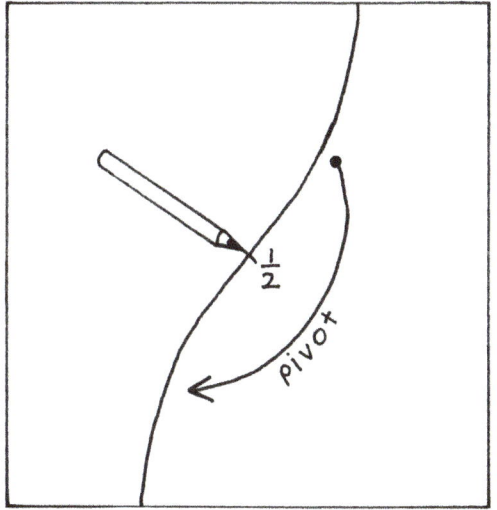

## Draw in the front neckline

**8.** In the top left corner, draw in the front neckline: Measure the **width** out *horizontally* from the corner. Make it 8.7 - 9 - 9.3 - 9.6 - 9.9cm and 9.9cm for all sizes thereafter.

Measure the **depth** 15cm *down* from the corner. Draw in the neckline with a smooth, pleasing curve. Measure 10cm down for the front slit.

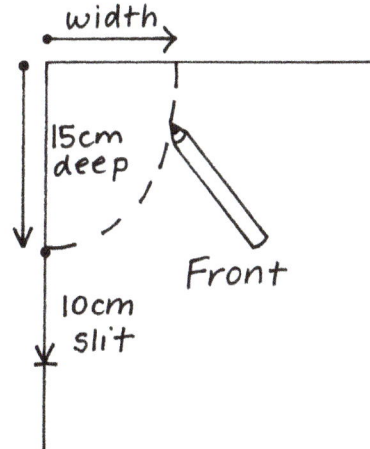

Tessellated

## Draw in the back neckline

**9.** In the lower right corner of the rectangle, draw in the back neckline:

Measure the **width** out *horizontally* from the corner. Make it 8.7 - 9 - 9.3 - 9.6 - 9.9cm and 9.9cm for all sizes thereafter (it's the same as the front).

Measure the **depth** 2.5cm *up* from the corner. If you have a large bust, increase the depth by an additional 2cm.

Draw in the neckline with a smooth curve, noting that you'll need to begin the curve 1cm up, as illustrated, to allow for the 1cm shoulder seam.

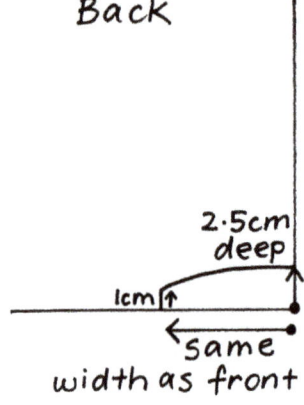

**10.** Two last things to do:
Add a 1cm seam allowance to the centre back.
Mark a notch 27cm from the end for the arm opening.

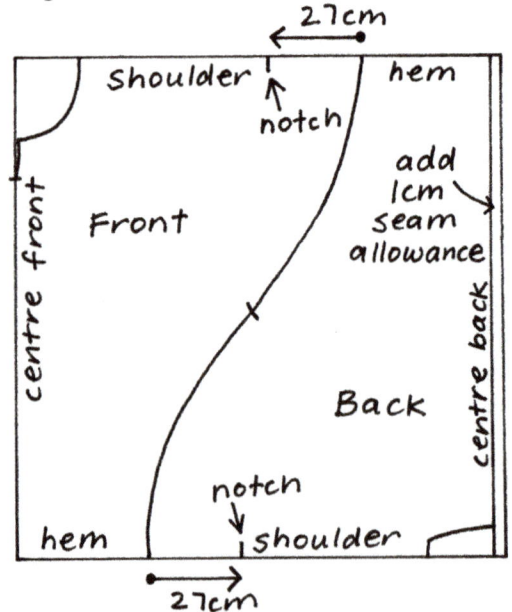

## To cut

**1.** Fold the fabric right sides together. Place the pattern onto the fabric, lining up the centre front on the fold. Pin the pattern to the fabric. You may find it easier to first cut the paper pattern so the front and back are separate.

When you cut the dress out, keep the front neck cutout intact—you'll use it for the back neck. The tiny back neck cutout is not used.

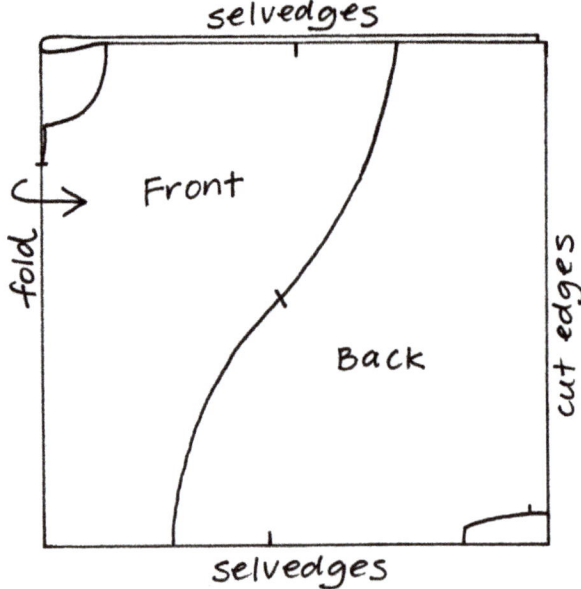

## To sew

**Seam allowances:** all 1cm.

**1.** Stay-stitch the front neckline to stop it from stretching while you sew everything else.

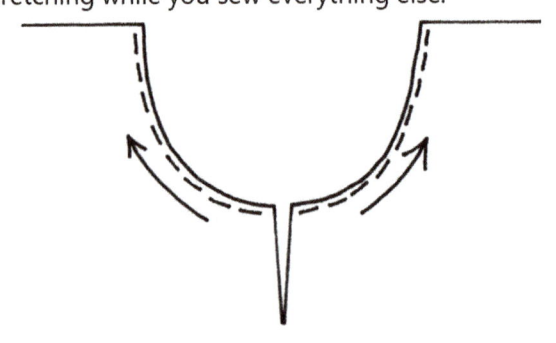

84   Zero Waste Sewing

**2.** Sew the centre back seam. Overlock and press it to one side.

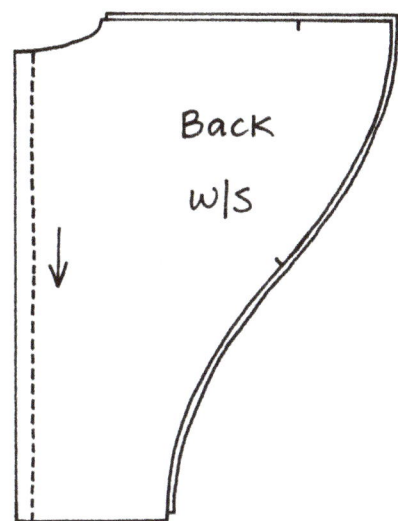

## Neck and shoulders

**3.** Take the front neck cutout and press under the curved edges 5mm.

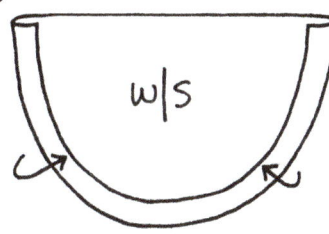

**4.** Position the front neck cutout *wrong* sides together on the back neck, matching the raw edges at the top. Trim to match the back neck if necessary. Sew around the edges.

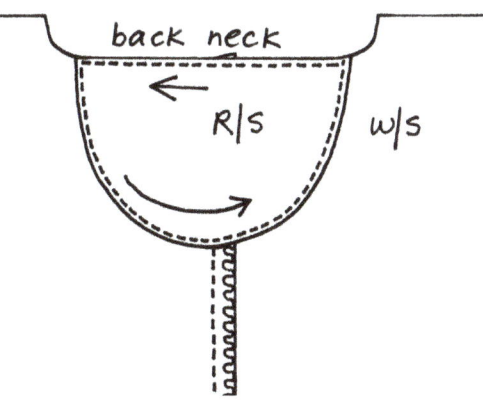

**5.** Sew the curved side seams and overlock.

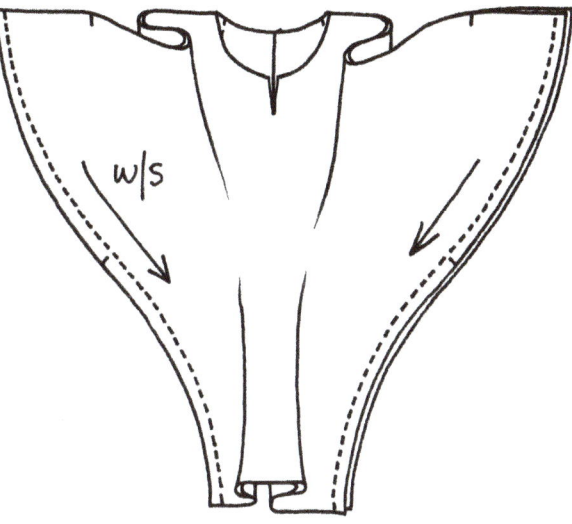

**6.** Sew the shoulder seams leaving a gap at each end for the arm openings. There's no need to overlock since this edge is the selvedge.

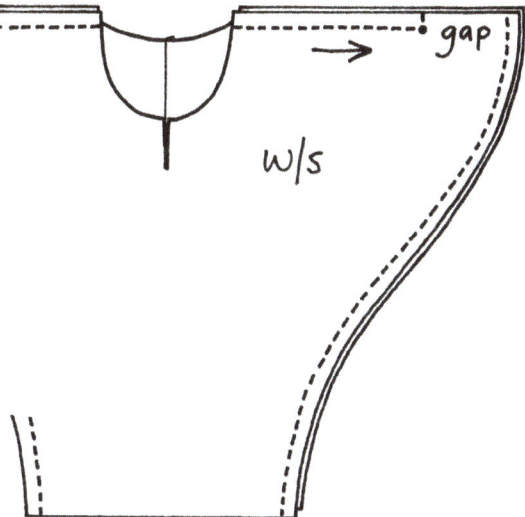

**7.** Hem the armhole openings with a 1cm hem.

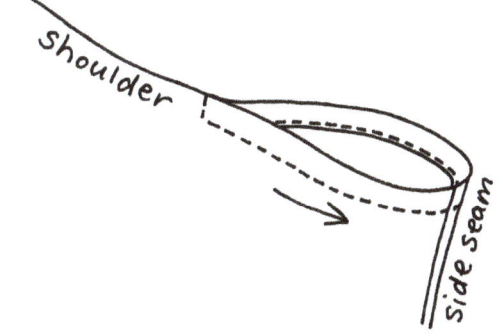

Tessellated

## Neck binding

**8.** Use the 12mm bias binding to bind the front slit and the neck. Bind the slit first (see specific instructions below). When you bind the neck, leave 25cm long ties at each end.

**To apply binding,** place the *right* side of the binding onto the *wrong* side of the fabric and stitch along the crease. Stretch the binding slightly around the curves of the neck—this helps it to sit flat when the binding is finished.

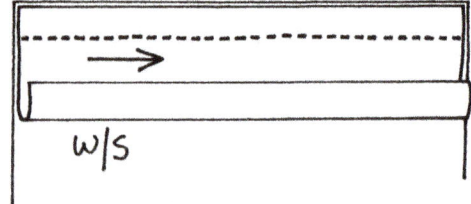

Bring the binding over to the right sides and stitch it down, just covering the first row of stitching. To avoid rippling, hold the fabric firmly towards you and let the binding "sit easy" on top as you stitch.

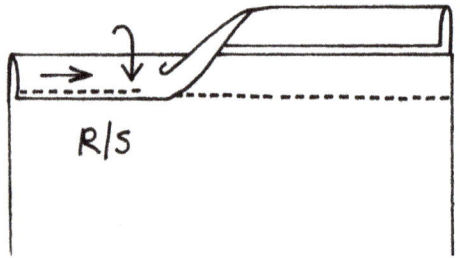

**To bind the slit,** hold the slit straight as you sew the binding. For the first row of stitching, position the slit so you just catch the point, but keep the seam allowance on the binding constant (the reverse side is illustrated).

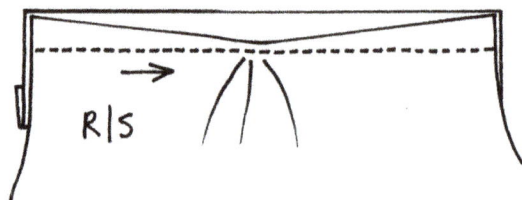

Fold the binding over to the right side to sew the second row as usual.

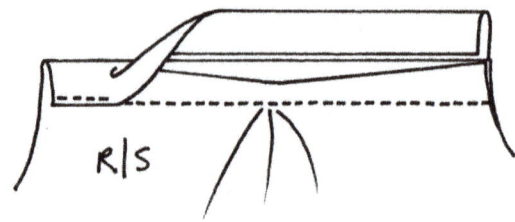

Fold the bound slit in half, right sides together, and sew across the corner at a 45 degree angle. Be sure not to sew across the binding's stitching, otherwise a pleat will form at the bottom of the V.

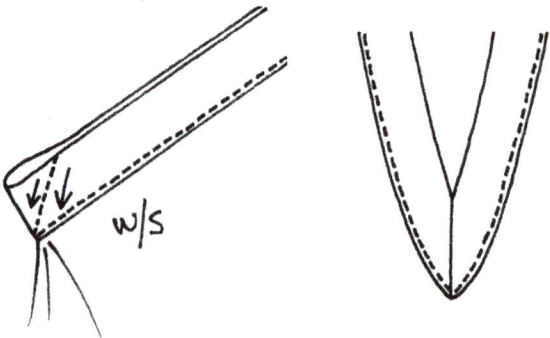

The finished neck should look like this:

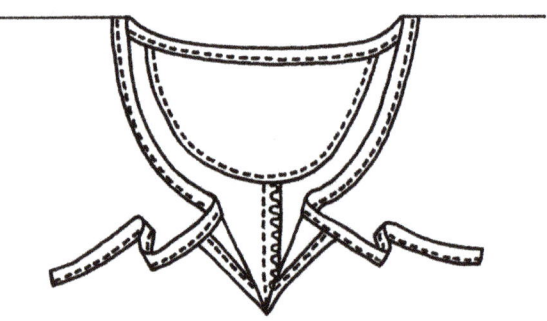

**9.** Try on the dress to check the length, then hem the dress to suit.

## Notes

✂ The dress may look good worn back to front.

✂ Got 150cm wide fabric? Try making a caftan. You'll need slits at the sides (or back) for easy walking. You'll need *exactly* half your hip measurement, plus 184cm. For sizes 8-16 this is 230 - 232.5 - 235 - 237.5 - 240cm.

1. In Step 1 on page 82, make the length 150cm or the width of the fabric.
Since the pattern is big, save paper by making the front and back the same pattern piece (don't forget to add a 1cm centre back seam).

2. In Step 2 on page 82, make the measurement a quarter of your hips, plus **15cm** *not* 5cm. Use the same measurement for Step 3 as well.

3. In Step 6 on page 83, curve the line out by about **6cm** instead of 7.5cm.

4. Sew, leaving 50cm side splits so you can walk.

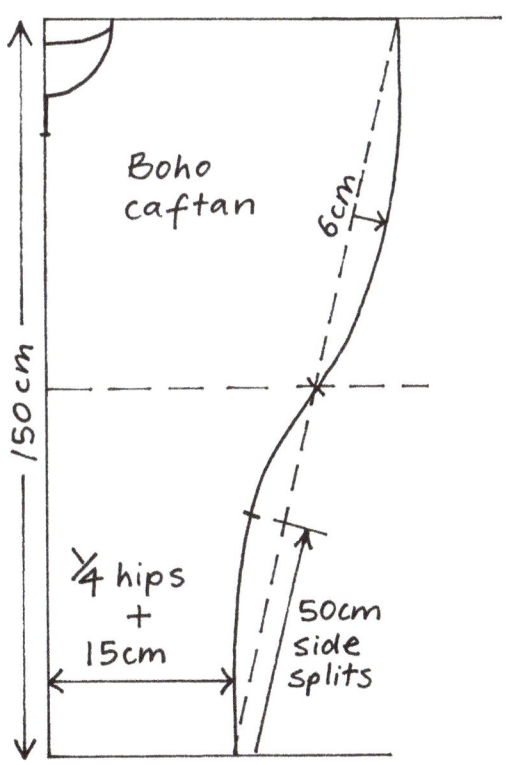

Tessellated

# wrap skirt

*A maxi wrap skirt with a generous underlap. This skirt can be made with 3, 5 or 7 gores. There is a very small amount of waste, caused by the curve of the gores, but the greater the number of gores the less curve and less waste.*

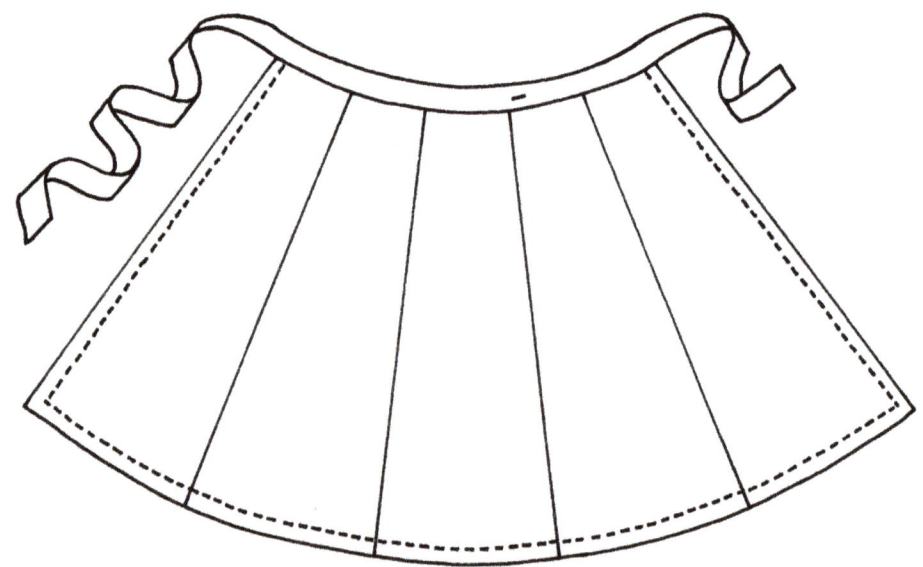

**Fabric** Woven fabric, approximately 115cm wide. If you're a short person you can use a narrower fabric width, because the fabric's width is used for the skirt's length. For the exact amount needed you'll need to make a pattern (pages 90-91) and measure a layout (page 92) because there are too many variables—it depends on your skirt length, size, number of gores and fabric width. As a guide though, a size 10 (3 - 5 - 7) gore skirt takes about (2.25 - 2.30 - 2.35) metres. Add or deduct 7.5cm per size. Suitable fabrics include medium weight cotton, linen, cotton drill, quilting cotton, chambray. Avoid thick fabrics—the skirt will be too heavy to wear. For large prints, make a 3 gore skirt so the design is uninterrupted.

**Notions** Thread. A strip of interfacing for the waistband.

**Sizes** Any.

**Finished length** To be decided by you. The skirt shown here is 105cm.

**Seam and hem allowances** **1cm** seams and **2.5cm** hem are included.

# Make a pattern

## Middle gore

**1.** On a large piece of paper, draw a rectangle.
Make the **length** 60cm long.
The **width** of the rectangle depends on how many gores the skirt will have.
For a 7 gore skirt: (1.5 x your waist) divided by 7, plus 2cm.
For a 5 gore skirt: (1.5 x your waist) divided by 5, plus 2cm.
For a 3 gore skirt: (1.5 x your waist) divided by 3, plus 2cm.
The 2cm is for the seam allowances.

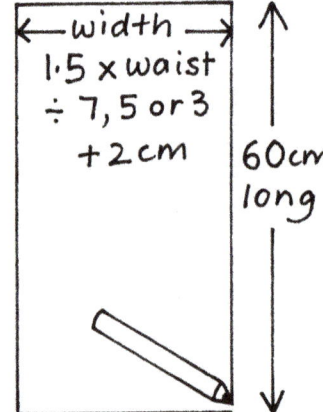

**2.** Add flare to each side of the rectangle.
For a 7 gore skirt add 8.5cm to each side.
For a 5 gore skirt add 13.5cm to each side.
For a 3 gore skirt add 27cm to each side.

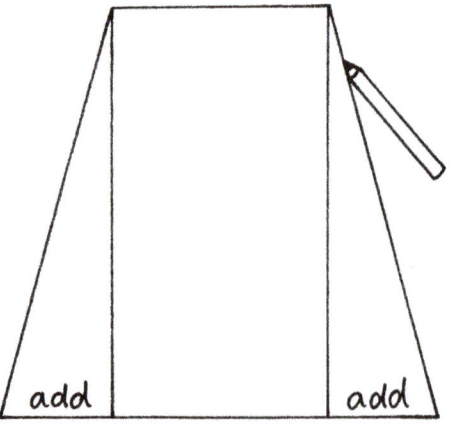

**3.** Add length to the bottom of the rectangle to make it your desired maxi skirt length plus 3.5cm. (The 3.5cm allows for a 1cm seam at the waist and 2.5cm for the hem.)
Extend the sides using a long ruler.

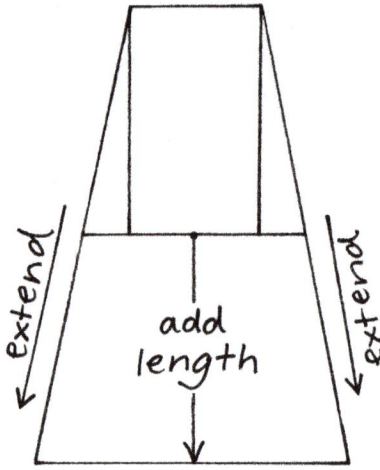

**4.** Curve the top and bottom edges.
For a 7 gore skirt, curve the top edges 3mm and the bottom ones 8mm.
For a 5 gore skirt, curve the top edges 1.3cm and the bottom ones 3cm.
For a 3 gore skirt, curve the top edges 3cm and the bottom ones 8cm.

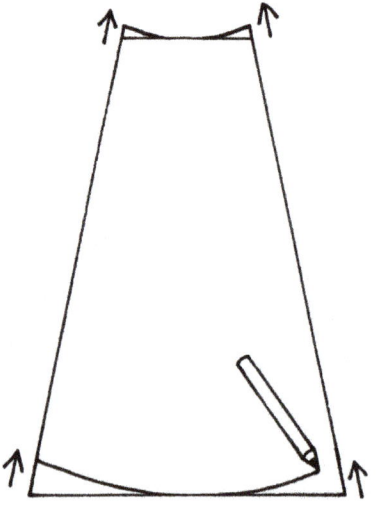

This completes the middle gore pattern. You'll need to cut five of them for a 7 gore skirt, three for a 5 gore skirt or one for a 3 gore skirt.

# End gore

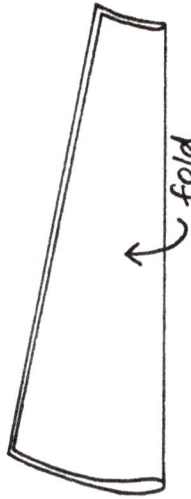

**5.** Trace off the middle gore pattern and put the middle gore aside.
Fold the traced gore in half to find the centre.

**6.** Draw a line parallel to the fold, beginning at the top corner.

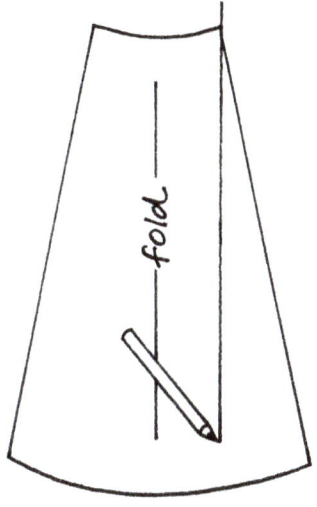

**7.** Add 1.5cm to the straight edge (to give you a 2.5cm hem; there is already a 1cm seam allowance here).

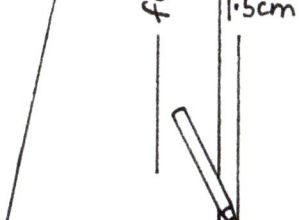

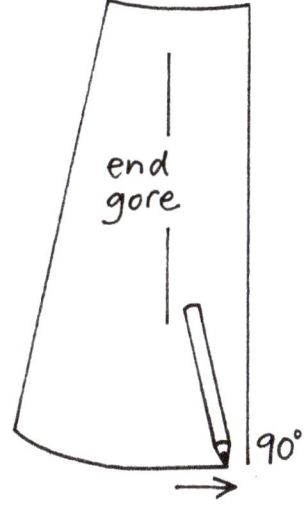

**8.** Square off the lower corner. This completes the end gore. You'll cut 2 (as a pair) of these.

**9.** The completed pattern pieces:

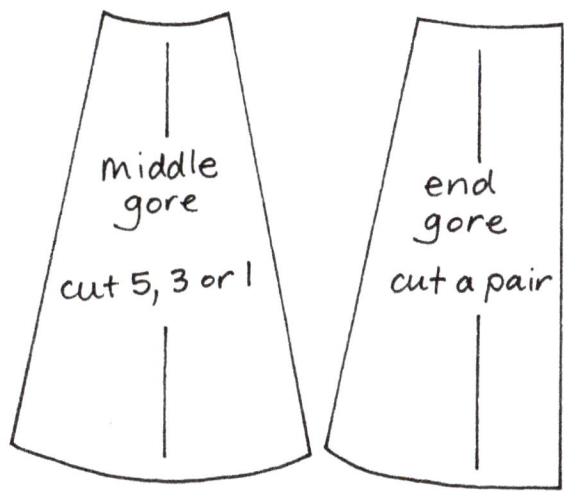

There's no pattern for the waistband/ties; they'll be marked straight onto the fabric prior to cutting.

Tessellated  91

## To cut

**1.** Mark in the skirt panels on a single layer of fabric. Put the end gores next to each cut end and "top and tail" the middle gores in between. The illustration shows a 5 gore skirt.

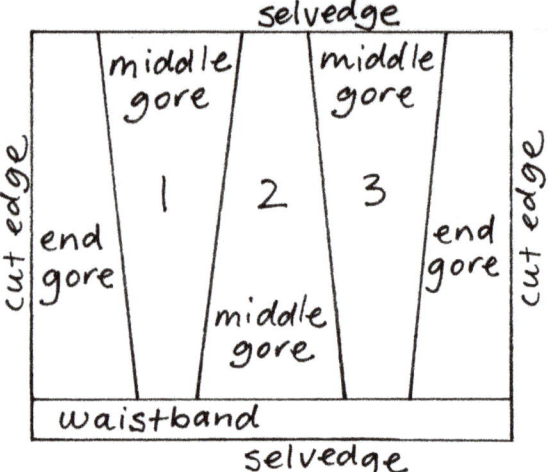

The spare strip of fabric (if any) along the selvedge edge is for the waistband/ties. It can be anything from 5cm to 12cm wide.

See pages 131-133 in *Sewing Techniques* for notes on cutting (and sewing) a waistband.

If there isn't enough for a waistband, cut 3 selvedge-to-selvedge strips instead:

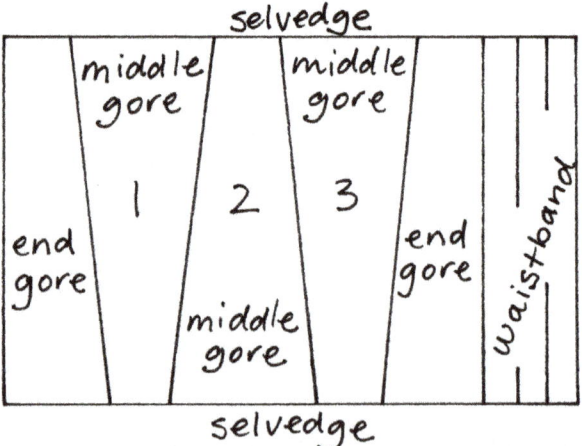

## To sew

**Seam allowances:** all 1cm.

### Skirt

**1.** Join all the panels together, stitching from the bottom to the top. Press the seam allowances to one side and overlock.

If you're topstitching the panels, stitch from the bottom to the top.

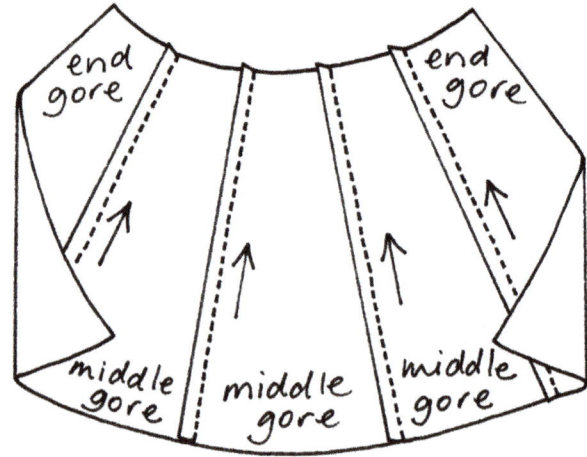

**2.** Overlock the lower edge and ends. Hem the sides of the end gores with a 2.5cm hem. Hem the lower edge, also with a 2.5cm hem (or if you prefer, you can wait until the skirt is finished to hem the lower edge, after you've tried it on).

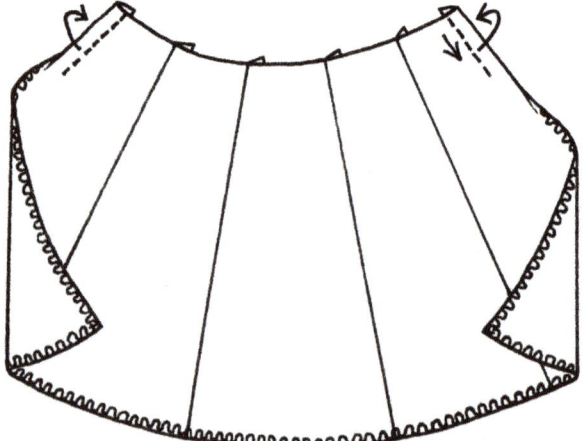

Zero Waste Sewing

## Waistband and ties

**3.** If the waistband is in three strips, join them together now, and press the seams open.

Lay the waistband next to the top of the skirt. The end ties need to be different lengths to allow for the wrapping. The one on the right should be at least 50cm long in order to tie a bow, and the other one should be half your waist longer. (If you don't want ties, see *Notes*, below.)

Mark on the waistband where it will be sewn to the skirt and interface that part. Don't interface the ties; they don't need it.

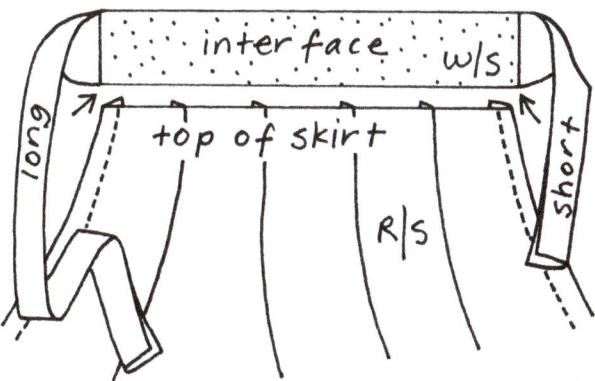

While you're at the ironing board, press the whole waistband/ties in half longways, with the wrong sides together.

**4.** Attach the waistband to the skirt by placing the waistband right sides together with the skirt. Make sure the ties are on the correct sides. Stitch. Press the seam towards the waistband.

Press up 8mm along the opposite side.

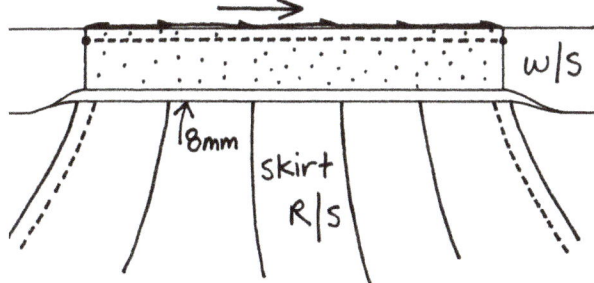

**5.** Make the ties by sewing the ends right sides together. Trim the corners, turn through, press.

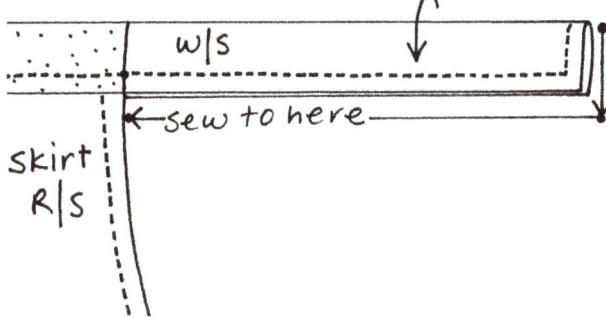

**6.** Fold the waistband into position and pin it from the right side, in the groove of the waist seam. Stitch-in-the-ditch (see page 12) on the right side to secure.

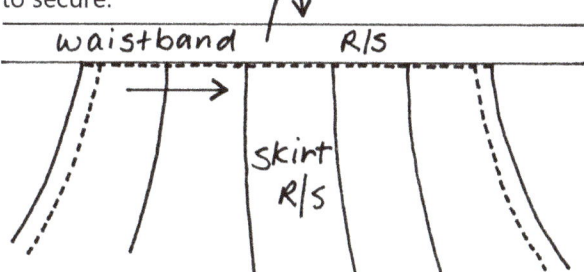

**7.** Sew a buttonhole in the waistband to pull the tie through. Position it a third of the way along from the end with the shortest tie—the sketch on page 88 shows the position.

## Notes

✂ Don't want ties? Just sew a regular waistband on the skirt (see pages 131-132) and fasten it with buttons and buttonholes, or use a length of press stud tape for an adjustable waist.

✂ Rather than hemmed edges, the front and hem can be bound with 25mm bias binding. The two lower corners can be curved or square. Bind the waist to match, leaving long ties for tying. There's no need for a buttonhole for such a narrow band.

✂ The skirt can have more gores than 7, provided it's an odd number. The more gores, the less curve is required on each, and therefore less waste.

# wrap trousers

*If you're an avowed trouser wearer and never wear skirts, you might like these wraparound trousers. They can be worn several ways. The trousers have concealed pockets.*

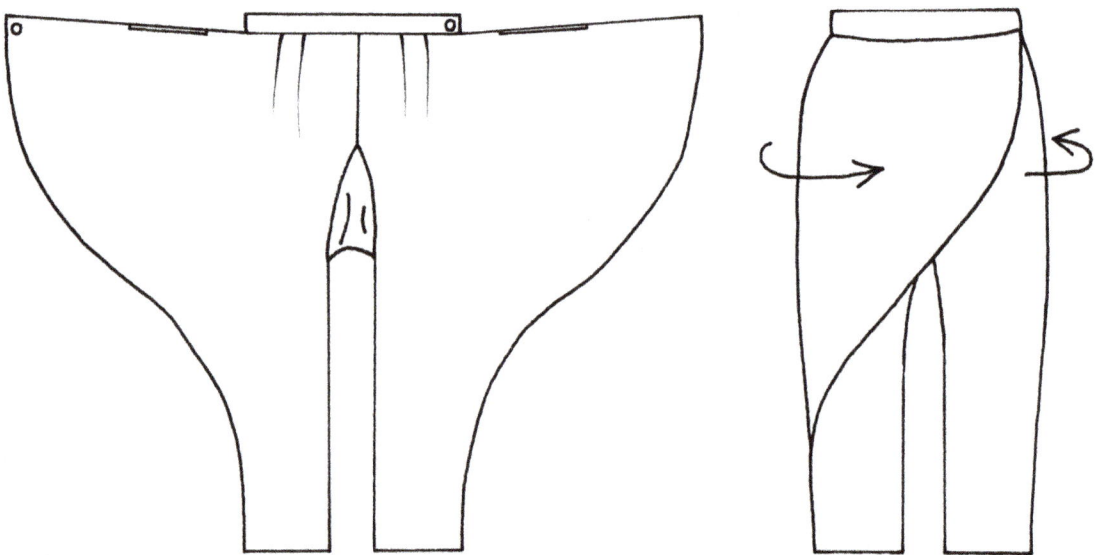

**Fabric** Woven fabric approximately 112cm-115cm wide. For "average" length trousers, sizes 8-20, you'll need *exactly* 248cm and size 22 will need *exactly* 258cm. (To calculate: for sizes 8-20, twice your length plus 7cm for seams and hems plus 30cm for the gusset and pockets. Add 10cm for a waistband for size 22. For sizes larger than 22, make the pattern first then review the cutting information on pages 97-98 to calculate the exact amount.) Suitable fabrics include lightweight silk, cotton voile and rayon. The fabric should be drapey and soft rather than crisp. Choose a lightweight fabric otherwise the trousers will be too heavy. Slightly transparent fabrics are fine to use since the upper trousers are three layers thick. One-way prints are unsuitable. Stripes will run vertically but for sizes larger than 22 they'll run horizontally and may not match.

**Notions** 1 x 25cm invisible zip. One button or hook for the waistband. 2 large 13mm press studs for the wrap-over. Sizes 18 and over will require a strip of interfacing for the waistband. Thread.

**Sizes** Any.

**Seam and hem allowances** **1cm** seams and **2.5cm** hems are included.

# Make a pattern

The trouser pattern is the same back and front.

**1.** On a large piece of paper, draw a rectangle. Make the **length** the *finished* trouser length plus 1cm for the waist seam plus a 2.5cm hem. For an "average" leg length this will be 105.5cm + 1cm + 2.5cm = 109cm.

Mark in the **width**: starting in the top left hand corner, first measure across a *quarter* of your waist, plus 12cm. This gets pleated into the waistband. Continuing on, measure *half* your waist, plus 6cm. This part will be the wrap-over.

**3.** Fold the paper in half to find the horizontal half-way point.

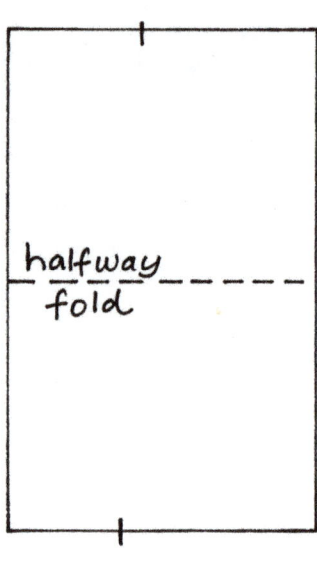

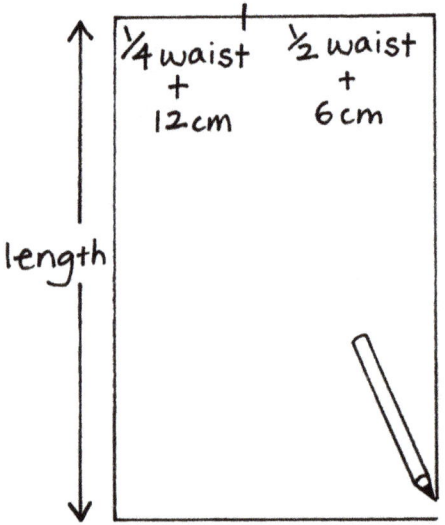

**2.** Mark in the ankle width. This needs to be *at least* 21cm so you can get your foot through. The one shown in this book is 25cm.

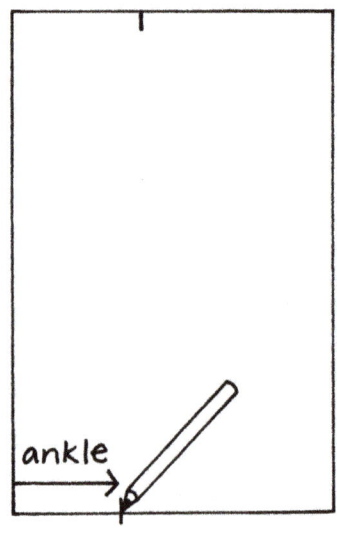

**4.** Rule a diagonal line across the paper from the ankle point to the wrap over. Mark where the two lines intersect.

**5.** Draw in a curved shape in the top half of the rectangle, as shown.
Curve it out about 6.5cm from the diagonal line.

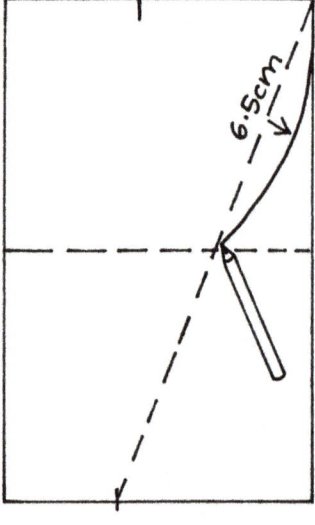

96  Zero Waste Sewing

## To cut

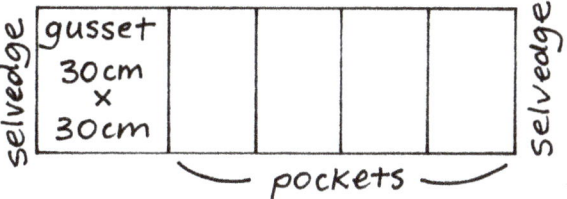

**1. For all sizes**, cut the crotch gusset and pockets from a 30cm wide strip of fabric. The crotch gusset is simply a square with 30cm sides. From the remainder, cut the pocket bags by dividing it into four. Each will be about 21cm wide.

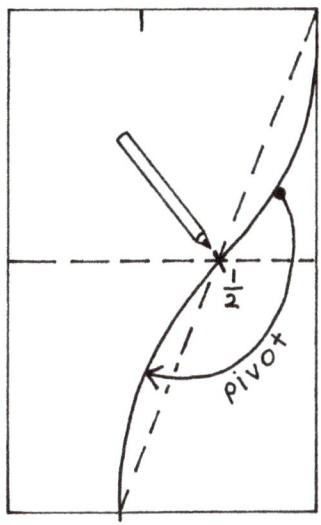

**6.** Pivot the curved line as described on pages 78-79 to make the tessellated shape. Mark the half way point as a notch to help when you sew the seam.

**2.** Fold the remaining fabric over so it's double, as shown. Lay the paper pattern on and mark it in twice, for the back and front. Put the back next to the selvedge.

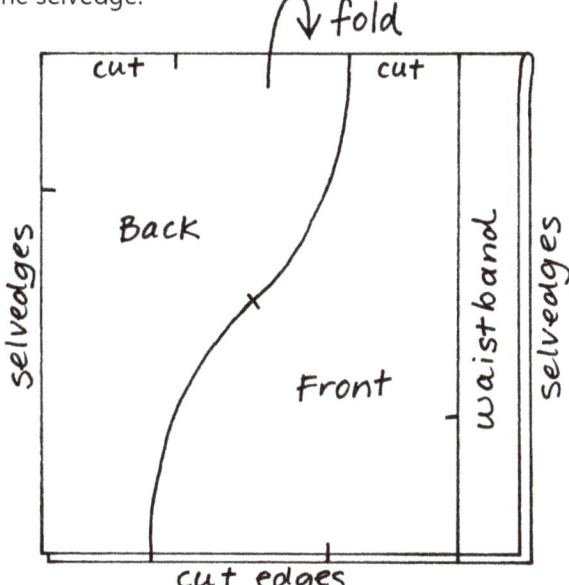

**7.** On the long straight side, mark a crotch notch 27.1 - 28 - 28.9 - 29.8 - 30.7cm down from the top. This line is the trousers' centre front and centre back.

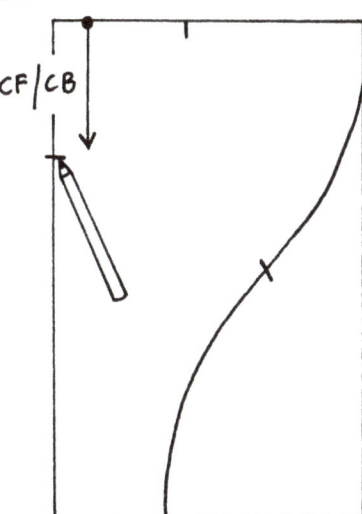

Sizes 8-16 should fit across with a double folded waistband at the side.

Sizes 18-20 will still fit but with a regular waistband at the side.

Size 22 will fit across but with a separately cut waistband (cut the waistband selvedge-to-selvedge at 10cm or your preferred width).

**8.** There's no pattern for the waistband; it's made from a strip left after cutting the front and back. Review the instructions for cutting and sewing a waistband in *Sewing Techniques* on pages 131-133.

Sizes bigger than 22 will need to be cut around the other way. Depending on the height of the wearer, a regular waistband should fit along one selvedge.

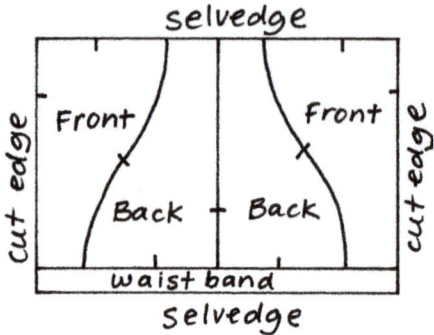

## To sew

**Seam allowances:** all 1cm.

### Zip and gusset

**1.** Sew a 25cm invisible zip at the centre back. You won't need to overlock the edge first, because this side has the selvedge. Sew the rest of the centre back seam down to the notch.

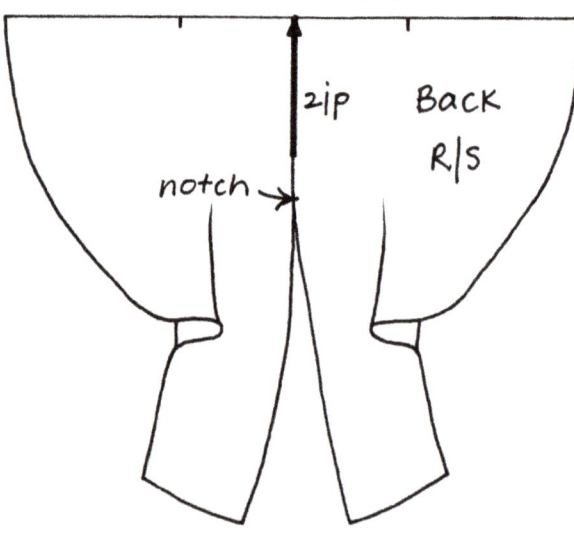

**Other options instead of a zip:** use any spare fabric to create a placket to be buttoned or press-studded closed—see page 130 in *Sewing Techniques*. Don't have an invisible zip? Use a regular one and take a bigger seam allowance if you need to. Note that no-one will see the zip when the trousers are worn wrapped over.

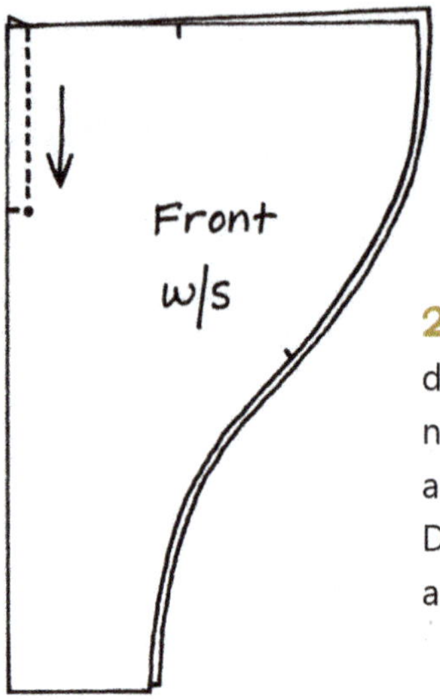

**2.** On the front, sew down to the crotch notch, backstitching accurately. Don't overlock anything until Step 5.

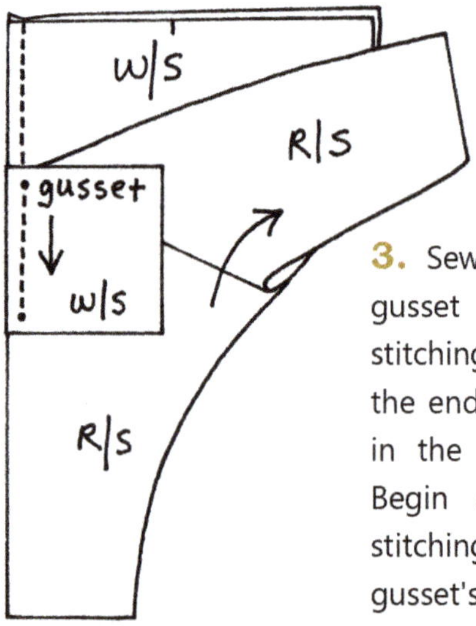

**3.** Sew one side of the gusset to the front, stitching *exactly* from the end of the stitching in the previous step. Begin and end the stitching 1cm from the gusset's raw edge.

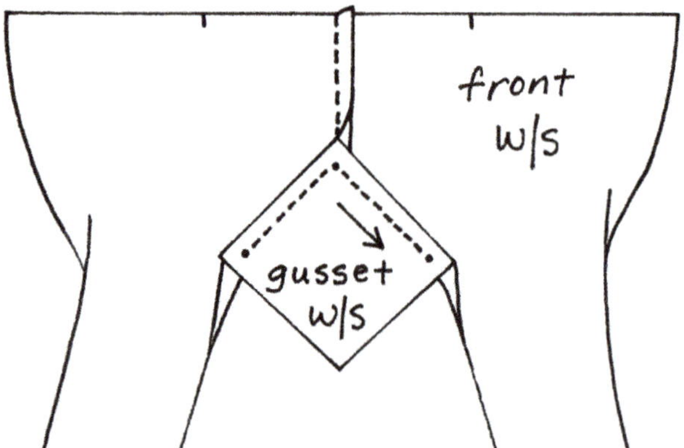

**4.** Do the same with the adjacent side on the other front leg.

98    Zero Waste Sewing

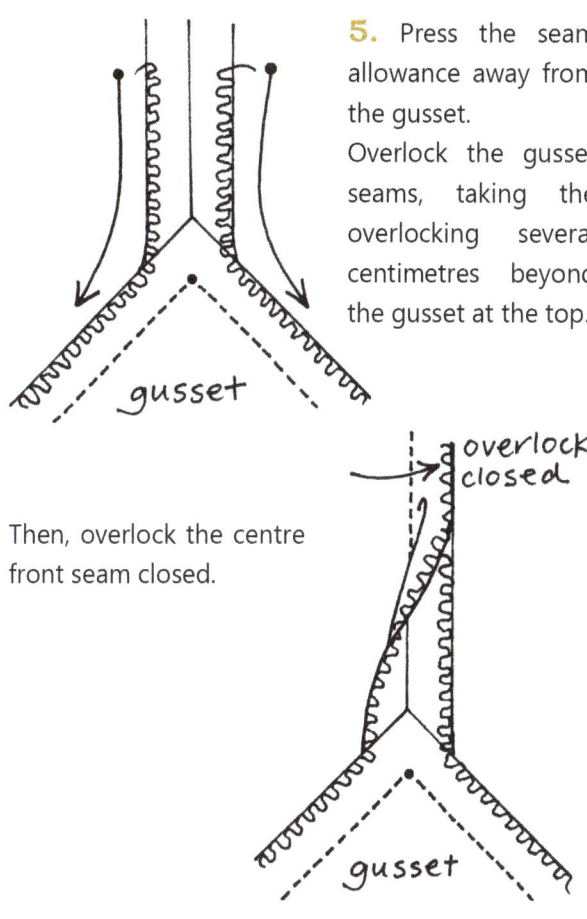

**5.** Press the seam allowance away from the gusset.
Overlock the gusset seams, taking the overlocking several centimetres beyond the gusset at the top.

Then, overlock the centre front seam closed.

**6.** Sew gusset on the back in the same way, but continue sewing down the inside leg.
Press the gusset seams away from the gusset and the inside leg seams towards the back. Overlock.

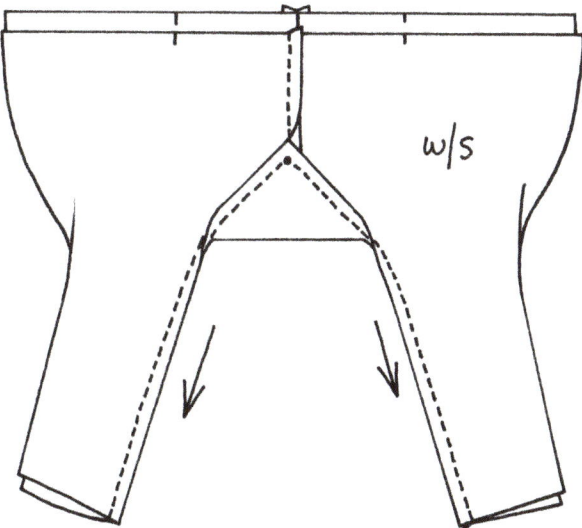

## Leg seams
**7.** Sew the outside legs and overlock them.

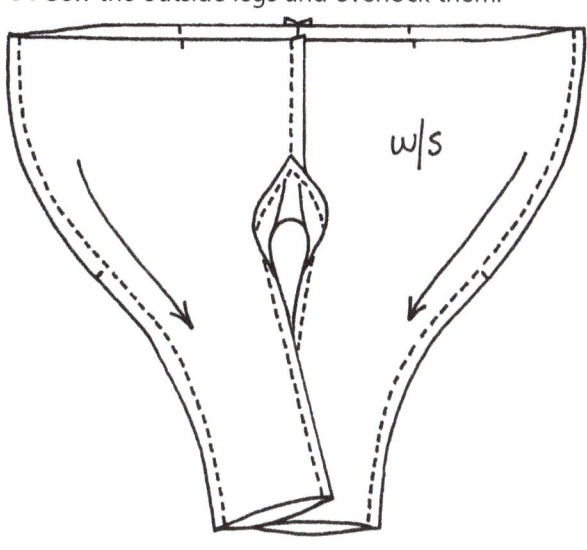

## Pockets
**8.** Position the pocket bags 2.5cm from the waist notch on the top edge, on each front and back. Sew, taking a 5mm seam allowance. Don't overlock.

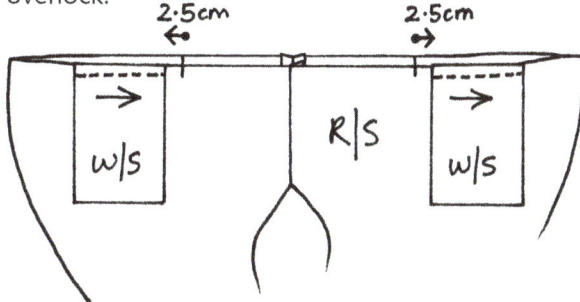

**9.** Press each pocket bag up and understitch (see page 12).

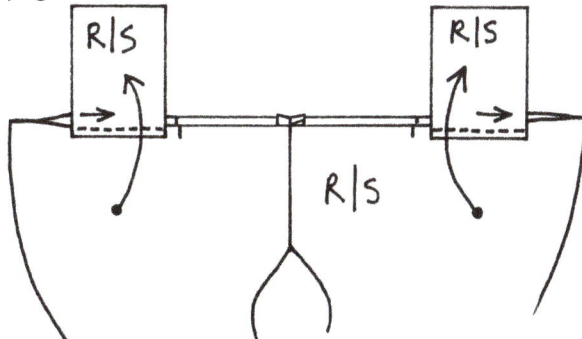

Tessellated

**10.** Turn the trousers inside out. Sew the tops of the trousers, stitching around the pocket bags, pivoting at the bag's corners. Finish sewing *exactly* at the waist notches. Snip in 1cm deep to the stitching *exactly* at the notches as shown.

Overlock where you've just sewn, stopping at the waist notches so that the centre/waist of the trousers remains raw.

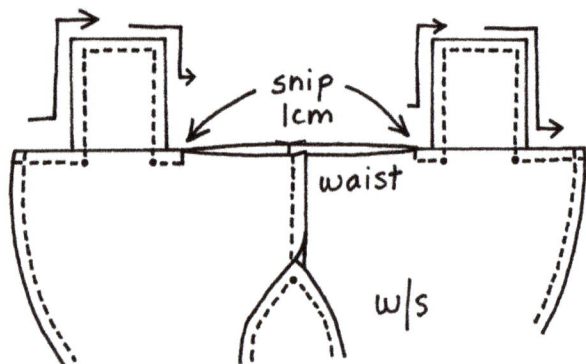

**11.** If you feel the pocket opening is too wide, stitch it smaller. The trousers in this book have a 14cm pocket opening.

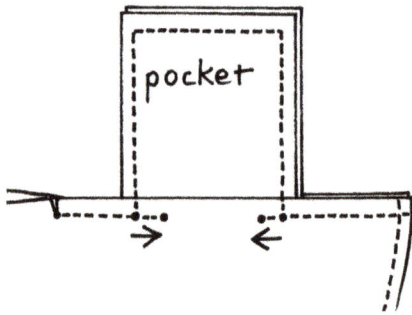

## Waistband

**12.** Take the strip of fabric for the waistband. Make the waistband as shown in *Sewing Techniques* on pages 131-133.

Sizes 8-16 should have enough fabric for a double folded waistband; otherwise make a regular waistband with interfacing in it.

Divide the (finished length of the) waistband into quarters and pleat each quarter of the trousers to fit the waistband. About 2-3 pleats per quarter should take up the excess fabric nicely.

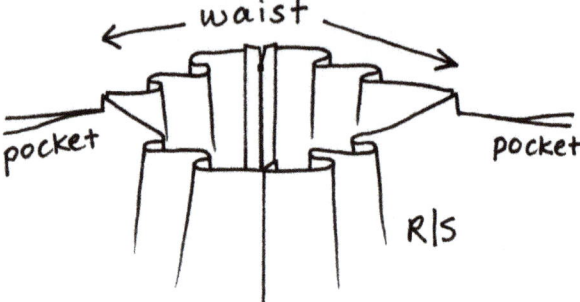

## Finishing

**13.** Sew a fastening to the waistband at the back, either a button/buttonhole or hook and bar.

**14.** Sew a large press stud to the corner of each back and front "wing" and the corresponding side of the trousers on the waistband.

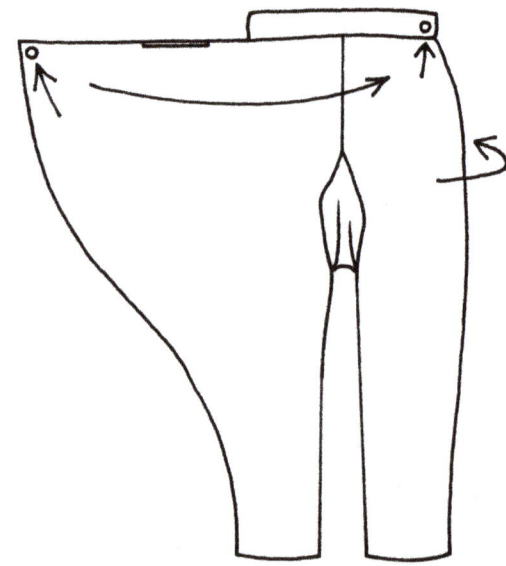

**15.** Hem the trousers.

## To wear

The trousers can be worn several ways: wrapped over as shown on page 95, unwrapped with the sides hanging loose, or with both wraps fastened at the back to create a bustle.

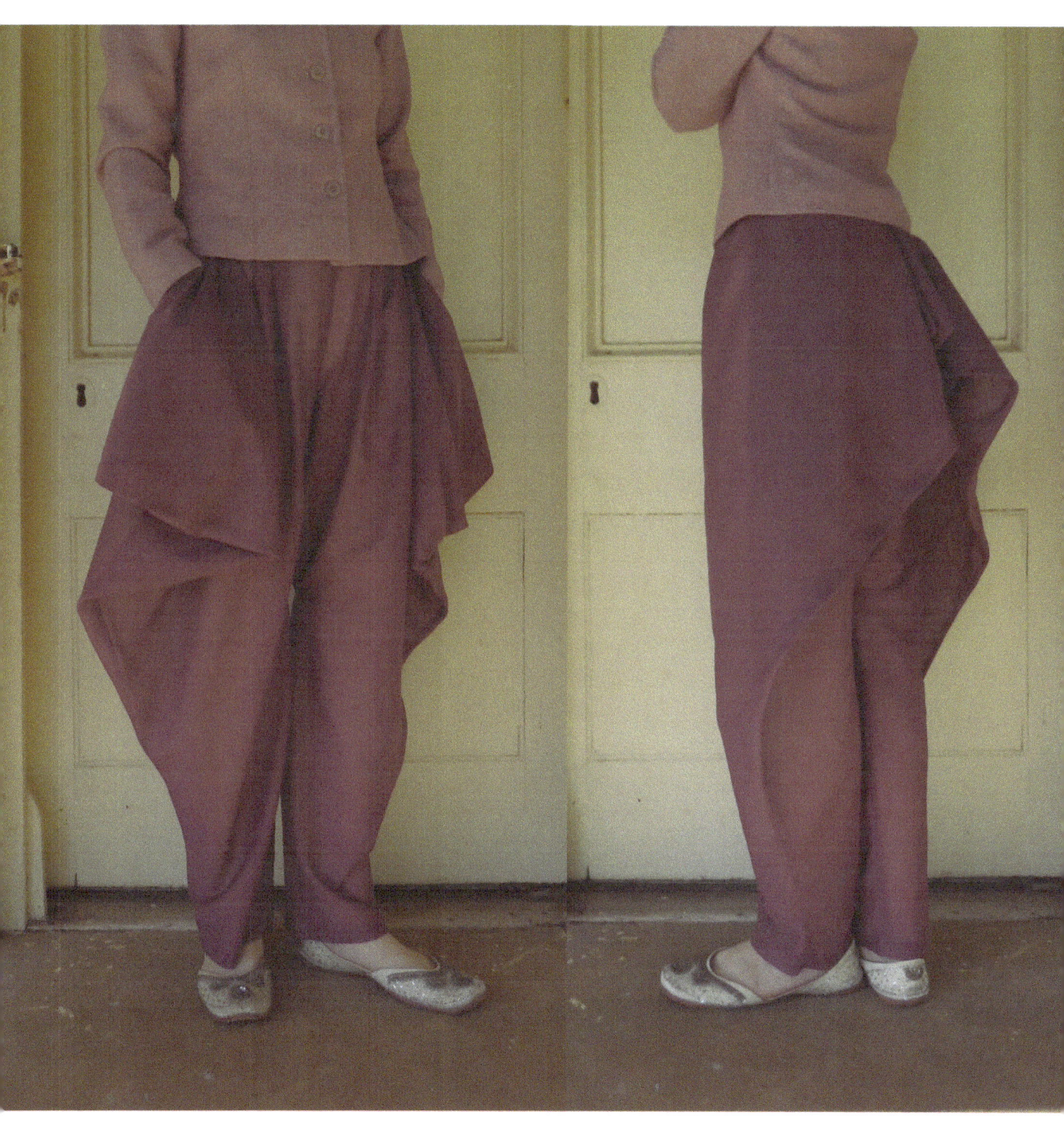

# dress + coat

*A summer dress and slim-fitting coat both cut from the same pattern. The coat is lined with the same fabric as the dress.*

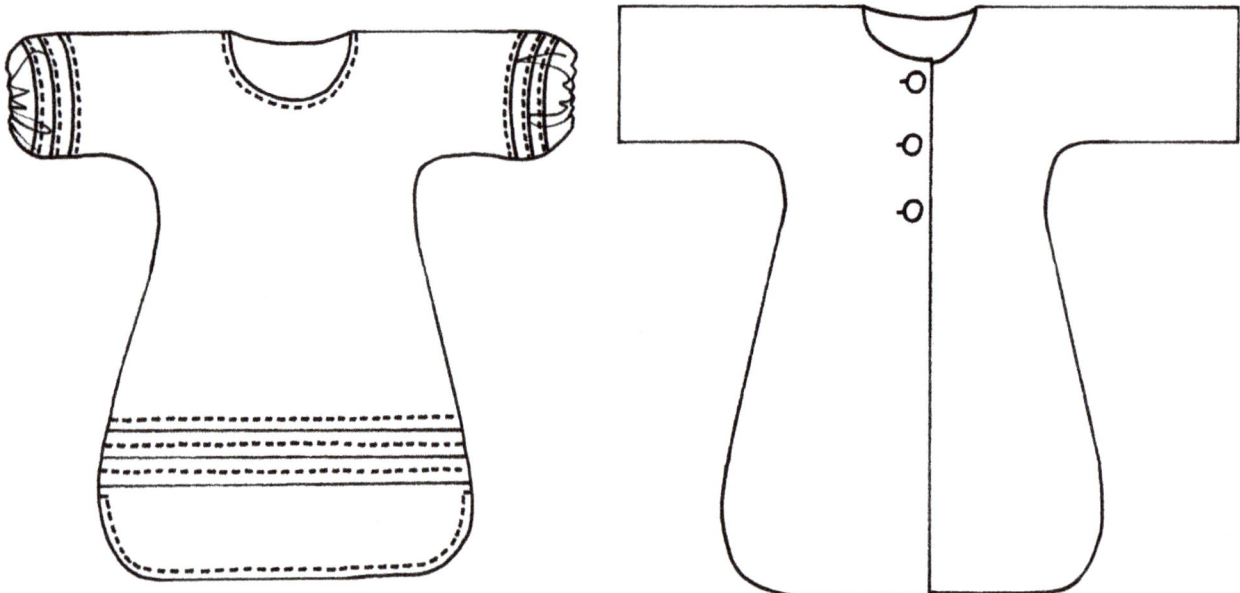

**Fabric** Woven fabric, a minimum of 130cm wide and up to 150cm wide. The coat and the dress require the same width. **For the dress/coat lining** sizes 8-16 you'll need *exactly* 252 - 262 - 272 - 282 - 292cm. For other sizes you'll need twice your bust measurement, plus 78cm. To make the dress on its own, see *Notes* on page 110. **For the coat** sizes 8-16 you'll need *exactly* 129 - 134 - 139 - 144 - 149cm. For other sizes you'll need your bust measurement plus 42cm. Suitable fabrics for the dress include light to medium weight cotton. For the coat, denim, linen, heavier weight cottons. Fabric can be plain or patterned but stripes and checks are unsuitable because they can't be matched.

**Notions For the dress:** approximately 60cm of 12mm bias binding to finish front neck. 2 lengths of 5mm elastic for the sleeves. Thread. **For the coat**: 3 x 30mm buttons. 2 strips of interfacing 5cm wide and approximately 1m long for the front edges. Interfacing for around the back and front neck. Thread.

**Sizes** Any, however, this is a simple style with no darts or shaping. See page 112 for a bust darts option.

**Finished length** The fabric width determines the length. For 130 wide fabric the dress is approximately 100cm long and the coat is 106cm long.

**Seam and hem allowances** 1cm seam and hems are included.

## Make a pattern

**1.** Draw a rectangle on a large piece of paper. Make the **length** the same as your fabric *width*. The dress and coat in this book used 130 wide fabric. Make the **width** half your bust measurement, plus 18cm. For sizes 8-16 this is 61.5 - 64 - 66.5 - 69 - 71.5cm.

Mark in the horizontal half way line.

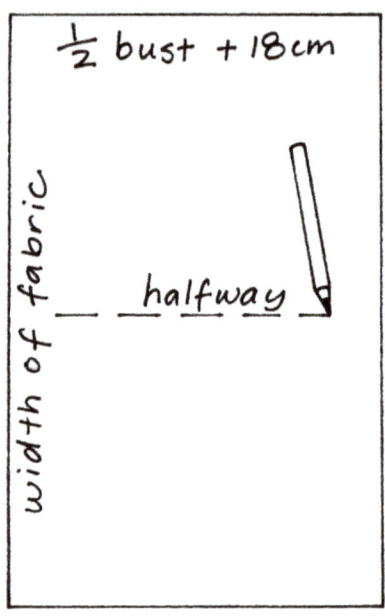

**2.** Mark in the sleeve width on both sides. For sizes 8-16 make it 21.4 - 22 - 22.6 - 23.2 - 23.8cm.

For other sizes, halve your upper arm measurement and add 9cm. You can also use this formula to check if the sleeve width is correct for you, regardless of your size.

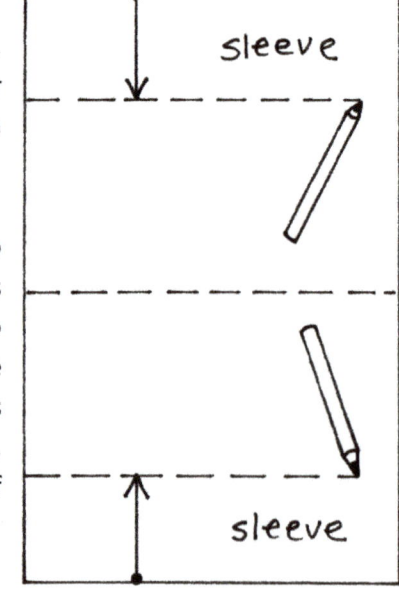

**3.** Mark in the front neckline in the top left corner. You'll be marking both the dress and the coat on the same pattern.

For the neckline's **width**, measure out *horizontally* from the corner. For sizes 8-16 measure 8.7 - 9 - 9.3 - 9.6 - 9.9cm for the dress and 8.2 - 8.5 - 8.8 - 9.1 - 9.4cm for the coat.

For the neckline's **depth**, measure *down* from the corner, 15cm for the dress and 12cm for the coat. Draw in a pleasing curve.

The back neckline will be drawn in the diagonally opposite corner later.

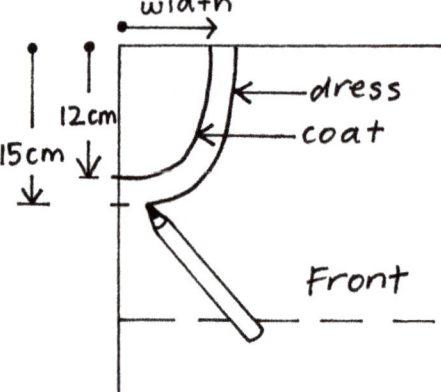

**4.** Measure out from the centre front (CF) a quarter of your bust measurement, plus 4cm. For sizes 8-16 this is 25.7 - 27 - 28.2 - 29.5 - 30.7cm.

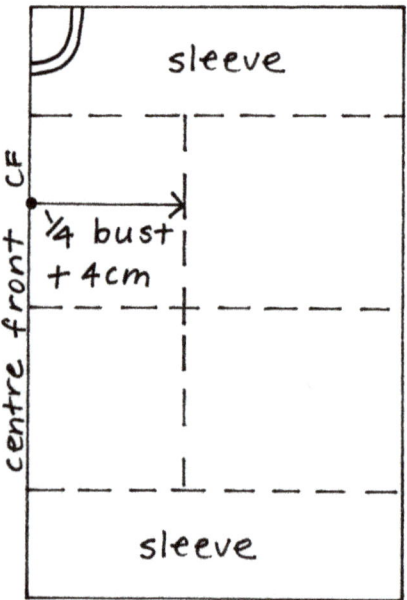

Zero Waste Sewing

**5.** Draw in the underarm curve: mark 10cm along each side of the corner as shown, then draw the curve coming 4cm out from the corner.

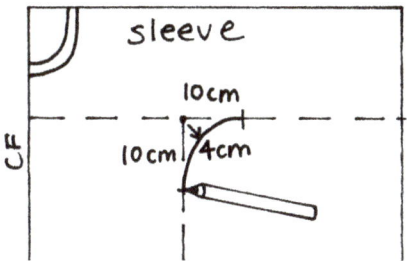

**6.** Place a mark 5cm to the right of the vertical line, on the rectangle's halfway line.

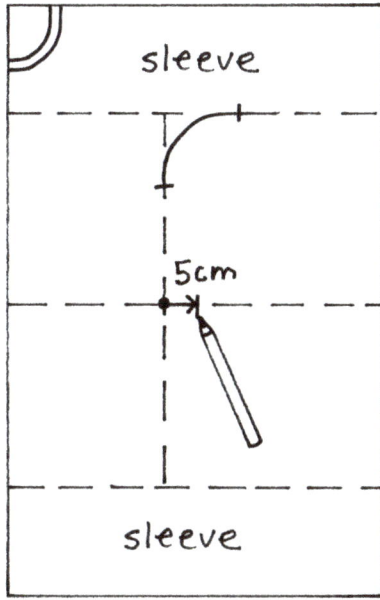

**7.** Connect the mark made in Step 6 with the curve.

Draw in a notch as shown—it's the mark you made on the vertical line back in Step 5.

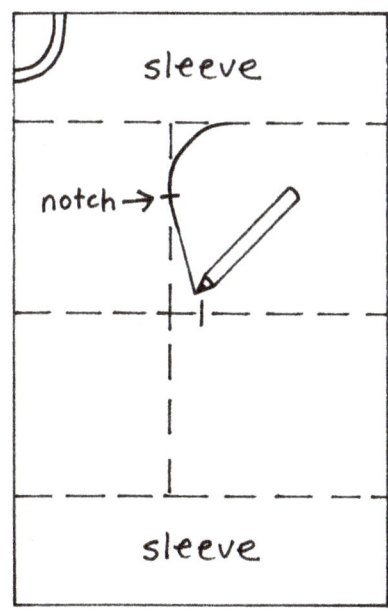

**8.** Pivot the curved line as described on pages 78-79 to make the tessellated shape. Mark the half way point as a notch to help when you sew the seam.

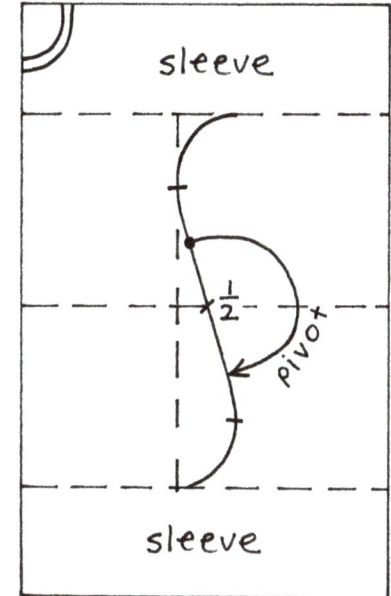

**9.** In the bottom right hand corner, draw in the back neck.

Measure the **width** out *horizontally* from the corner and make it the same as the front.

Measure the neckline's **depth** *up* from the corner and make it 2.5cm for the dress and the coat.

Draw in the neckline with a smooth curve, noting that you'll need to begin the curve 1cm up as illustrated, to allow for the 1cm shoulder seam.

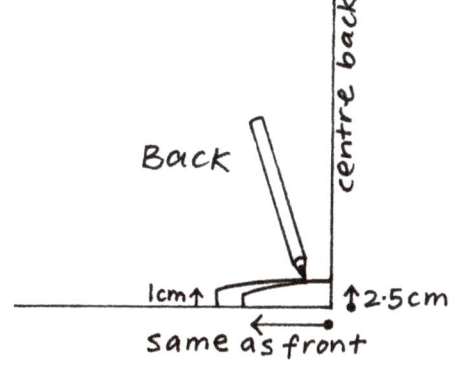

Tessellated  105

## To cut

### Coat

**1.** Fold the coat fabric in half, right sides together, so the cut edges sit on top of one another.

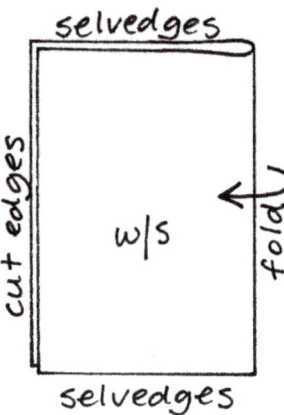

**2.** Position the pattern so the centre back is on the fold. Add 3cm to the centre front.

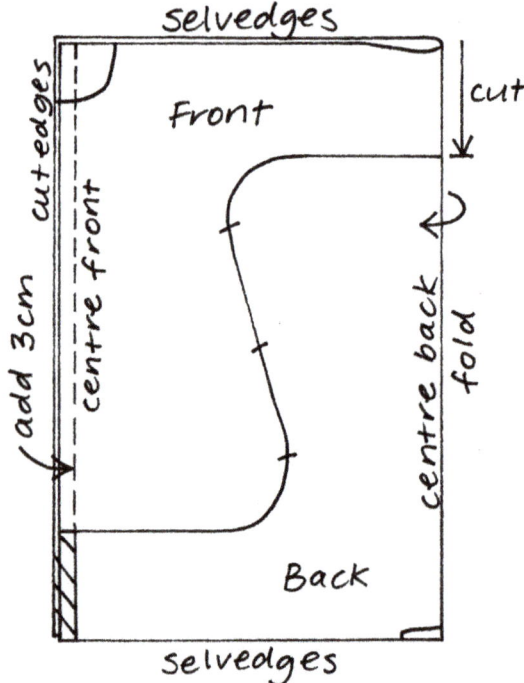

You may like to cut apart the paper pattern to separate the front and back to make it easier to cut the fabric.

### Dress/coat lining

**3.** The dress and coat lining are cut out together so that the dress has no centre back or front seams.

Fold the fabric in half, wrong sides together, so the cut edges sit on top of one another.

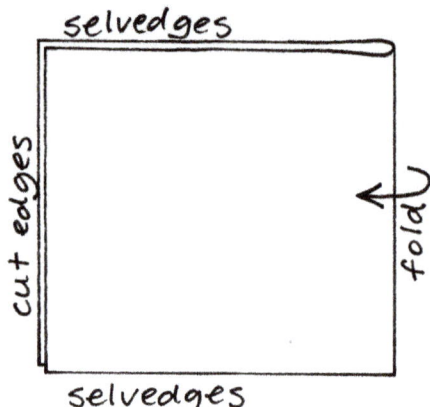

**4.** Position the coat's back lining on the centre back fold.

The dress is cut in one piece.

Position the coat's front lining next to the fabric's cut edges—add 3cm to the centre front, same as you did for the coat.

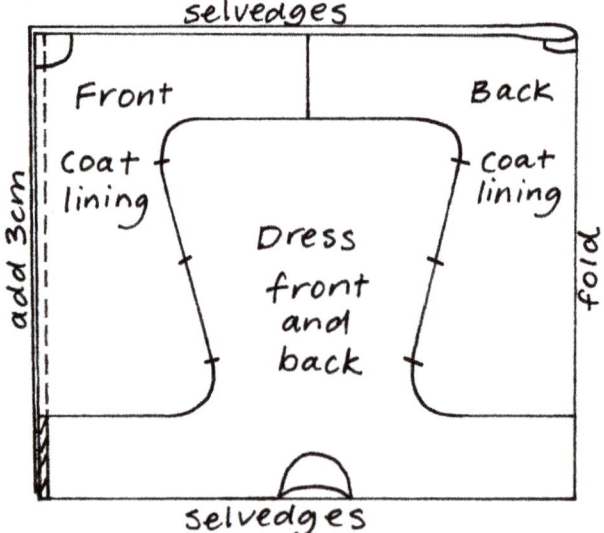

# To sew the dress
**Seam allowances:** all 1cm.

## Shoulders and neck
**1.** Sew the shoulder seams and overlock.

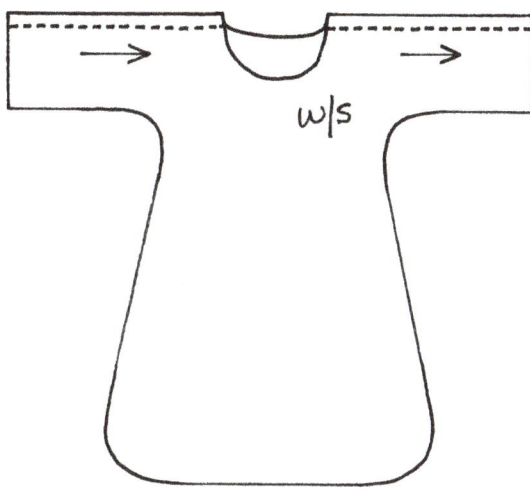

**2.** Finish the neckline with a bias binding facing as described in *Sewing Techniques* on pages 127-128. Use the front neck cutout as a back neck facing. The neckline is big enough to pull on over the head.

## Side/underarm seam and hem
**3.** Sew the side/underarm seam, beginning at the top of the curved side splits.

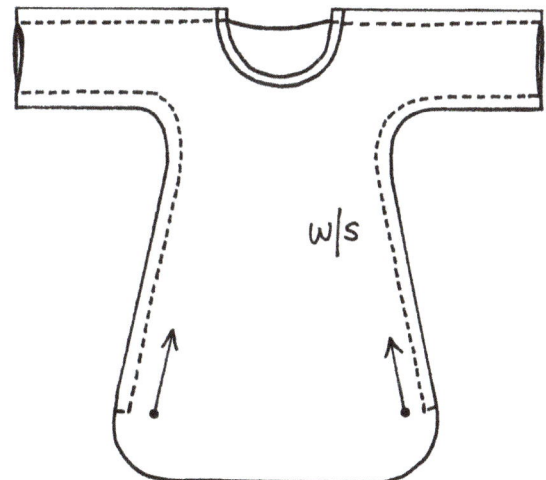

Overlock: do the hem first, beginning several centimetres up the sides. Then overlock the sides seams together, running off at the top of the side splits.

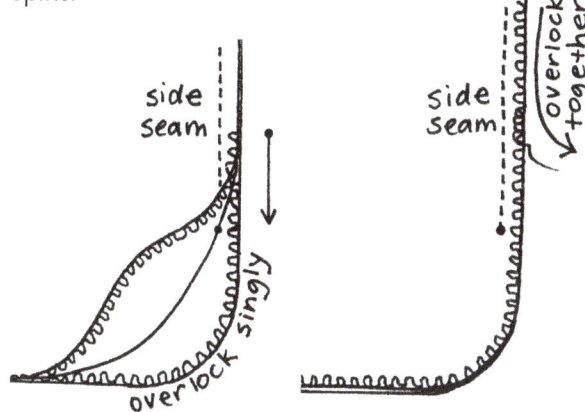

**4.** Hem the dress with a 1cm hem (overlocking not shown for clarity).

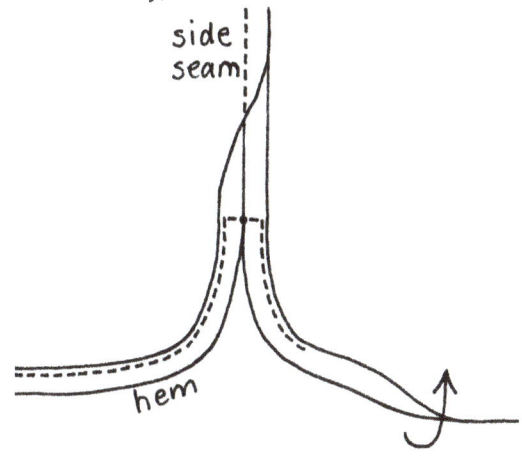

## Hem the sleeves
**5.** Turn the sleeve edge up 5mm then 1.5cm and stitch to form a casing. Leave a tiny gap to insert 5mm wide elastic later.

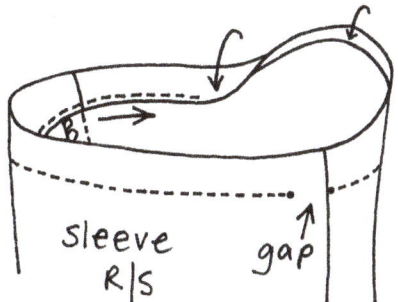

Tessellated

## Tucks

**6.** For the **sleeve tucks**, turn the sleeve inside out. Fold back the already-hemmed sleeve 6cm and sew 6mm from the folded edge. Press the tuck flat towards the casing. It's best to press from the wrong side.

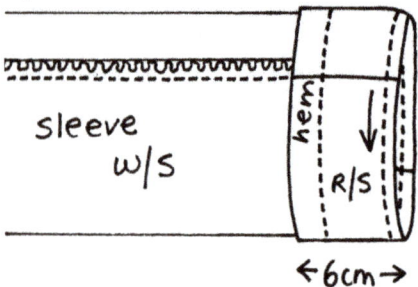

For the second tuck, fold back the sleeve further, 3.5cm from the first tuck's folded edge. Sew 6mm from the folded edge and press as before. Make the third tuck the same way.

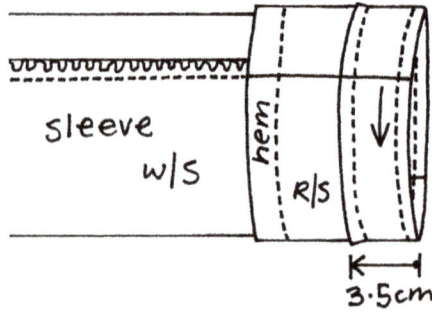

**7.** For the **hem tucks**, turn under the hemmed edge 13cm and sew 1cm from the folded edge. The tuck should clear the curved edge. Press the tuck towards the hem in the same way as you did for the sleeves.

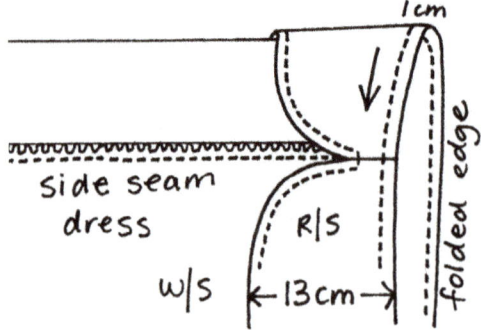

For the second tuck, fold the fabric 5cm from the first tuck's fold and stitch 1cm from the folded edge. Repeat for the third tuck.

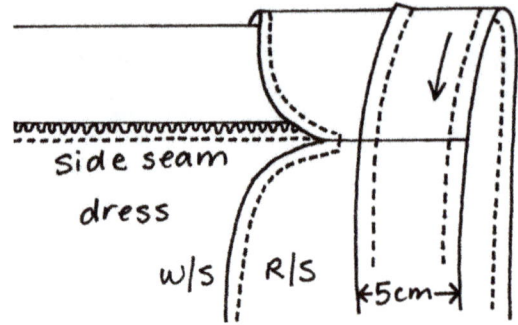

## Sleeve elastic

**8.** Cut two pieces of 5mm elastic long enough to comfortably go around each upper arm. Thread them through the sleeve casings.

## To sew the coat

**Seam allowances:** all 1cm.

There are no tucks on the coat. The coat is stitched to the lining at the edges, so there are no bias binding facings around the neck.

## Interfacing

**9.** On the coat's front lining, iron a 5cm strip of interfacing on each front edge. Cut some interfacing to the shape of the neck and press it on with the iron.

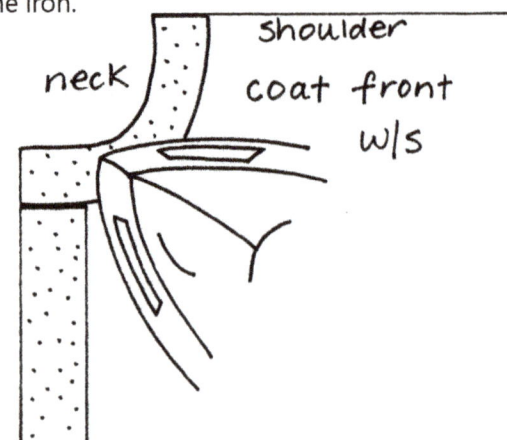

**10.** Interface around the neck of the back lining too.

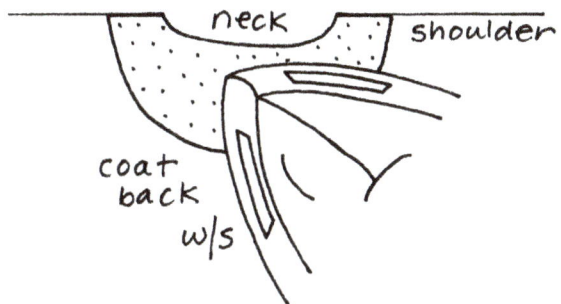

## Seams

**11.** Sew the shoulder and underarm/side seams of both coat and lining. There's no need to overlock either of them because the coat is lined. Press the seams open.

**Important:** make sure the side seams of both coat and lining finish exactly at the notch above the curved hem.

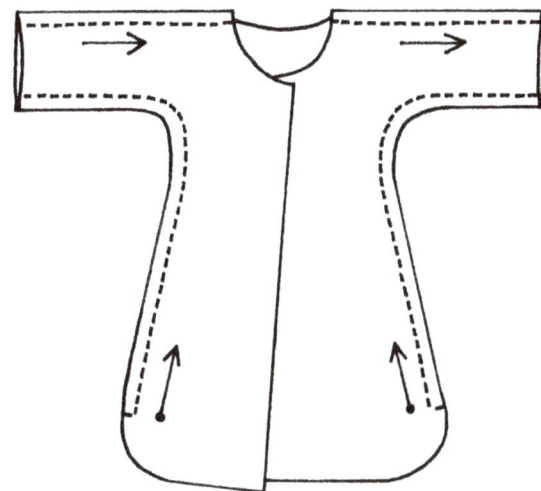

## Interior pockets

**12.** Make interior pockets of your own design from the neckline cutouts and apply them to the coat lining. Try the lining on (carefully) to check the best position for the pockets.

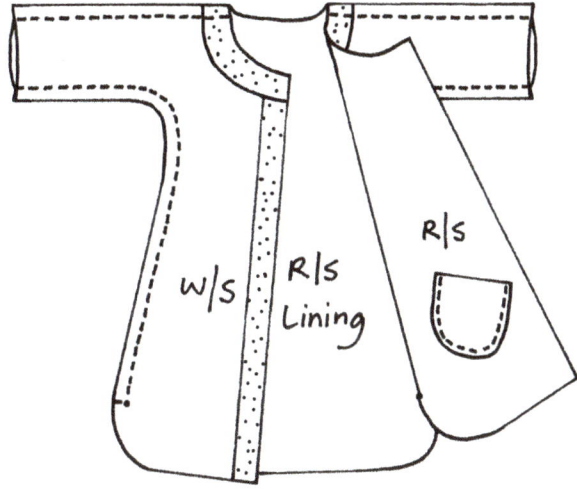

## Attach the lining

**13.** Lay the coat and lining right sides together and sew around the neckline and front edges. Understitch (see page 12) as far as you can and press. (Interfacing not shown for clarity.)

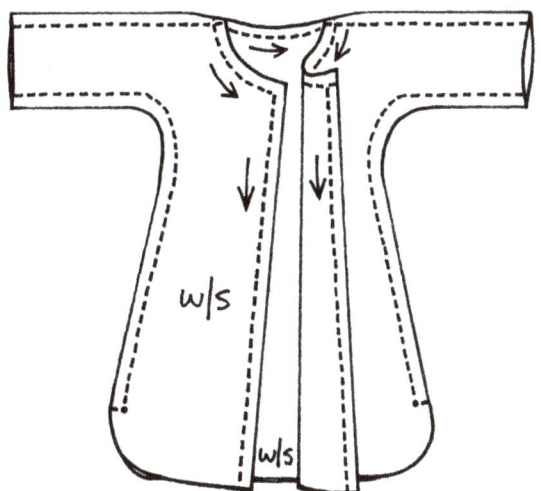

**14.** Access the sleeves via the lower edge and sew the wrist edges together.

**Important:** DO NOT just put the whole coat right sides together and stitch the edges; it won't work!

Take a 5mm larger seam allowance for the lining than the main fabric, to allow the lining to remain hidden. Understitch if possible.

**15.** Sew the lower edges and curved side splits together. You'll have to start and stop stitching at the curves. Leave a small gap at the centre back so you can access the seams. Understitch the seams if possible. Sew the gap closed by hand.

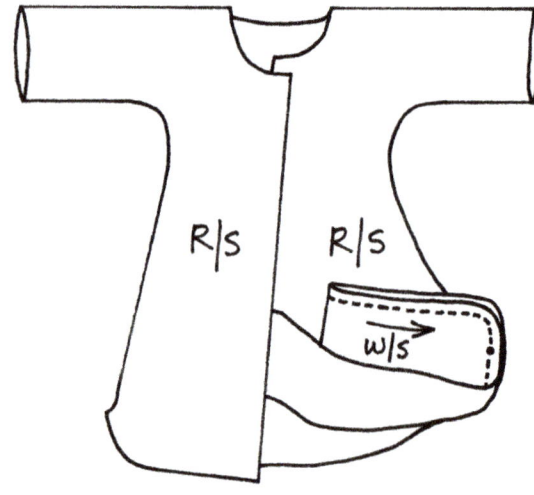

## Finishing
**16.** Press thoroughly.
Topstitch around the edges if desired.
Make the three front buttonholes about 11.5cm apart and horizontal. Sew the buttons on.

## Notes

✂ Do you want to change the neckline? Go ahead, but note that the front neckline needs to be *at least* 9cm deep and 6.7 - 7 - 7.3 - 7.6 - 7.9cm wide which will give you a close fitting neckline. The coat and the dress can have the same neckline or not. If you're undecided, you can always cut it lower later.

✂ Alternative closures for the coat: hooks, ribbon ties, single button with loop, nothing, belt. For an edge-to-edge finish, add only 1cm (ie a seam allowance) when you cut it out, not 3cm.

✂ Cutting a dress by itself? You'll need your bust measurement plus 38cm of fabric. For sizes 8-16 this is 125 - 130 - 135 - 140 - 145cm. Place the centre front of the dress on the fold and have a seam at the back (remember to add a 1cm seam allowance at the centre back when you cut it out).

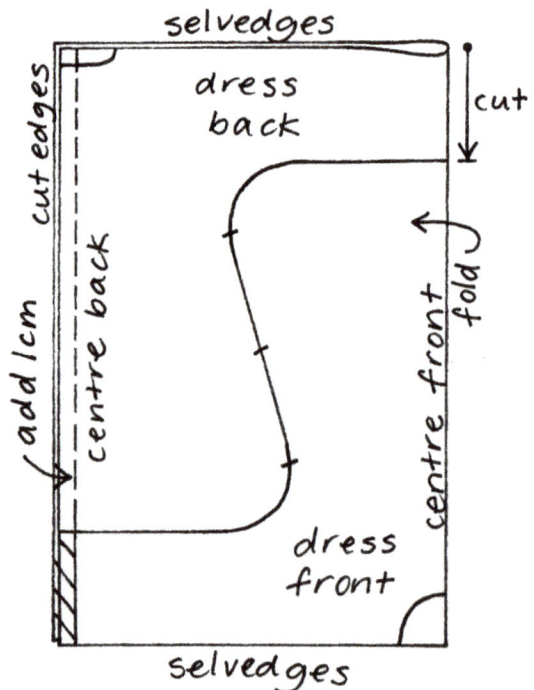

✂ To lengthen or shorten according to the fabric width, you don't need to make a whole new pattern. Simply fold out a pleat or add at the existing pattern's horizontal half way line and draw in a new side seam.

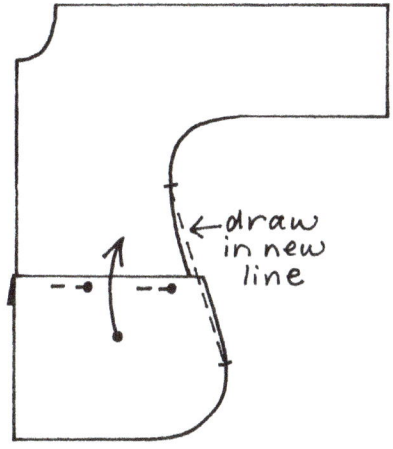

✂ For a quicker, simpler-looking dress, omit the tucks and sleeve elastic.

✂ For central pleats or gathers, add extra fabric along the centre front and centre back when cutting out.

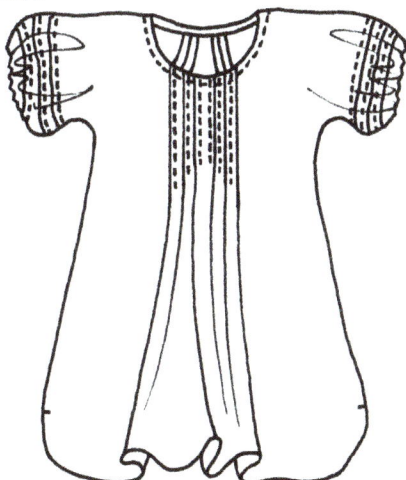

Adding to the body width equally on the front and back will yield longer sleeves.

✂ Want to make a collarless shirt dress? You'll need your bust measurement plus 47cm of fabric. For sizes 8-16 this is 134 -139 - 144 - 149 - 154cm. Complete the shirt dress with sleeves tabs, pockets and optional belt cut from extra fabric.

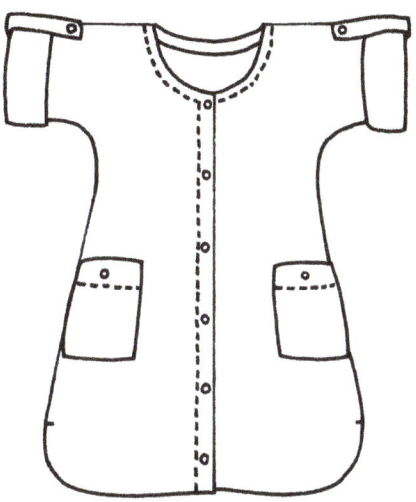

**1.** Cut the centre back on the fold and add 5.5cm to the front edge.

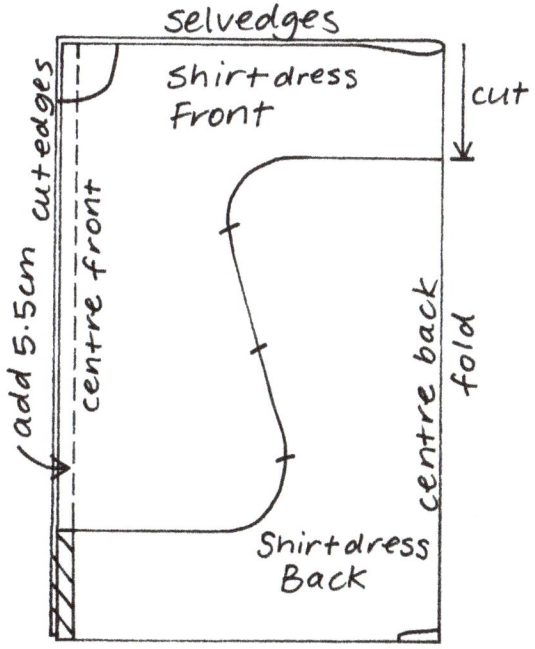

Tessellated    111

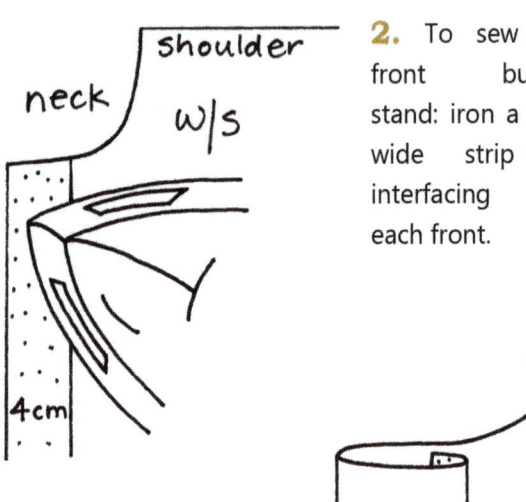

**2.** To sew the front button stand: iron a 4cm wide strip of interfacing on each front.

**3.** Press the (now interfaced) front edge under 1cm then 3cm.

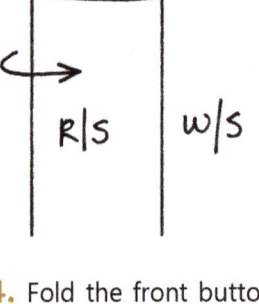

**4.** Fold the front button stand back on itself and stitch across the top 5mm down from the raw edge. Don't turn it through to the right side yet.

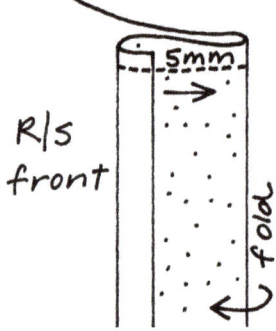

**5.** Finish the neckline with a bias binding facing as described on pages 127-128 in *Sewing Techniques*, overlapping the end onto the button stand.

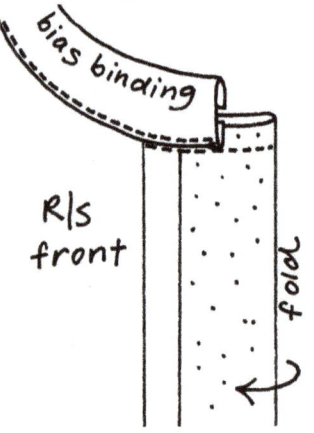

Turn the corner through to complete the final row of stitching on the bias binding; the end will be neatly covered by the button stand. Stitch the button stand down in the same operation.

## Adding a bust dart to the dress

It's possible to add bust darts to the dress. It results in a dress with a high-low hem.
You'll need 4cm more fabric.

**1.** Make the pattern as described on pages 104-105 BUT in Step 4, measure out a quarter of your bust measurement, plus *5cm*, not 4cm.

**2.** Sew the dress up to Step 3 on page 107. Sew only the *underarm* seam for now, not the sides.

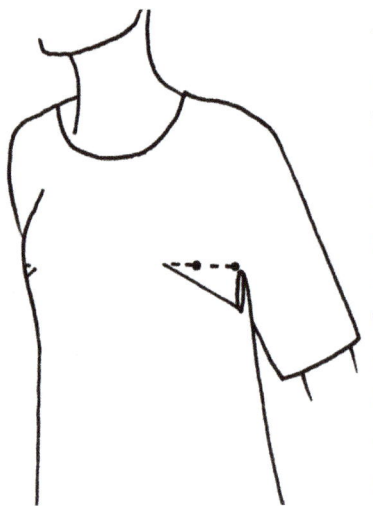

Turn the dress right side out and try it on. Pin a bust dart on each side. Make the point of the dart 2.5cm back from the actual bust point. Try and keep the dart as horizontal as possible.

**3.** Lay the dress flat on the table and remove all the pins except three: the point and each end. Compare the left and right sides and even them up so they're the same.

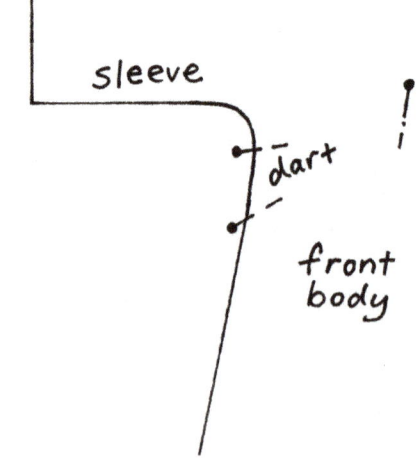

Zero Waste Sewing

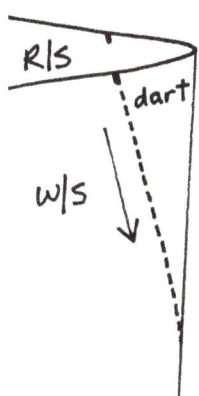

**4.** Sew the darts. Note that one side (the lower side) will be longer, making it tricky to line up each side. It helps to rule a chalk line for each side of the dart to match them perfectly.

Press the darts pointing down. If the darts are large, consider trimming them back to 1cm and overlocking.

**5.** Pin the side seams together before sewing them. There'll be an overhang on the front below the dart, but keep the sides parallel. Take a total of 4cm seam allowance - 1cm on the back and 3cm on the front or whatever will total 4cm. It will vary depending on the size and angle of the dart taken. After stitching, trim off the overhang and re-shape the front hem curve.

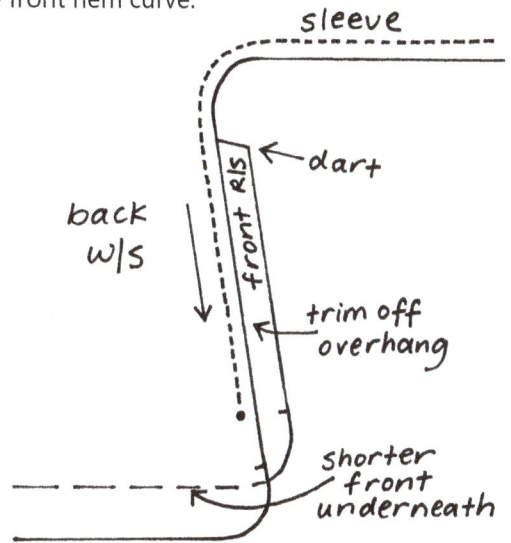

# playsuit

*One of the more involved projects in this book, this playsuit has flattering culottes-style legs, front buttons and in-seam pockets.*

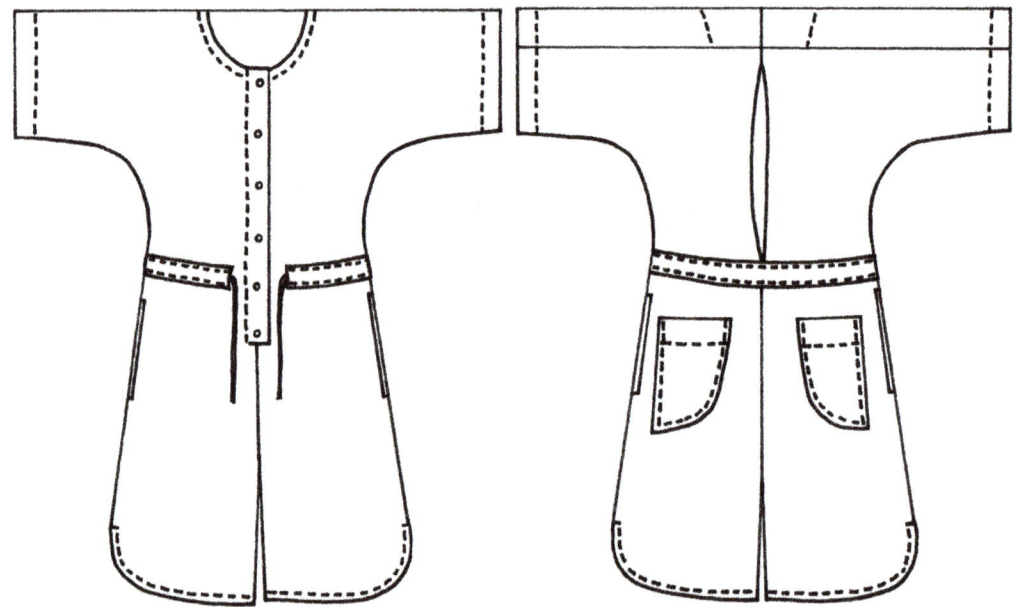

**Fabric** Woven fabric, approximately 112cm-115cm wide. For sizes 8-16 you'll need *exactly* 175.3 - 181.3 - 187.7 - 193.7 - 200.1cm. Suitable fabrics include crisp cottons, for example chambray, quilting cotton, lightweight denim, lightweight cotton drill. Plains or prints are fine but avoid stripes, checks, napped fabrics and one-way designs.

**Notions** 6 x 15mm buttons. Approximately 50cm of 12mm bias binding for the neck. Thread.

**Sizes** 8-10-12-14-16. Pick a size based on your hip measurement. Note that there is no provision for bust shaping.

**Finished length** Approximately 90cm.

**Seam and hem allowances** All **1cm** except neck **5mm**, inside leg **2cm** and sleeve hem **2.5cm**.

# Make a pattern

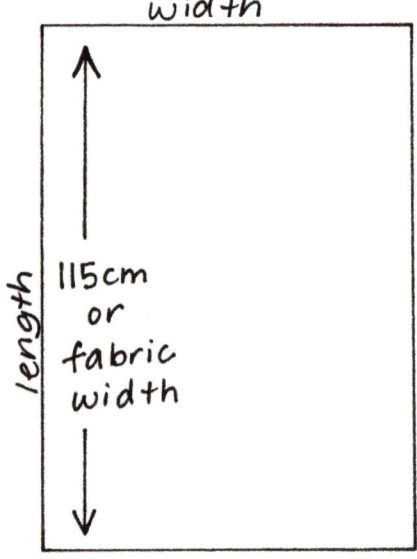

**Extra measurement:** this playsuit is designed for a 155.5 - 160 - 164.5 - 169 - 173.5cm full U.

To take a full U measurement, begin with one end of the tape measure on your shoulder. Pass the tape measure between your legs and up to the shoulder again.

Compare your full U measurement according to the one for your size as listed above. Divide any difference by 2 and raise or lower the crotch by this amount. For example, if you're a size 10 with a full U of 163cm, you would lower the crotch by 1.5cm.

Note that the crotch can be lowered (by stitching it lower when the playsuit is finished) but not raised, so err on the side of higher.

**1.** Draw a rectangle on a large piece of paper. Make the **length** the same as your fabric *width* (for example 115cm). Make the **width** 83.4 - 86.4 - 89.6 - 92.6 - 95.8cm.

**2.** Mark in the sleeve depth of 19.7 - 20.3 - 20.9 - 21.5 - 22.1cm on both sides.

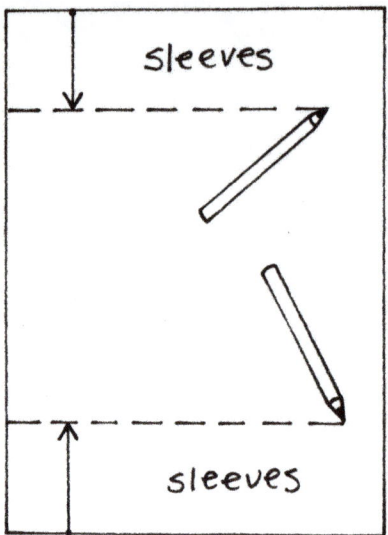

**3.** Mark in the centre front/centre back (CF/CB): measureced out from the left 14.7 - 15 - 15.3 - 15.6 - 15.9cm.

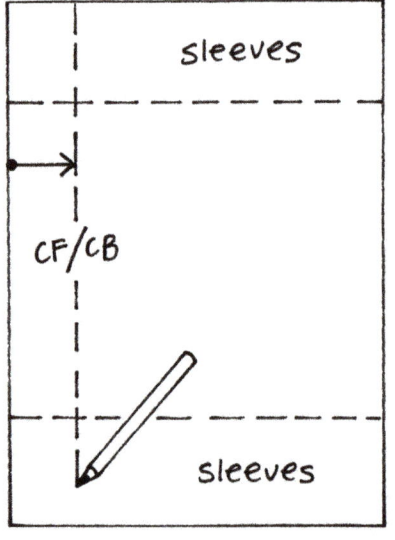

**4.** Draw in the crotch depth: measure down 72.5 - 74.3 - 76.1 - 77.9 - 79.7cm. If you need to alter the crotch depth based on your full U measurement, do it here.

Draw a horizontal line to 1cm short of the CF/CB line.

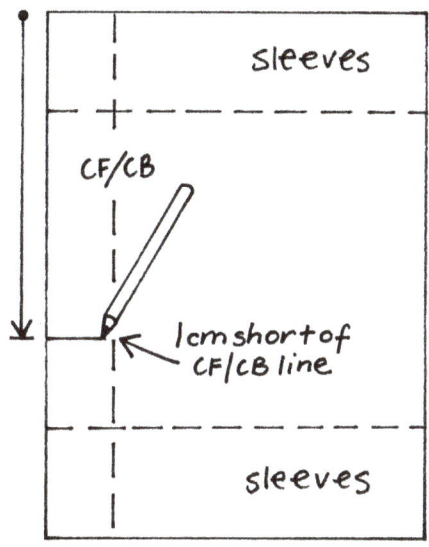

**5.** Measure down 62 - 62 - 63 - 63 - 64cm from the top and 1cm to the left of the CF/CB line. Mark a point.

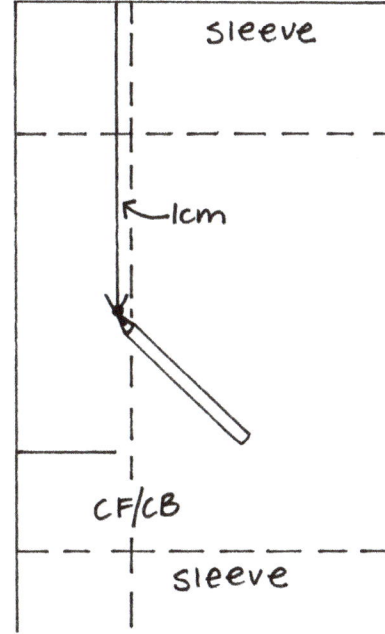

**6.** Draw in the crotch curve, coming 4cm out from the corner.

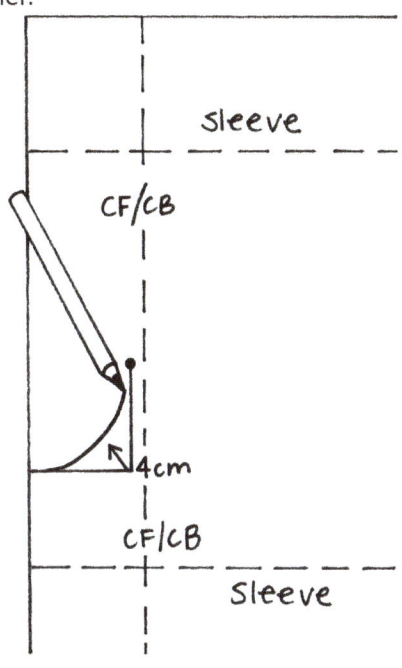

**7.** Measure out 27 - 28.2 - 29.5 - 30.7 - 32cm from the CF/CB line to find the side seam (you're actually measuring a quarter of your hip measurement, plus 4cm ease).

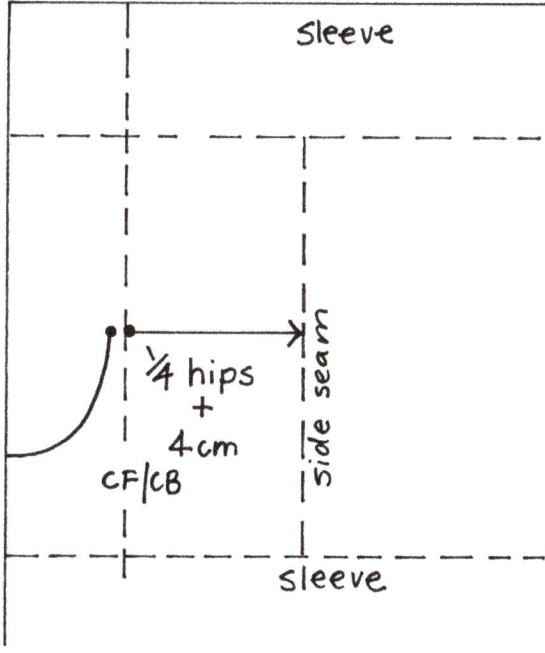

Tessellated

**8.** Angle the side seam 2.5cm each way and mark the half way point.

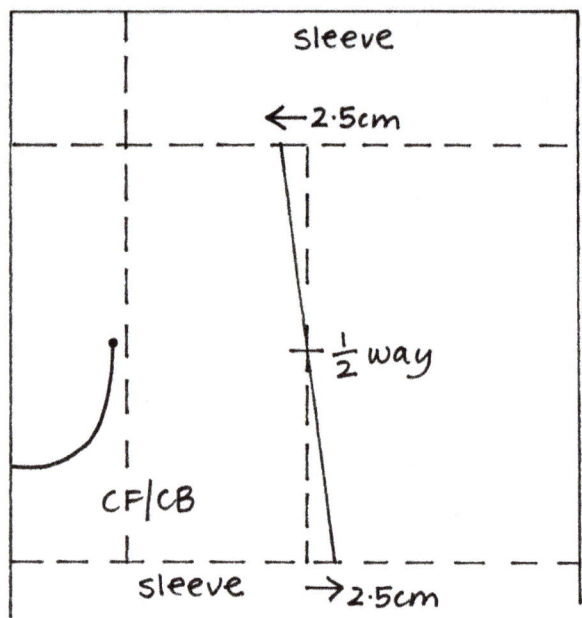

**9.** Draw in the underarm curve: mark 9cm along each side of the corner as shown, then draw the curve coming 4cm out from the corner. Place a notch at the bottom of the curve, on the 9cm mark.

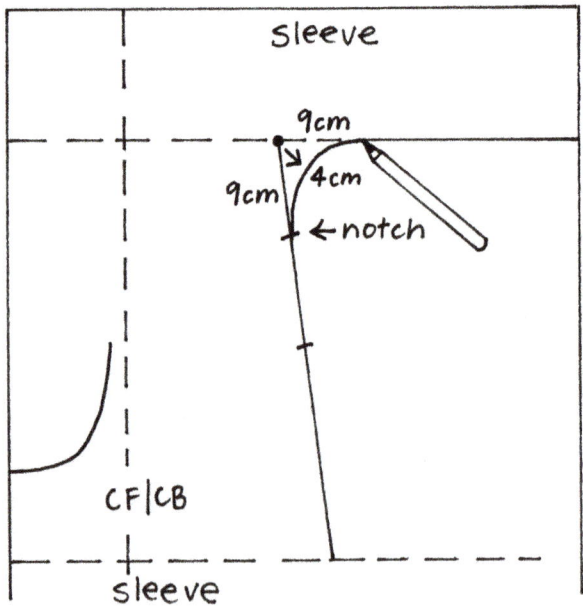

**10.** Pivot the curved line as described on pages 78-79 to make the tessellated shape. Mark the half way point as a notch to help when you sew the seam.

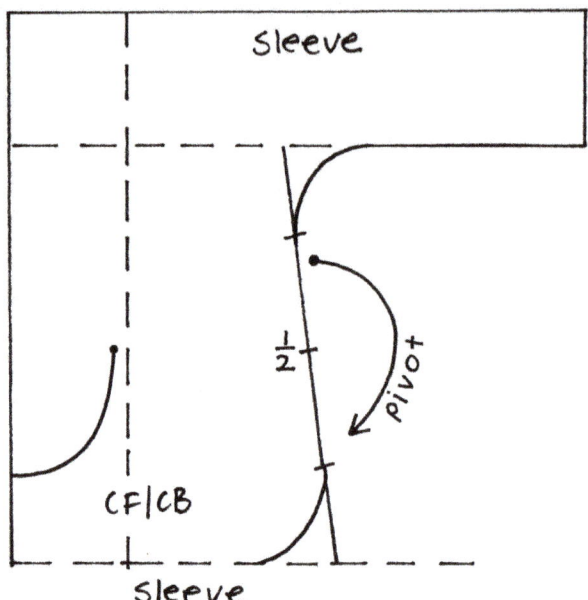

**11.** Draw in the casing position: mark a line 11.5cm up from the "half way" notch on the side seam. Then mark another line 2.5cm higher. This is the approximate casing position, which you'll check when the playsuit is nearly finished.

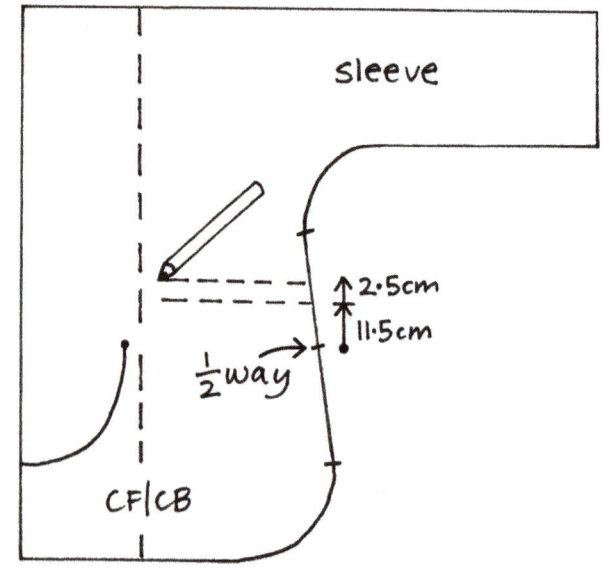

118    Zero Waste Sewing

**12.** Draw in the cut line for the short sleeve. Measure in 25cm from the end of the sleeve. The end piece will be used for in-seam pockets. (This is optional; if you want long sleeves and no pockets, don't do this step).

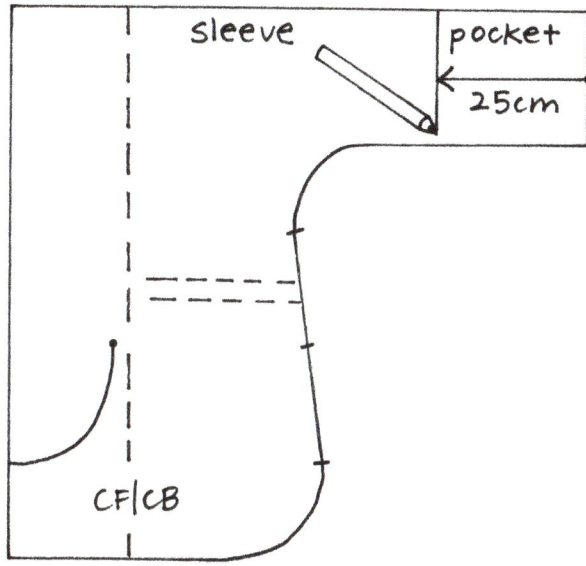

**13.** The same pattern piece will be used for cutting both the back and the front playsuit, but with a few changes.

*For the front only*, mark a line 7cm from the CF to form the front button stand. The remainder of the fabric will be used for the back yoke.

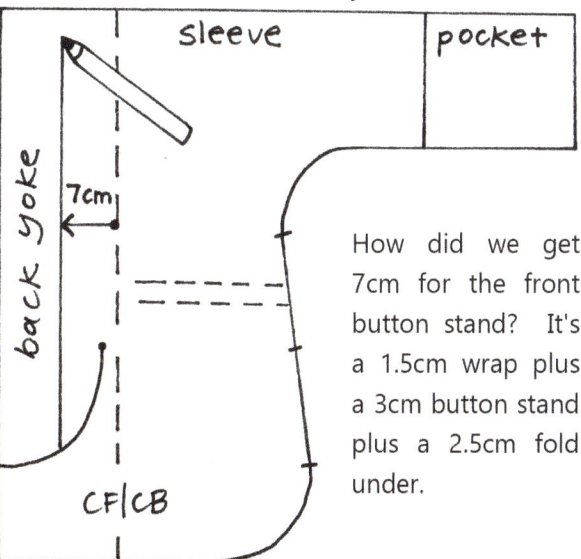

How did we get 7cm for the front button stand? It's a 1.5cm wrap plus a 3cm button stand plus a 2.5cm fold under.

**14.** *For the front only:* in the top left corner, draw in the front neckline. Make the **depth** 14cm as shown, and make the **neck width** 7.7 - 8 - 8.3 - 8.6 - 8.9cm.

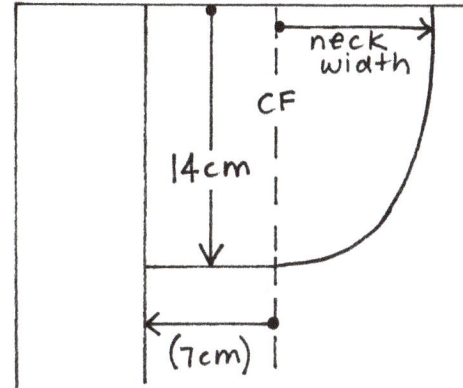

**15.** *For the back only,* extend the crotch curve up to level with the bottom of the casing, then draw horizontally across. This section will become the back patch pocket.

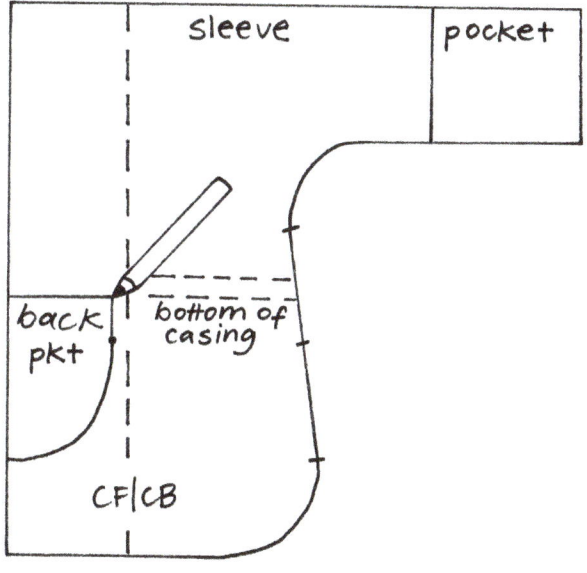

Tessellated   119

# To cut

**1.** On the straightened, cut edge of the fabric, mark two strips running from selvedge-to-selvedge, one 4.5cm wide and the other 4cm wide. The 4.5cm strip will become the drawcord casing and the 4cm strip will become the drawcord. Before plunging in with scissors, check that you have *exactly* 166.8 - 172.8 - 179.2 - 185.2 - 191.6cm of fabric remaining. To be sure, you can leave these marked and cut them after everything else is cut.

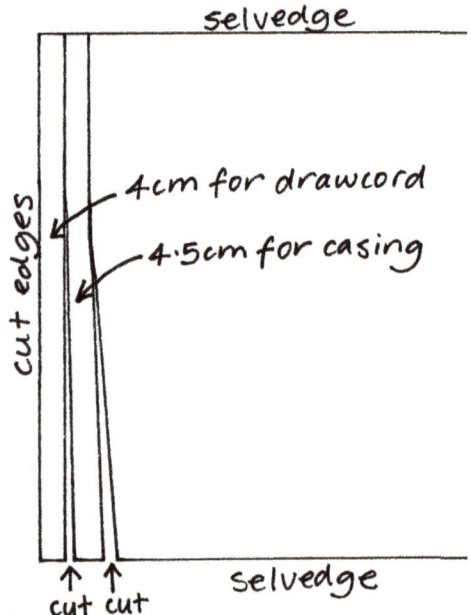

**2.** The back and front are cut using the same pattern but the back has no neckline or button stand/back yoke.
Fold the fabric in half, right sides together, and position the back on the fold.

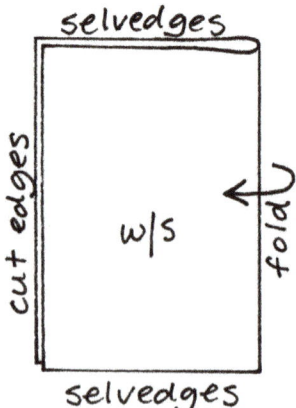

Mark in the back and the front nestled together. Mark the centre front (CF), centre back (CB) and drawcord casing position in removable tailors chalk on the *wrong* side of the fabric.
Cut on all the solid lines and mark in the broken lines.

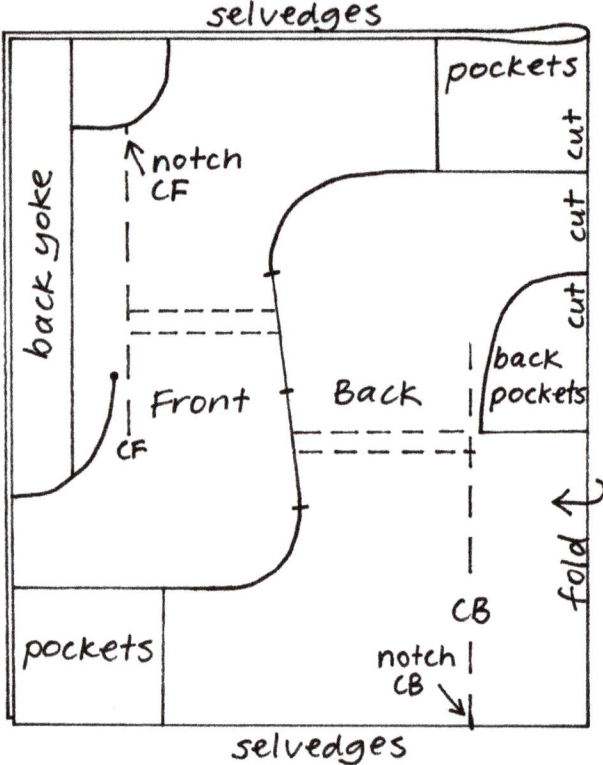

If you don't want short sleeves (or if you're not sure), don't cut the pocket pieces. Leave them as an extension of the sleeves and decide later (on page 124, when you check the fit).

## To sew

**Seam allowances:** all 1cm except front neck 5mm and inside leg 2cm.

## Back pleat

1. Open out the back and overlock the crotch curve and the lower edge of (what will be) the inverted pleat.

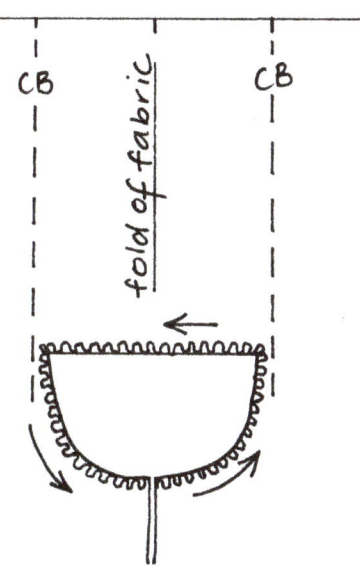

2. Re-fold the back in half, right sides together (overlocking not shown for clarity). Stitch the back inverted pleat ON the centre back (CB) line. Sew down 2.5cm from the top, then resume stitching 36cm below that, continuing down and around the crotch. Don't sew right to the end just yet.

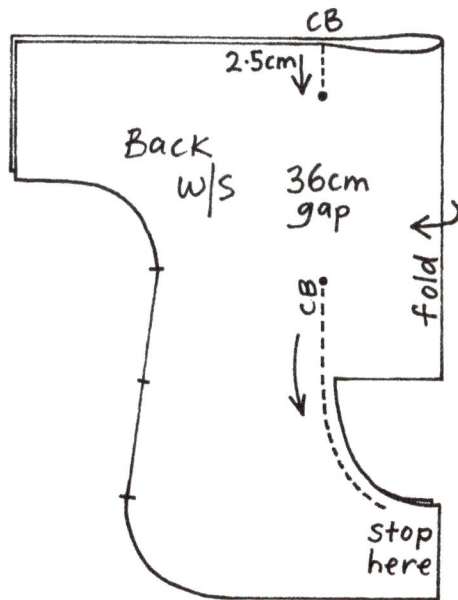

3. Press the pleat, centring the seam. *On the wrong side*, stitch the back folds of the pleat to hold it in place after laundering. Just stitch through the folded edges, not the actual back.

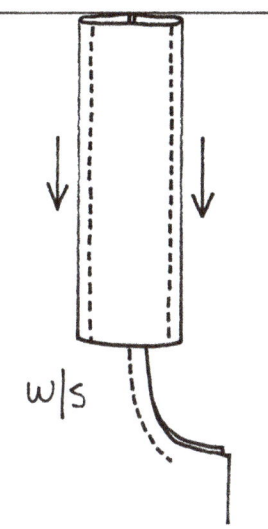

4. Stay-stitch across the top of the pleat. The bottom of the pleat will be held in place by the waist casing.

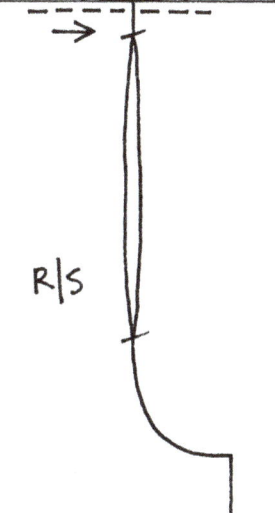

## Back yoke

5. Sew together the two short ends of the back yoke. Press the seam open and overlock each seam allowance separately.

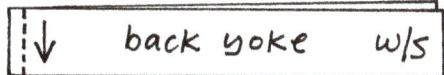

**6.** Lay the back yoke right sides together onto the top of the back, centring the seam. Stitch across. Trim the back yoke at the ends. Press the seam towards the back yoke. Overlock. Topstitch the seam if desired. (Don't overlock or topstitch just yet if you're undecided about the sleeve length —wait until you've tried it on.)

**9.** Take the right front (the right as it would be worn to the wearer) and stay-stitch the bottom of the stand as shown, 1cm from the raw edge. The stitching should pivot exactly in the centre of the band.

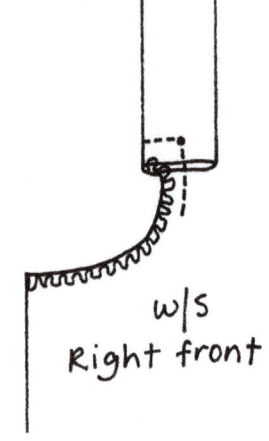

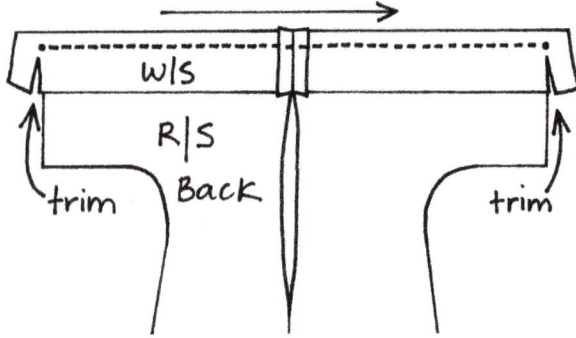

Snip diagonally to the pivot point. (Overlocking not shown for clarity.)

## Front button stand

**7.** On the fronts, accurately press under 2.5cm then 3cm to make the button stand. Don't stitch it yet.

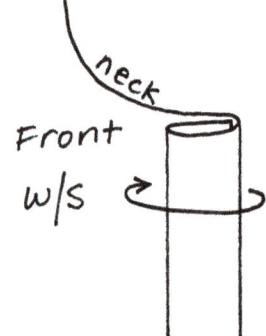

**8.** At the bottom of the button stand, trim off the pointy part so it's level. Overlock each crotch curve, overlocking *on top of* the folded front band.

**10.** Lay the two fronts right sides together matching the button stand and crotch curve. Begin stitching several centimetres from the crotch end, and sew up *exactly* to the pivot point, backstitching securely at the end.
Note that the illustration is now around the way you'll face it sewing it on a machine.

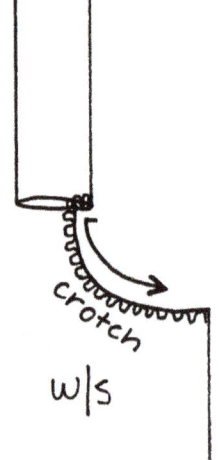

122    Zero Waste Sewing

**11.** Place the playsuit right side up on a flat surface and lay the front stands on top of each other as they would be worn, the right front over the left front. Tuck the end of the button stand under neatly - it can be horizontal or angled like this one. Topstitch a box to hold it in position.

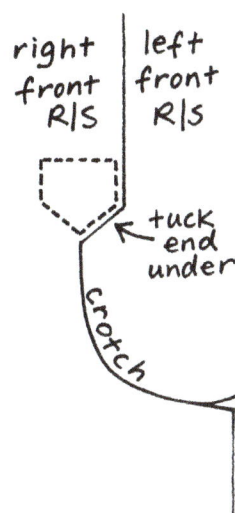

If you plan to sew extra topstitching on the front button stand, do it now.

## Back neck

**13.** Pin the back to the front at the shoulders, right sides together.

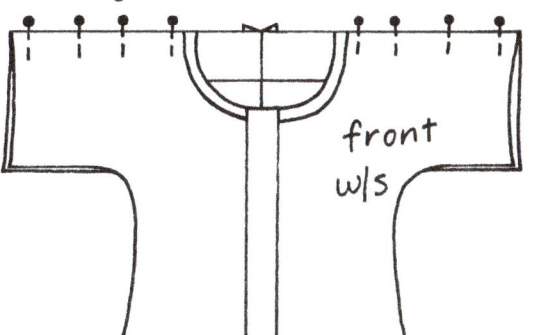

## Front neck

**12.** Face the front neckline with bias binding as described in *Sewing Techniques* on pages 127-128. At the front, fold the front stand back on itself and lap the bias over the top. Sew around the entire front neckline.

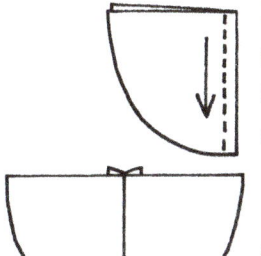

**14.** Take the pair of front neck cutouts and sew them together. Leave the edges raw.

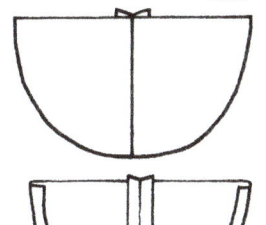

Press the seam open.

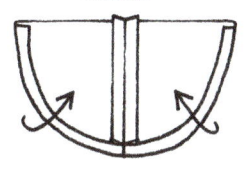

Press under 5mm around the long curved edge.

When you stitch the bias binding down in the final step, go on to sew the front button stand down too.

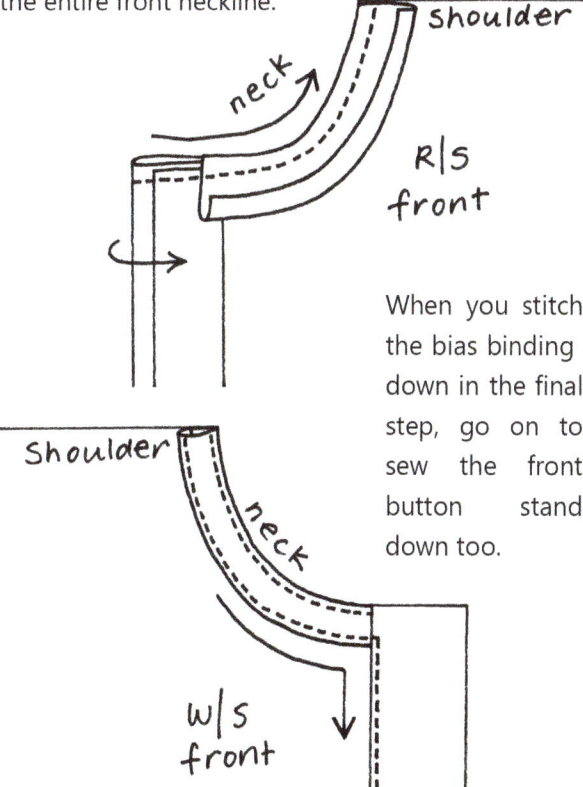

**15.** Lay the shape face down on the front (which is pinned right sides together to the back) and sew across the entire top from wrist to wrist. Press the seam towards the back. Don't overlock yet.

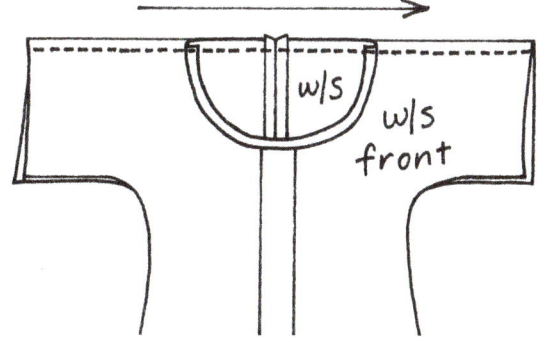

## Check the fit

**16.** Pin the playsuit's side/underarm seams, crotch seams and inside leg seams together (or baste, if you're allergic to pins). The inside legs have a 2cm seam allowance.

Flip the back neck facing from Step 15 to the inside of the playsuit.

Try on the playsuit.

Tie a tape around your waist and confirm the position of the drawcord casing which you marked with removable chalk. Change it if necessary.

Now's the time to decide on the sleeve length if you haven't already. If you're having short sleeves, cut off the excess now, leaving a 2.5cm hem. You can use the offcuts as in-seam pockets, provided they're about 18cm or longer. Alternatively, use them for front patch pockets if you prefer.

## Finish the back neck

**17.** Overlock the back yoke from Step 6 and the shoulder seam from Step 15.

Flip up the back neck facing and understitch (see page 12).

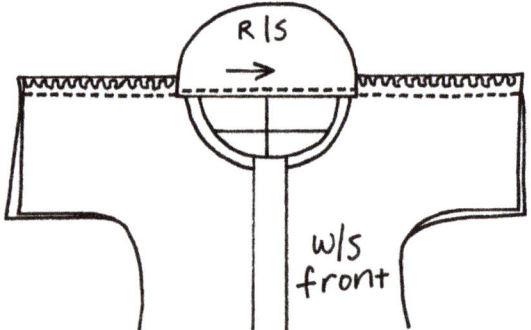

**18.** Fold the back neck facing down onto the inside of the back, tucking the excess under so it meets the back yoke seam.

Stitch the sides onto the yoke.

Turn it over and sew the long edge down from the right side, pinning through the layers first to make sure you catch the yoke. Either edgestitch or stitch-in-the-ditch, depending on whether you want the stitching to be visible or not.

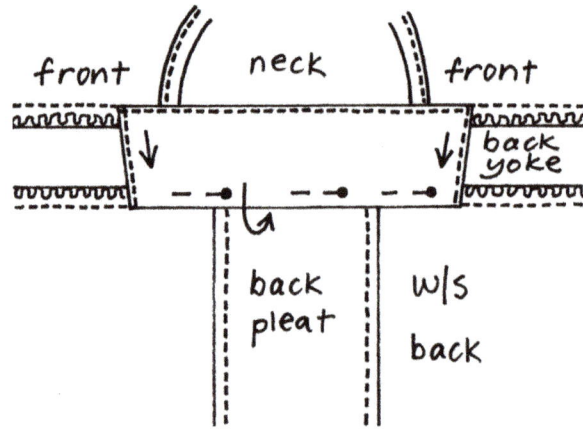

## In-seam pockets

**19.** On the front and back side seams, mark a 15cm pocket opening with tiny 3mm snips in the seam allowance.

Make the top snip 1.5cm down from the bottom line of the drawcord casing.

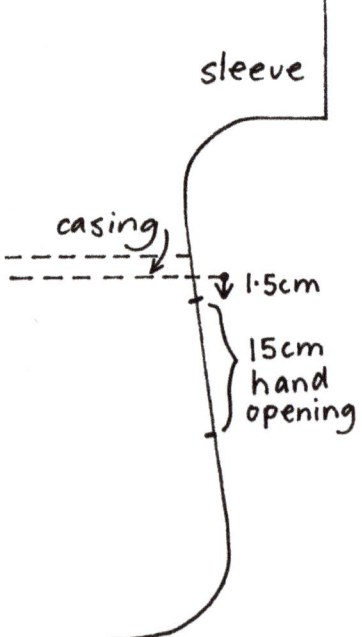

124  Zero Waste Sewing

**20.** On the pocket pieces, mark the 15cm hand opening on the longest side, 3cm down from the top.

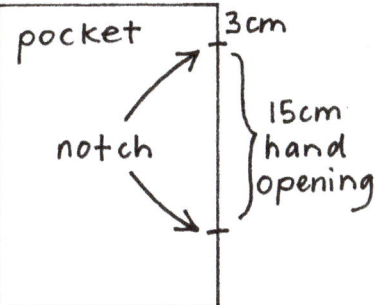

**21.** Lay a pocket piece on the side seam, matching the notches, and stitch 5mm away from the edge.
Stop and start 1cm in from the ends.
Overlock.
Do this for all four pocket bags.

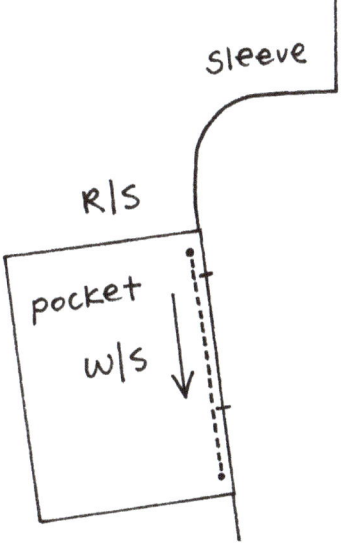

**22.** Understitch the *front* pocket bags.

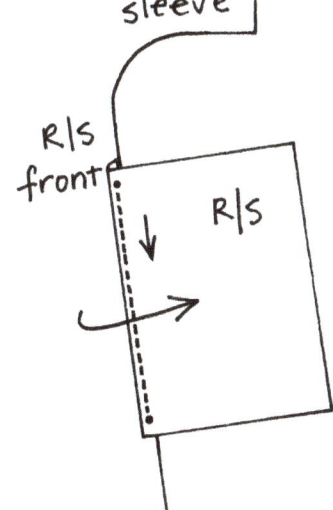

**23.** Lay the front and back playsuit together and stitch the underarm/side seam. Leave a gap between the pocket notches, which you should still be able to see under the overlocking. Stitch separately around the pocket bag.

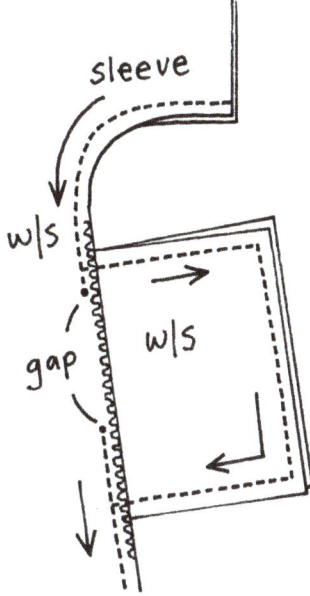

**24.** Overlock around the hem, finishing several centimetres above the hem curve at the sides. Then, overlock the underarm/side seam (and pockets), running off above the hem curve notch, so that the hem can be pressed up and open at the side.

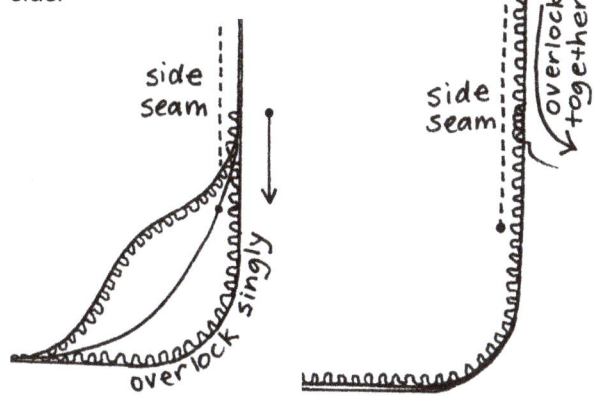

**25.** Sew the inside leg seams taking a **2cm** seam allowance.

Tessellated

If you feel the crotch is too baggy or too tight, take a wider or smaller seam allowance. Overlock.

**26.** Sew the remainder of the curved crotch seam. This can be sewn lower and trimmed if the crotch is too high.

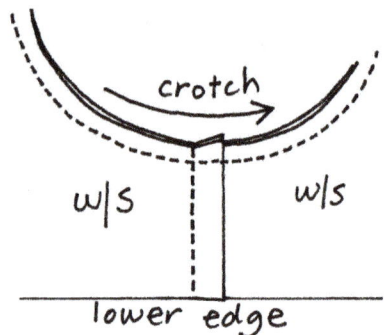

## Drawcord casing

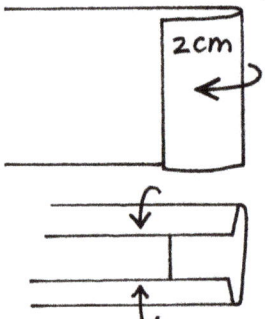

**27.** Take the 4.5cm wide strip and press back 2cm at one of the short ends. Press under 1cm on the long edges.

**28.** Position the casing on the placement lines, beginning 6cm in from the edge of the front stand. Catch the tops of the in-seam pocket bags in the lower edge of the casing. Trim any excess length off the drawcord casing and fold the second short end back 2cm to match the first.
Edgestitch the drawcord casing in place.

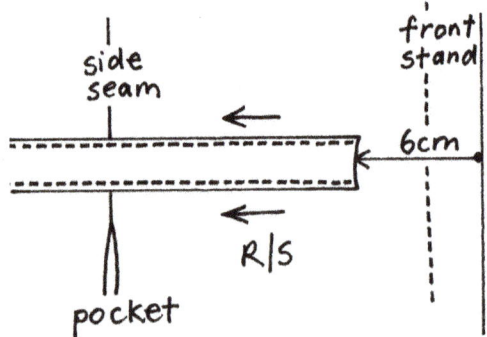

**29.** Make a drawcord by folding the 4cm wide strip like a beltloop: fold the edges into the centre then fold it in half. Stitch.

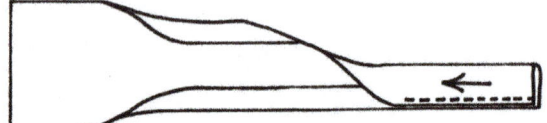

Thread the drawcord through the casing, cut it to the correct length and knot the ends.

## Back pockets

**30.** Overlock and fold over the top edge approximately 8cm (or the best amount for a well proportioned pocket).
Fold under the other sides 1cm. Position the back pockets in a pleasing position and sew them on.

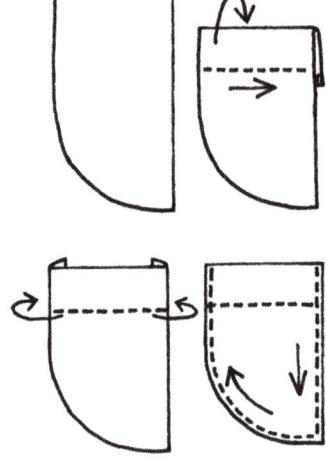

## Finishing

**31.** Hem the sleeves with a 2.5cm hem and the legs with a 1cm hem.

**32.** Button and buttonhole the front stand. Position the buttons about 8.5cm apart and sew the buttonholes vertically.

# Sewing Techniques

These are some specific sewing techniques you will encounter in this book. Included are some other useful ones you may decide to use if you vary a pattern. Omitted are "ordinary" techniques such as inserting zips or making buttonholes, which you can easily find in any good sewing book, such as *The Dressmaker's Companion*.

## Finishing a neckline using bias binding as a facing

This is a frequently-used finish for the necklines in this book, using purchased 12mm bias binding. Please don't attempt it with wider 25mm bias; the curves are too tight.

It's easiest to do early on in the garment's construction because the neckline can be laid flat. This technique also works really well as a finish for other curved edges such as armholes and pocket openings.

The key is pressing: press the bias binding into a matching curve first (essential), press after attaching it, then press again after the final row of stitching.

You'll be taking a 5mm seam allowance on the edge.

**1.** At the ironing board, arrange the neckline *right* side up, flat. Lay the bias binding around the neck, *wrong* side up and 5mm from the raw edge.

Use a steam iron to stretch/shrink the bias binding to the same curve as the neckline. Press down and use the weight of the iron to hold it as you position the bias binding.

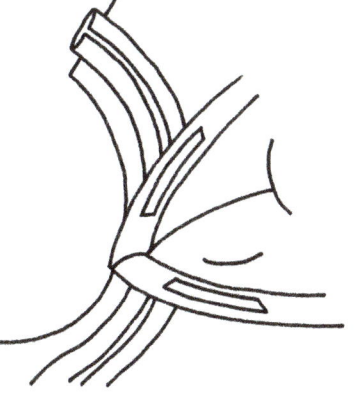

If you can't shape the bias binding easily around the sides of the neck because it's too curved, trim the neck a little to straighten it off.

**2.** Before moving the bias binding, open out the fold and match it to the neckline's raw edge. Pin in the bias binding's crease line.

**3.** Stitch along the crease line where you've pinned.

**4.** Flip the bias binding and the seam allowance away from the garment. Understitch the bias binding (see page 12 for understitching).

**5.** Turn the binding and facing to the wrong side of the neck, where it will sit perfectly flat due to the curved shape you pressed it in. Press.

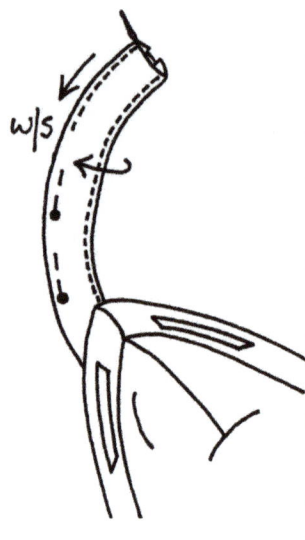

Pin, then stitch in position with the binding side up. Watch the seam guide on the machine so that the stitching for the bias binding is an even distance from the edge. If you don't want a visible line of stitching, this can be sewn invisibly by hand.
Press again for a flat neckline edge.

**4.** Prepare the bias binding on the neck as described on page 127 in Steps 1 and 2. Overlap the ends onto the back neck facing.

**5.** Stitch in the binding's crease, all the way around the neck.

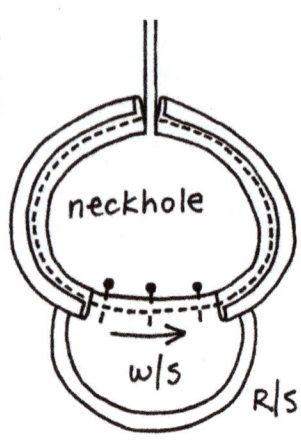

### ...with a back neck facing

**1.** Use the neck cutout for the back neck facing.
Lay the cutout underneath the neck hole and trim the top to match the back neck.

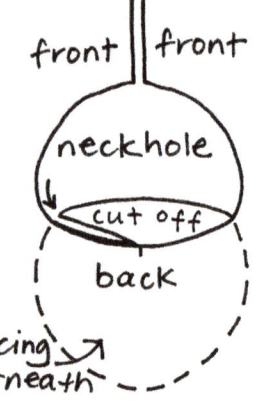

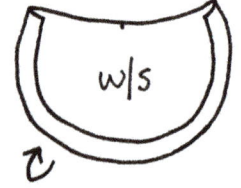

**2.** Press under the curved edge 5mm.

**6.** Push the bias binding and the seam allowance away from the garment. Understitch the bias binding THEN understitch the facing, to hold everything to the inside.

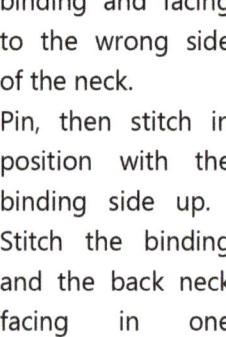

**3.** Lay it on the back neck, right sides together. Match the centres of the neckhole and the back neck facing. Pin.

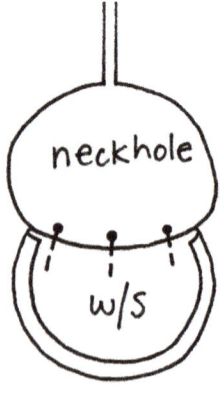

**7.** Turn the binding and facing to the wrong side of the neck.
Pin, then stitch in position with the binding side up. Stitch the binding and the back neck facing in one operation. Press.

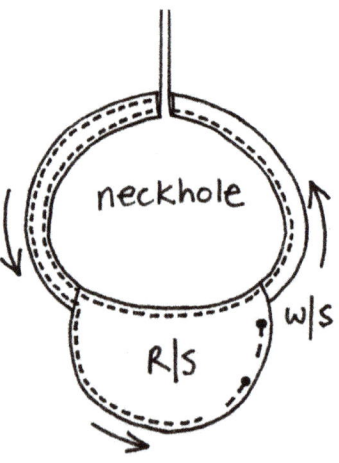

# Plackets

A placket can be fastened with buttons, studs, hooks or nothing, and requires no more than a slit cut in the garment and a strip of fabric or tape. It can be an alternative to a zip and be barely noticeable.

A placket can also be added to a gap in the seam. If you're able to organise it, the placket could be cut as a folded-back extension of the garment - no separate pattern pieces required.

There are many ways to cut and sew a placket but here are a few simple ones:

## Continuous lap placket (in a slit)

**1.** Cut a strip of fabric. The **length** needs to be twice as long as the slit plus 5mm. You can also just use a longer strip and cut it to length after sewing. The **width** of the strip needs to be at least 4cm.

For a button stand, make it 7cm wide so you can fit the buttons/buttonholes on (finished width 3cm) and interface half.

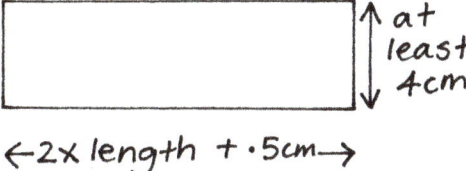

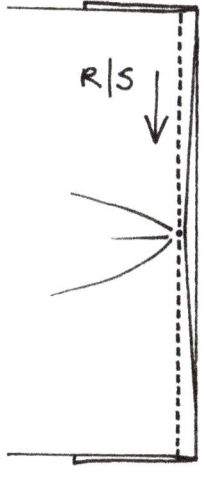

**2.** Lay the strip under the slit so both are facing right side up. Stitch using a 5mm seam allowance. As you approach the point of the slit, spread it so it's straight and just catch the point with the stitching.

If the placket has interfacing on it (for a button stand), sew the *un*-interfaced side.

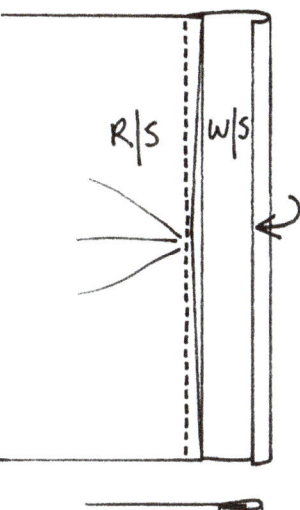

**3.** Press the seam towards the strip. Press under 5mm on the other long side.

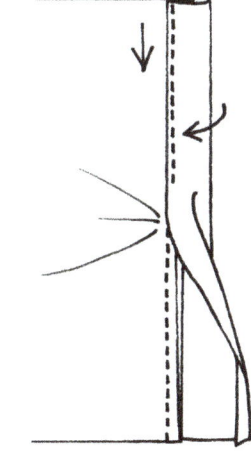

**4.** Bring the remaining long edge over and edgestitch it in place.

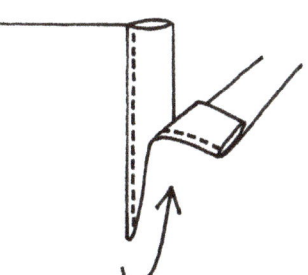

**5.** Fold the placket into position and press.

## Tape placket (in a slit)

**1.** Cut a length of herringbone twill tape or heavy ribbon twice as long as the slit plus 5mm. Alternatively, just use a longer strip and cut it to length after sewing.

**2.** Lay it on the straightened slit, both right side up. Lap the edge of the tape 5mm over and edgestitch it on, ensuring you catch the point of the slit and avoiding any pleats.

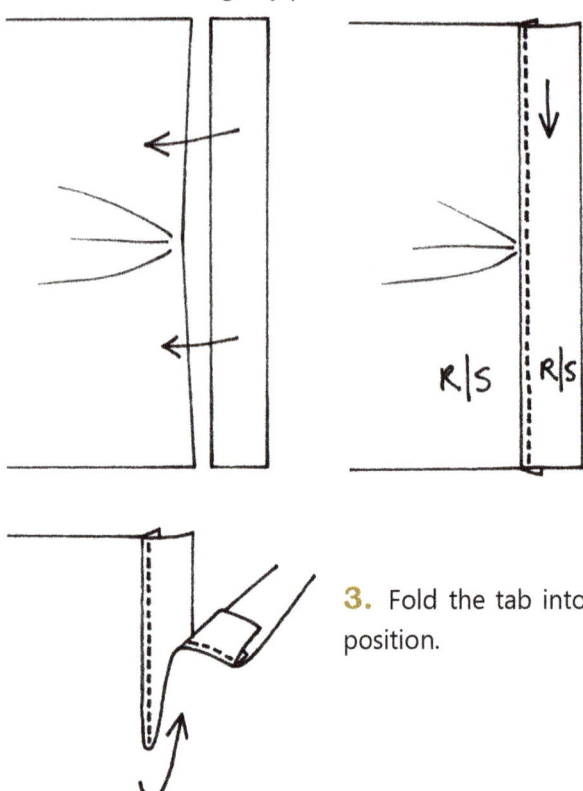

**3.** Fold the tab into position.

## Placket in a seam's gap

**1.** Sew the seam leaving an opening where you want the placket to be. The seam can be open at the top (for example on a skirt) or simply a gap (for example on a dress's side seam). Don't overlock yet.

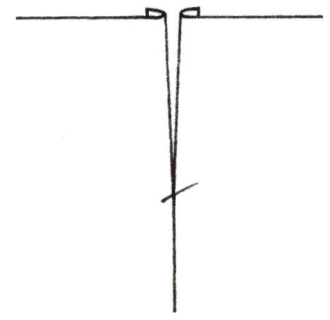

**2.** Cut two strips of fabric, each the length of the opening plus 2cm, and between 4cm-7cm wide. Iron them in halves longways, wrong sides together.

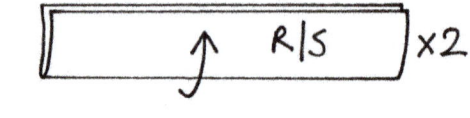

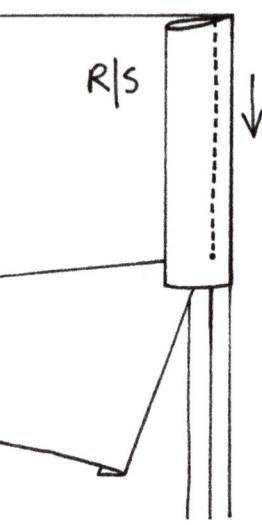

**3.** Stitch a folded strip to each side of the gap, taking the same seam allowance as the gap's. Overlock the seam allowance, overlocking the strips at the same time.

**4.** Press the strips so they lie on top of one another and stitch across the bottom to hold them together.
If the placket is sewn in a gap in a seam, sew across the top *and* the bottom.

# Waistbands

## Regular waistband

**1.** Cut a strip of fabric for the waistband. The **width** should be twice the finished width plus two seam allowances. For example, an 8cm wide strip will become a 3cm wide waistband, and a 10cm strip will become a 4cm wide one.

About the narrowest width you could cut a waistband would be 5cm (= 1.5cm wide finished) and the widest 12cm (= 5cm wide finished).

The waistband will be cut to the correct length in Step 3, below.

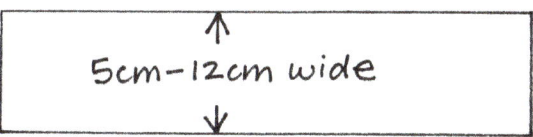

**2.** Iron on some interfacing. Iron the strip in half longways, wrong sides together.

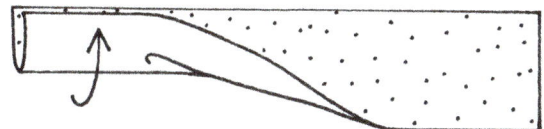

**3.** Notch the finished waistband **length**.
To find the finished length, either:
wrap it around your waist and mark the beginning and end (good if you wear your skirts/trousers below your actual waist)
or
take your waist measurement and add an amount of ease, anywhere from 1.2cm to 2.5cm depending on if you wear clothes tucked in or like your waistbands loose or tight. I like to have 1.5cm ease for skirts and 2.5cm for trouser waistbands.

Trim the ends of the waistband, leaving a 1cm seam allowance at one end and a 4cm extension at the other. The trimmings could be used for beltloops, pen pockets, loops or anything else you can think of.

Obviously the garment's waist needs to be the same length as the waistband, so check that too.

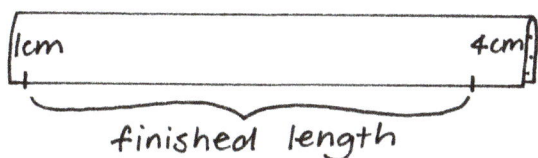

**4.** Quarter the waistband to find the centre front and sides.

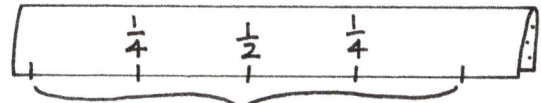

**5.** Place the waistband onto the waist, right sides together. Match all the notches, ensuring there's the correct overhang at each end.

✂ Before you sew, you can check the fit by pinning the waistband on, on the *garment* side, using pins without heads. Flip the waistband up to hide the pins and try the garment on.

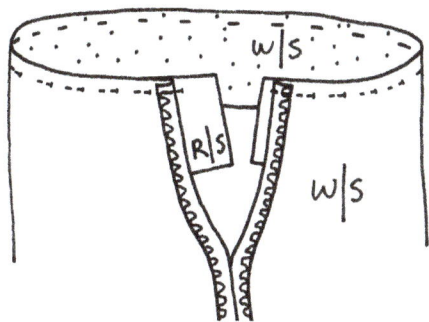

When you're happy with the waistband, sew, with the waistband uppermost and the garment underneath.

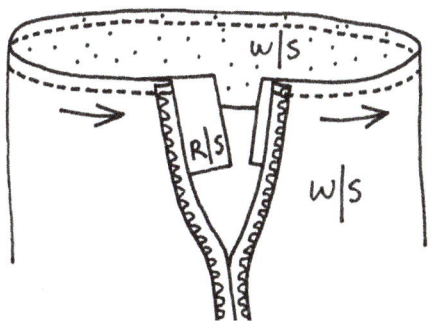

Sewing techniques

**6.** Press the seam up, towards the waistband. Overlock the other long edge of the waistband.

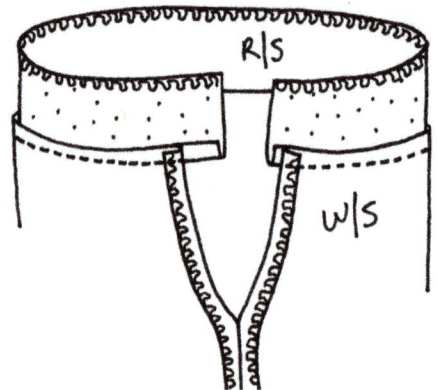

**7.** Finish the ends: fold the waistband back on itself and stitch the end level with the garment. On the end with the extension, take a 1cm seam.

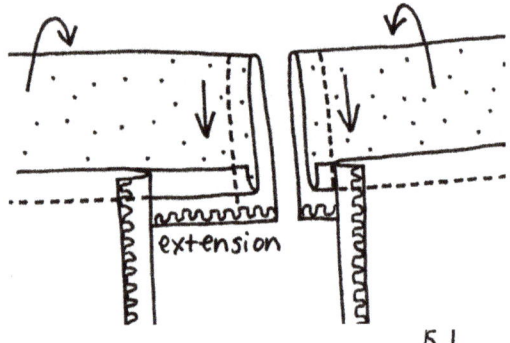

Turn through and fold the ends in neatly, making each fold square and definite.

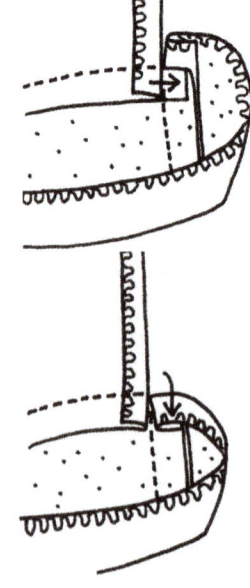

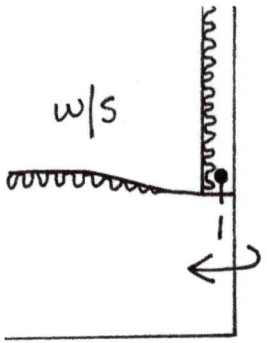

Secure the final fold with a pin.

**8.** Fold the waistband down into position and pin on the right side. With the garment right side up, stitch-in-the-ditch (see page 12) to secure the waistband.

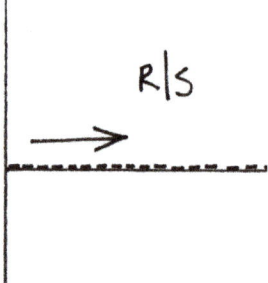

## Double-fold waistband

As you know, interfacing is essentially just an extra layer of fabric. A double-fold waistband uses its own fabric for the interfacing. While I've never seen this type of waistband in any sewing book nor in any factory, it's the same principle as double folded binding except that it's cut on the straight grain rather than the bias. The same technique can also be used for cuffs.

This type of waistband doesn't require an overlocker and looks very neat on the wrong side; both sides look the same. It's also a bit quicker to make than a regular waistband.

A double-fold waistband is good if:

✄ the fabric is light to medium in weight—it doesn't work for thick fabrics.

✄ you've got enough fabric (this waistband is cut wider than a regular one).

✄ you've run out of interfacing.

✄ the interfacing won't fuse or you're worried about how it will perform.

1. Cut a strip of fabric for the waistband four times the finished width plus two seam allowances. For example, cut it 14cm for a 3cm wide waistband, or 18cm for a 4cm wide one.
The minimum size to cut is 8cm (= 1.5cm wide finished) and maximum 22cm (= 5cm wide finished).

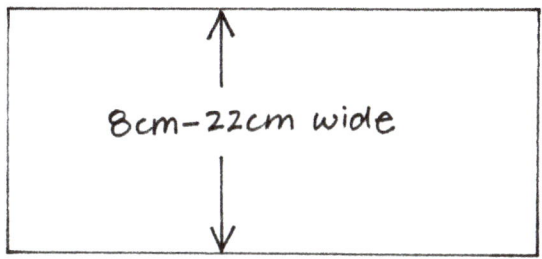

2. Iron the strip in half longways, wrong sides together.

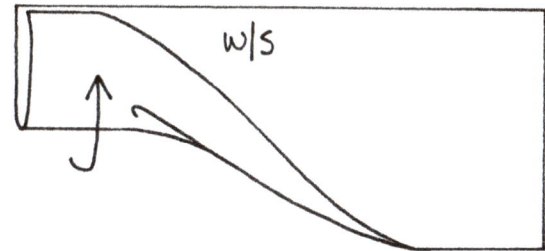

3 & 4. Same as Steps 3 and 4 for a regular waistband, described above.

5. Place the still-folded-in-half waistband onto the *wrong* side of the waist. Match all the notches, ensuring there's the correct overhang at each end. Sew, with the waistband uppermost and the garment underneath.

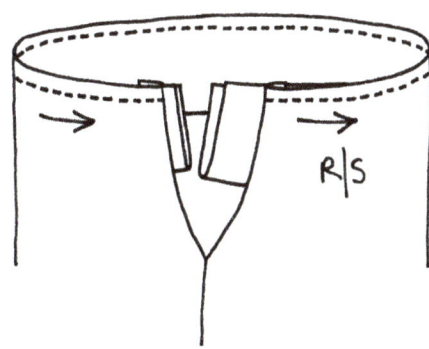

6. Press the seam and the waistband both up.

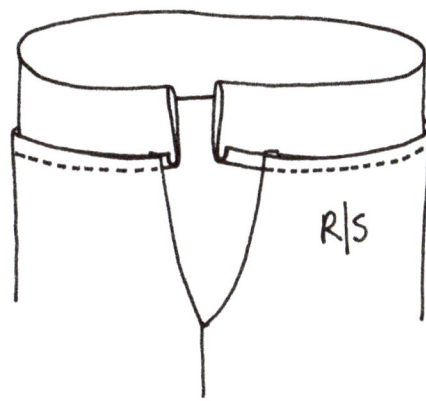

7. Finish the ends: fold the waistband back on itself and stitch the end level with the garment. On the end with the extension, take a 1cm seam. Trim the corners and turn through.

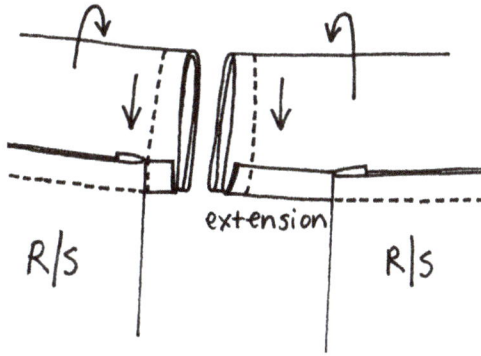

8. Bring the waistband over to the right side and edgestitch into position.
For a smooth, ripple-free waistband, hold the garment firmly as you sew, and let the waistband "sit easy" on top.

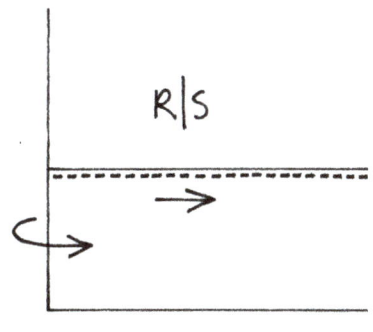

Sewing techniques     133

# Belts

## Tie belt

1. Cut a strip of fabric, long enough to go around your waist and tie. 150cm will probably do it; check by tying a tape measure around your waist. Make the strip's **width** double the finished belt plus 2cm for seam allowances. Fabric cut 6cm wide will yield a narrow 2cm belt, and 12cm wide will yield a 5cm wide finished belt. Tie belts don't require interfacing.

2. Fold the strip in half longways, wrong sides together. Stitch around the edge, leaving a gap in the centre to turn through.

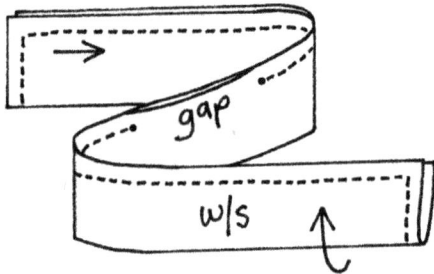

3. Trim the corners to no closer than 3mm, turn through and press. A pair of hemostats makes it quick to turn through to the right side. Sew the gap closed by hand, or leave it if you're edgestitching around the belt.

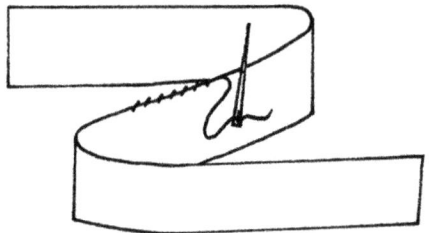

## Buckle belt (slip-through buckle)

The same method for a tie belt is used to make a belt with a slip-through buckle. The belt will need interfacing to support the weight 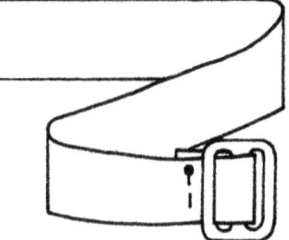 of the buckle. Note that the width of the buckle determines the belt's width.

If you find a buckle you like but it has a prong, the prong can be removed and the buckle used as a slip-through buckle.

If the buckle needs to be removed before the garment is laundered, use velcro to attach it.

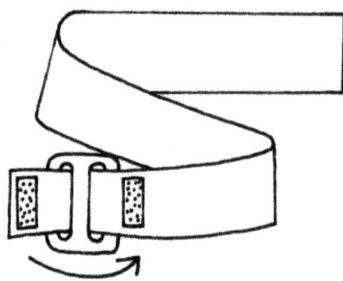

To keep the end of the belt in place, slide it through a loop of beltloop on the belt.

## Beltloops

Cut a long strip approximately 4cm wide and fold the long edges into the centre, then fold them together and stitch. Cut the beltloops to length.

If the fabric is light, you could sew a tube and press it flat.

If the fabric is thick, overlock and turn under the edges.

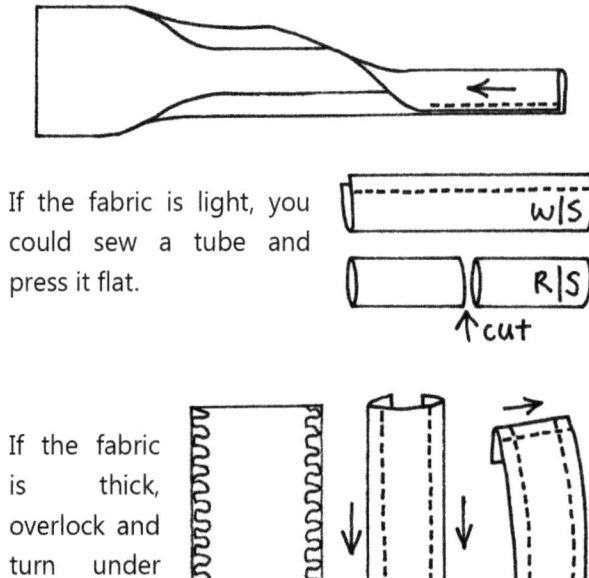

Cut and sew the beltloops individually if works out better for zero waste.

# Making zero waste patterns

I got started with zero waste patternmaking after reading *Shaping Sustainable Fashion* (see book list on pages 138-139) and then *Zero Waste Fashion Design*. I immediately clicked with it.

I had imagined that making zero waste patterns would be difficult but instead I found it to be exciting and unexpectedly freeing. Normally, patternmakers have a sketch or photo to adhere to, or sometimes (to my displeasure) are asked to make a pattern from a finished garment. Although the design is discussed, it's usually pretty much final. Therefore, it's exciting watching the pattern develop around the other way from usual - rather than making a pattern to match an idea, the idea comes as the pattern is made. I could compare it to creative writing versus journalism. Not knowing the outcome adds an element of risk and excitement, yet at the same time I feel confident that everything will come together and all fit and design issues will be resolved. Ideas emerge from one another, the fabric giving clues as to which direction to take. Actually, the fabric dictates much of the design, encouraging greater respect for the materials we use.

There's no one way to go about making zero waste patterns, but here are some things that might be helpful.

- Pattern drafting experience will really help, even if you've only done a bit. The more patternmaking you do, the more intuitive it will become; you'll be able to just look at a pattern and tell if it's the right shape or size. You'll also be able to recognise potential garment shapes. The ability to picture three dimensional shapes in your head from the pattern is also an asset, as is a solid knowledge of sewing and garment construction.

Experience with creating cutting layouts is also a big help, whether the layouts are made manually or on computer.

- Start with the width of the fabric, so that you're making your pattern in the right dimensions. 115cm or 150cm or another width. Which way around are you going to use it? Can you use the selvedges (either visibly or as a seam finish) or are they too rough?

- It can be helpful to start with an existing block or basic pattern to use as a guide. I find I need to refer to one often. Keep in mind whether you need to add or remove seam allowances.

- Find a method of working that works best for you. I start by drawing the pattern pieces/layouts in my sketch book and then chalking it onto some fabric, referring to a basic block to help with the size. I keep very detailed notes and sketches. A considerable amount of time is spent thinking before cutting it out. Rather than use calico, I prefer to use a wearable fabric (but not too special, in case I've got it all wrong). When it's cut out, I pin the entire thing together and carefully try it on. I can then see whether the idea is worth pursuing, needs big changes or needs abandoning. Some people find that graph paper is useful to draw the layout to scale. Other people work by cutting some shapes from fabric, draping them on a mannequin and seeing what emerges. You may prefer working on a half-scale mannequin (which Vionnet did—the advantage is you can see the effect without standing back all the time, however you're going to have to scale it up to 100% afterwards).

Decide whether you're going to (or need to) make a paper pattern or draft straight onto the fabric. If you draft onto paper you can make corrections and make another garment later.

Zero waste patterns can be drafted on a computer using pattern drafting CAD, Illustrator or Inkscape, and some people start all their patterns that way.

✂ Zero waste layouts can be simple or complex, but they don't have to be complex to work well. An old senior cutter gave me some good advice when I was a fresh-faced factory junior. He said *The simplest markers are usually the best. Mark out half and mirror it if possible.* This can apply to zero waste layouts too.

Decide on the main/large pieces first then take a look at the smaller spaces around them. These remaining spaces are where you'll cut the garment's details. Creativity here will often inspire the design.

It's important to think of all the pieces you'll need to complete the garment (facings, pocket bags, waistbands etc) because you can't just cut them out later; they need to be in the layout.

✂ Try not to have set ideas about what the outcome will be. The designing happens as you make the pattern, so you won't need a traditional fashion sketch before you start. Begin with a very loose design brief which is inspired by the fabric, for example: a jumpsuit, a jacket with a great statement collar, a dress from a single pattern piece or a red carpet gown. The fabric will inform the design direction.

✂ Do try to think outside the box. If you have formal training or a great deal of experience it can be hard to change from how you usually do things. On the other hand, experience brings a certain intuitiveness to patternmaking and you may find it as freeing as I did.

✂ While creating a garment with zero waste is a worthy goal, it shouldn't be at the expense of fit and appearance. If there's a choice between zero waste and a better fit, always pick fit. You may end up with a pattern that's almost zero waste instead, or you may be able to improve on it in the future.

✂ Can you adapt a pattern you already have for zero waste? Spread out the fabric and position the big pieces first, just as you normally would when doing a cutting layout. You'll be able to see which garment areas you can adjust and which ones are non-negotiable. Review the small areas left. You might be able to add pockets, change the shape of any facings, make tabs, epaulettes, ruffles, ties, invent a new collar shape and so on.

Again, don't have fixed expectations of the outcome; be prepared for something new.

✂ You may be able to use the projects in this book as a starting point to create different designs.

✂ Two garment pieces don't have to be the same shape to sew together—they just have to be the same length. Even then, ease, pleats, tucks, darts and gathering can help adjust pieces to the correct size.

✂ Use some interesting closures. It could be part of your design brief, either the fastening itself or how it's used/positioned. It's also possible to change most fastenings if you plan ahead. If you don't want to use a zip because it's plastic (or a metal zip with a synthetic tape), consider a placket instead—see *Sewing Techniques* pages 129-130.

✂ Experiment with some interesting ways to control fullness. For example, stitched folds, wrapping, pleats, tucks with embroidery on top, gathers, darts, smocking, shirring, belts.

✂ Using shapes:
**Circles** can be used for facings, patch pockets, in-seam pockets, collars and plackets.
**Triangles** can be used for gussets, godets and sleeves. Triangles can be hard to use, but try and think outside of "front" and "back" garment pieces, because triangles can wrap around in a spiral seamed tube and be used for bodies and sleeves. Triangles can be used for X-over bodices.
**Squares and rectangles.** Some designers only use squares and rectangles, and it can yield some beautiful minimalist shapes.
**Appliqués.** If embellishment is your thing. Or, fabric can be appliquéd to provide the strength of a double layer.

✂ Kimono sleeves (sleeves cut in one with the body), with or without a gusset, are an easy shape to begin with.
Putting an armhole or sleeve in an unexpected place can create drape or an unusual silhouette.

✂ Consider tessellated patterns. The projects in this book demonstrate the use of simple tessellations, but there's much more potential for developing sophisticated garment patterns. What if several edges were tessellated? Could you rotate a tessellation around a single point? Could you design a garment with multiple tessellated pieces (for example, sleeves, body and collar) and fit them all on the same piece of fabric?

# Sizing

Is the garment going to be only one size or multiple sizes? You'll need to plan for sizes as you make the pattern. Some solutions to sizing:

✂ One size. The person simply wears the clothes tighter or looser. This can work for bias-cut clothes in fluid fabrics or loose, oversized clothes. The garment could also be made adjustable in some way.

✂ Take bigger or smaller seam allowances—this could create up to 3 sizes.

✂ Tucks or pleats down the centre of a garment could be adjusted to give bigger or smaller sizes.

✂ Cutting across the fabric will give you space to make the garments wider, because garments grow in width more than length as the sizes increase. Therefore the *garment's length* is dictated by the *fabric's width*. The garment's width can be any size provided you have enough fabric. The tessellated and one seam projects in this book are examples of this.

✂ Belts, button bands, waistbands or collars cut parallel or perpendicular to the selvedge can give you more freedom to make the garment pieces bigger or smaller. For example, if a waistband is cut next to the selvedge for a smaller size, it could be cut perpendicular for a bigger size to give more fabric width for the main pieces. The tessellated wrap trousers in this book use this idea.

✂ Using 115 wide fabric instead of 150 wide may give sizes suitable for children.

# Further reading

## Sewing books

Find some good reference books on sewing. These will help you choose the way you construct the garment and therefore make the pattern.

**The Dressmaker's Companion—A practical guide to sewing clothes** by Elizabeth M Haywood (*Cooatalaa Press* 2017) A comprehensive sewing reference including fitting advice and sewing troubleshooting. You simply *must* own a copy.

**Reader's Digest Complete Guide to Sewing** (*Reader's Digest Services Pty Ltd* 1977) The 1977 edition is still considered the best.

**The Art of Manipulating Fabric** by Collette Wolff (*Krause Publications* 1996) An encyclopedia of techniques for the three dimensional manipulation of fabric.

## Patternmaking books

There are very few books specifically on zero waste patternmaking, however the concept exists in books on ethnic clothing, folk costumes and historical clothes. It's not all aprons and peasant blouses! Books on patternless sewing may also have styles that can be adapted to zero waste.

**Zero Waste Fashion Design** by Timo Rissanen and Holly McQuillan (*Bloomsbury Publishing Plc* 2016) Offers strategies and techniques for zero waste pattern cutting. Written for fashion design students.

**Cut my Cote** by Dorothy K Burnham (*Royal Ontario Museum* 1973) A slim book describing traditional clothes cut with zero waste to fit the width of the cloth.

**The Medieval Tailor's Assistant—Common garments 110-1480** by Sarah Thursfield (*The Crowood Press Ltd* 2015 edition) Historical evidence combined with practical cutting and sewing. Written for re-enactors and costumers.

**Madeleine Vionnet** by Betty Kirke (*Chronicle Books* 1998) Not zero waste, but shows Vionnet's innovative cutting and construction.

**Vionnet** by Bunka Fashion College, Japan (2009) In Japanese, a companion volume to Betty Kirke's book. You'll need it if you want to try her patterns.

**Bias Cut Blueprints—A geometric method for clothing design and construction** by Julianne Bramson and Susan Lenahan (*Fashion in Harmony* 2014) Directions for making tops and dresses based on rectangles sewn to form bias-cut tubes.

**Creative Dressing: the unique collection of top designer looks that you can make yourself** by Kaori O'Connor (*Routledge Kegan & Paul* 1983) Cutting and sewing instructions for classic late 70s ethnic inspired fashion.

**The Folkwear Book of Ethnic Clothing: Easy ways to sew and embellish fabulous garments from around the world** by Mary S. Parker (*Lark Books* 2002)

**Make Your Own Japanese Clothes** by John Marshall (*Kodansha International* 1989) A creative sourcebook for cutting and sewing Japanese clothes.

**Ethnic Costume—clothing, designs and techniques with an international inspiration** by Lois and Diane Ericson (*Simon & Schuster* 1984)

**No Pattern Needed** by Rosie Martin (*Laurence King Publishing Ltd* 2016)  A book of 15 patternless styles and variations that could be adapted to zero waste.

**Vintage Menswear—A collection from the vintage showroom** by Josh Sims, Roy Luckett and Douglas Gunn (*Laurence King Publishing Ltd* 2012)  Not a patternmaking book, but an excellent sourcebook of ideas for garment details.

**Designing Tessellations: the secrets of interlocking patterns** by Jinny Beyer (*McGraw-Hill* 1999)  A great book on understanding and designing tessellating shapes.  Written for quilters.

## Sustainable fashion books

There are new books on sustainable/ethical/slow fashion being published all the time; these are some favourites.

**Shaping Sustainable Fashion—Changing the way we make and wear clothes** edited by Alison Gwilt and Timo Rissanen (*Earthscan* 2011)

**Slow Clothing—Finding meaning in what we wear** by Jane Milburn (*Textile Beat* 2017)

**Wardrobe Crisis—How we went from Sunday best to fast fashion** by Clare Press (*Skyhorse* 2018)

**Overdressed: The shockingly high cost of cheap fashion** by Elizabeth L Cline (*Portfolio 2013*)

## Zero waste fashion websites

www.studiofaro.com
Patternmaking discussion including zero waste by educator Anita McAdam in Australia.

www.milanavjc.com
Zero waste sewing patterns from French patternmaker Mylène L'Orguilloux.

www.mysomapatterns.com
Sewing patterns including zero waste by Sylvie Privat in California.

www.fashion-incubator.com
Patternmaking discussion including zero waste by Kathleen Fasanella.

@aryanicreativitynest
Zero waste patternmaking courses in Indonesia. She's only on Instagram, translation required.

www.makeuse.nz
A research project led by Holly McQuillan exploring the concept of zero waste user modifiable clothing.  Free downloadable templates and patterns for zero waste clothes.

www.zerowastedaniel.com
Zero waste clothes made from waste fabric in NYC.

www.majastabel.com
Norwegian designer Maja Stabel uses repurposed textiles for zero waste garments.

www.editionalicesutton.com
Aussie zero waste fashion label.

www.lizhaywood.com.au
My website - please visit!

# Index

**a**
abbreviations 12

**b**
beltloops 134
belts 134
bias binding as a facing 127-128
binding 86
bog jacket 44

**c**
coat, hooded 76

**d**
dresses   boho 80-87
          boho caftan 87
          tessellated 102-113
          coat dress 56-63
          simple one seam 48-53

**e**
edgestitching 12

**f**
fabric advice 11
fabric, straightening edge 11-12

**j**
jackets/   tessellated coat 102-110
coats      cardi jacket 64-69
           hooded robe 70-76
           simple one seam 54-55

**m**
metric-imperial conversions 10-11
moebius scarf 69

**o**
one seam, about 44-47
one seam, fitting 47

**p**
plackets 129-130
playsuit 114-126
pockets, in seam on playsuit 124-125
patternmaking advice 135-137

**r**
resources 138-139

**s**
seam allowances 11
sizing chart 10
sizing options for zero waste 137
skirt, wrap 88-93
stitch-in-the-ditch 12

**t**
tessellating, about/how-to 78-79
tops      geometric 38-42
          tie front 14-21
          hooded blouson 22-29
          draped jersey 34-37
          yo yo 30-33
trousers, wraparound 94-101

**u**
understitching 12

**w**
waistband, double fold 132-133
waistband, regular 131-132

# Acknowledgements

To my dear family, who suffered piles of fabric everywhere and Mum banging on about her book all the time.  Bless you for thinking this book was called *Zero Waist Sewing*.

My informal "focus group" Anthea Martin, Melanie Michael, Niki Rimmer, Lisa Koo, my mum Val and my husband Grant, who weren't afraid to tell me my early attempts looked like nighties, hospital gowns, rapper pants, canteen lady uniforms, bad relics from the 1980s, "hilarious" or simply "boring".  Thanks for all your encouragement too!

My sewing students, in particular Leonie and Rae for trying projects and giving me valuable constructive criticism.

Thank you historian Mary Warner, for conversations on one seam garments—it was more helpful than you probably realise.

The ever-helpful staff at Clare library, where I've ordered so many fashion books through inter-library loans that I even have my own spot on the holds trolley.

Thank you to the models in this book: Irene Grigg, Viv Lamshed, Rachel Sanders, Lydia Sanders, Lisa Koo, Melanie Michael and Claire Freebairn.  You were all such great sports!

Thanks to The Valleys Lifestyle Centre for allowing us to photograph there.

Two very important people: tech editor Anthea Martin and general editor Nan Berrett.  Your uninhibited constructive criticism and advice gave this book clarity.

Thank you for another beautiful cover, Stu Nankivell.

I'm a dwarf standing on the shoulders of giants: thank you Timo Rissanen and Holly McQuillan for writing *Zero Waste Fashion Design*.

# About the author

Elizabeth Haywood trained as a patternmaker, combining her love of maths, drawing, fabric and stationery.  She was fortunate to find something she loved doing early on in adult life and remained passionate about patternmaking over a twenty year career in clothing manufacture.

She now writes and teaches sewing, and is the author of the award-winning *The Dressmaker's Companion—A practical guide to sewing clothes*.

The sewing machine on the cover is her "everyday drive" and was used to sew every garment in this book.

Visit her sewing and fashion blog at
www.lizhaywood.com.au
instagram @lizhaywood3754
facebook @thedressmakerscompanion

Also by Elizabeth Haywood:
*The Dressmaker's Companion*
*—A practical guide to sewing clothes*
(978-0-646-98547-3)

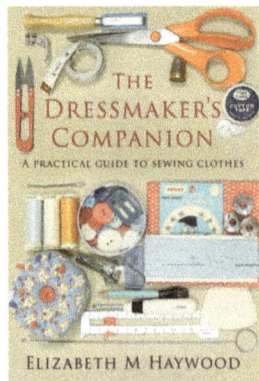

www.ingramcontent.com/pod-product-compliance
Lightning Source LLC
Chambersburg PA
CBHW061820290426
44110CB00027B/2931